Making the Grade

Evaluating Student Progress

Making the Grade

Evaluating Student Progress

Prentice-Hall Canada Inc.
Scarborough, Ontario

Canadian Cataloguing in Publication Data

Main entry under title:

Making the grade: evaluating student progress

Bibliography: p.
Includes index.
ISBN 0-13-547191-5

1. Educational tests and measurements.
2. Students, Rating of.   I. Etobicoke Board of
   Education.

LB3051.M35 1987   371.2'7   C86-094714-9

Prentice-Hall Inc., Englewood Cliffs, New Jersey
Prentice-Hall International, Inc., London
Prentice-Hall of Australia, Pty., Sydney
Prentice-Hall of India Pvt., Ltd., New Delhi
Prentice-Hall of Japan, Inc., Tokyo
Prentice-Hall of Southeast Asia (Pte.) Ltd., Singapore
Editora Prentice-Hall do Brasil Ltda., Rio de Janeiro
Prentice-Hall Hispanoamericana, S.A., Mexico

ISBN 0-13-547191-5

Production Editor: K.C. Bell
Design: Robert Garbutt Productions
Production: Irene Maunder
Composition: Cundari Group Ltd.
Printed and bound in Canada by Webcom Limited

    4 5 6 W 91 90 89 88

The publisher of this book has made every reasonable effort to trace the
ownership of data and visuals and to make full acknowledgement for their
use. If any errors or omissions have occurred, they will be corrected in
future editions, providing written notification has been received by the
publisher.

Contents

Preface   ix
Acknowledgements   xi
Introduction   xiii

What Is Student Evaluation?   1

Introduction   2
Why We Evaluate Students   3
Significant Factors Affecting Student Evaluation   4
Characteristics of an Effective Evaluation Program   7
Types of Student Evaluation   8
Is the Intended Evaluation Taking Place?   10
Intended Evaluation and Students of Other Cultures, Languages or Dialects   12
Factors to Consider Before Using an Evaluation Procedure   14
Factors to Consider After Using an Evaluation Procedure   15
Now What Do I Do?   16
No Surprises!   17
Developing a Program for Student Evaluation   18
Developing a School Policy for Student Evaluation   19
Developing an Evaluation Policy for a Grade, Subject, or Department
  Within a School   20

Learning Objectives and Student Evaluation   27

Introduction   28
Objectives and the Three Domains   29
Suggestions on How to Write Objectives   33

Stages of Cognitive Development from Kindergarten to the End of Secondary School   35

Introduction   36
The Four Stages   38
Conclusion   42

Study Skills and Student Evaluation   43

Introduction   **44**
Suggestions for Teaching Study Skills   **44**

A Variety of Approaches to Evaluation   55

Introduction   **56**

Observation   59

Introduction   **60**
Advantages and Disadvantages of Observation   **60**
Tips on Using Observation as a Method of Evaluation   **61**
Guideposts for the Construction of Observational Checklists   **62**
Examples of Observation Techniques and of Methods
   of Recording Observations   **63**

Projects   95

Introduction   **96**
Advantages of the Project Assignment   **96**
Disadvantages of the Project Assignment   **97**
Guideposts for Assigning and Marking Projects   **98**
Sample Outline of a Project Assignment Sheet   **100**
Suggested Evaluation Criteria for Projects   **101**
Examples of Project Assignment Sheets   **102**

Tests and Examinations: Written and Oral   109

Introduction   **110**
Planning Evaluation   **110**
Balance and Integration   **111**
88 Key Questions to Ask About Tests and Examinations   **112**
Now What Do I Do?   **118**
No Surprises!   **118**

Essay-Style Questions   119

Introduction   **120**
Advantages and Disadvantages of Essay-Style Questions   **120**
Guideposts for Essay-Style Questions   **123**
Five Steps in the Construction, Use and Marking of Essay-Style Questions   **123**
The Use of "Directing" Words in Formulating Essay-Style Questions   **135**
Directing Words and Levels of Thinking   **140**

Essays   143

Introduction   144
Essay Assignments and Objectives   144
Objectives and Evaluation Criteria   144
Objectives, Evaluation Criteria and Levels of Ability   145
Frequent Short Essays   145
Selective Evaluation   145
Need for Clear and Detailed Instructions   146
The "First Draft Syndrome"   147
Marking the Essay   148
Peer Evaluation of Essays   153
Different Types of Essays   153

Objective-Style Questions   155

Introduction   156
Advantages of Objective Types of Evaluation   157
Disadvantages of Objective Types of Evaluation   157
Types of Objective-Style Questions   158
The Multiple-Choice Question   159
The True-False Question   167
The Matching Question   175
The Short-Response Item   178

Diagnostic Techniques in Evaluation   183

Introduction   184
Examples of Three Diagnostic Techniques   184
Modified Miscue Analysis   184
Cloze   193
Human Figure Drawing   198

Modifying Evaluation Procedures and Methods for Exceptional Students in the Classroom   203

Introduction   204
Exceptionalities   204
Modification of Evaluation Procedures for Exceptional Students   205
Factors to Consider in Evaluating Exceptional Students   206
Factors to Consider When Reporting on the Evaluation of Exceptional Students   206
Samples of Modification in Evaluation for Exceptional Students   208
Communications Exceptionality — Learning Disability   208
Behavioral Exceptionality   212
Intellectual Exceptionality — Giftedness   220
Intellectual Exceptionality — Slow Learner   223

Differentiating Evaluation for Different Levels of Ability   227

Introduction   **228**

Evaluation Procedures for Students Experiencing Difficulty in Regular
Classroom Programs: Grades 7 to 12   **229**

Differentiating Evaluation — A Teacher Checklist   **232**

Additional Considerations for Evaluation of Students
Taking Basic-Level Courses   **235**

Examples of Evaluation Procedures Differentiated for Different
Levels of Ability   **237**

In Closing   259

Endnotes   **260**

Credits   **261**

Bibliography   **263**

Index   **269**

Preface

In June 1983, the Director of Education for the City of Etobicoke, Canada, commissioned a committee on student evaluation to prepare materials which would be of assistance to both elementary and secondary administrative and teaching staffs whenever they examine and review their policies and practices regarding the evaluation of student progress. *Making the Grade* is the result.

Making the Grade addresses many significant issues related to the evaluation of student progress. It provides an abundance of practical ideas, suggestions, illustrations and examples, all of which are based upon sound teaching principles.

We tried to create for teachers a book which would be both practical and easy to read. To this end, we avoided as much as possible the use of technical terms, educational jargon and statistical analyses. For example, because teachers generally use the term "evaluation" rather than "assessment," the former term is used throughout this book, even though the latter term is more correct. It was not our intention to attempt to cover completely the vast topic of student evaluation. We recognized, for example, that such important matters as reporting to parents would require a treatment almost as extensive as this one on student evaluation. However, we did attempt to concentrate on those particular approaches which constitute the largest part of a teacher's evaluation repertoire.

Individual school staffs, whole school systems and / or teacher organizations may wish to consider what form of professional development program would best fit their needs when deciding how to implement some of the concepts outlined in this book. School staffs, for example, may wish to plan for professional development activities centered around a broad review of their current student evaluation policies and practices. Similarly, individual teachers may wish to review their own specific evaluation procedures and methods in the context of the many ideas presented in this volume.

The authors wish to express sincere appreciation to the administration, the Program Department and the teaching staff of the Board of Education for the City of Etobicoke for their willing assistance, suggestions and support in the development of this book. Special thanks are extended to the authors of the Etobicoke booklet *Student Evaluation in History,*[1] which provided a foundation for the present work.

R. J. C.
K. M. C.
B. D.
K. McC.
J. P.
G. W. S.

Acknowledgements

Making the Grade: Evaluating Student Progress was first conceived and published as a resource document for the teaching and administrative staffs operating under the Board of Education for the City of Etobicoke, Canada. Prentice-Hall Canada recognized that its great practical value made *Making the Grade* deserving of a larger audience and requested revisions. These revisions were undertaken by the authors and, we believe, have made *Making the Grade* applicable to teachers and administrators across Canada and the United States.

Prentice-Hall Canada gratefully acknowledges the contributions of the Board of Education for the City of Etobicoke and, in particular, to S.S. Sauro, Director of Education and Secretary-Treasurer, A.L. Kozakavich, Superintendent of Program, and Karl M. McCutcheon, who chaired the writing committee.

Prentice-Hall Canada is also deeply indebted to the officers and staff of the Ontario Secondary School Teachers' Federation, without whose support this edition of *Making the Grade* would not have been possible. We especially wish to thank Raymond Primeau, Executive Assistant, and Kevin Crouse, Director, Resource Booklets.

Others who assisted with the publication of *Making the Grade* were Gordon R. Thomas, Alberta Teachers' Association, Robert Morrow, Jr., Wentworth County Board of Education, Peter L. McCreath, Nova Scotia Teachers' Union, Dr. Myrle Vokey, Newfoundland Teachers' Association, Dwaine McLean, New Brunswick Teachers' Association, and James W. MacKay, Prince Edward Island Teachers' Federation.

Introduction

As teachers, we have made considerable progress over the years in improving our programs and teaching techniques. During this time, however, we have generally continued to use the same old evaluation techniques to assess student progress in our new programs. *Making the Grade* is based on the assumption that evaluation's role in the teaching-learning process is both *active* and *fundamental.* It is therefore essential for teachers and principals constantly to review their evaluation strategies to make them more effective. When reviewing evaluation practices, it is especially important to remember that *students will judge which elements of the curriculum are important by the emphasis placed on them by the evaluation process.*

Making the Grade is intended to aid teachers in refining their evaluation skills and to encourage them to augment traditional methods with other ones. For example, teachers whose student assessments have tended to rely on *product*-oriented evaluation programs will be interested in the numerous discussions and practical examples designed to evaluate the learning *process* itself. We have found that giving due attention to the learning *process* can lead to the early identification of problems, clarify their nature and source, and facilitate the teacher's adjustment of objectives and teaching methods in order to resolve them.

Teachers and principals who look to *Making the Grade* for help in clarifying and structuring their evaluation programs will find that it deals with:

- the necessary relationship between educational objectives and the evaluation of student progress;

- practical, teacher-prepared classroom activities for evaluating an individual student's progress within the student's program;

- the evaluation of program; the evaluation of student progress necessarily reflects upon the suitability of the program.

Making the Grade does *not* deal with:

- the evaluation of teachers;

- formal assessment for the potential identification of exceptional students;

- formal assessment for early identification from Junior Kindergarten to Grade 3.

A conscientious attempt has been made by the authors to ensure that *Making the Grade* is relevant to all grades and subjects. It is hoped that it will increase awareness of the evaluation techniques that all students experience. We believe that it is necessary to the continuity, fairness and effectiveness of evaluation programs that teachers be alert to the overall pattern of evaluation practices their students experience. For primary teachers this means an awareness of the evaluation procedures his or her students will meet in subsequent years, just as secondary teachers should have a sense of which procedures their students will — or will not — have already encountered.

When considering evaluation strategies, several important factors should be kept in mind, a number of which are addressed in this book. These include:

- the need to regard evaluation as a positive component of the student's learning experience;

- the need to relate evaluation activities to the student's level of development;

- the need to use only evaluation activities appropriate to each particular grade, division or subject;

- the need to recognize and address the relationship between stated objectives, learning activities and evaluation activities;

- the need to develop evaluation practices which support learning-as-process as well as learning-as-product;

- the need to modify evaluation procedures for exceptional students and to differentiate evaluation for students at different levels of ability;

- the need continually to re-examine evaluation practices, and to be open to changing them should it prove necessary;

- the need to determine whether or not we are truly evaluating what we *think* we are evaluating.

Making the Grade is designed for personal, practical use by teachers. It contains many useful suggestions for reinforcing classroom programs by adopting more effective evaluation procedures.

The first section, "What Is Student Evaluation," provides the foundation upon which all later sections are developed. After studying the rest of the book, teachers may consider adding to, deleting from or modifying some of the evaluation techniques they are presently using.

Teachers who perceive the need to modify their evaluation procedures to meet the special requirements of exceptional students will find a chapter devoted to that purpose near the end of the book (pp. 227-257). It is important to remember, however, that the evaluation practices suggested for exceptional students are simply a special case of the principles developed and illustrated throughout the rest of *Making the Grade.* The final section suggests ways of differentiating evaluation practices for students with different levels of ability.

What Is
Student Evaluation?

Introduction

The word "evaluation" is often used narrowly as a synonym for "testing." More appropriately, the term includes *all* available methods of obtaining information regarding what the students are learning and how effective the teaching is.

Much evaluation carried out in the classroom is of a casual nature; that is, teachers frequently observe the behavior or performance of students and make informal evaluations. This aspect of evaluation is important, but it is not the focus of this document. While this book does not ignore such "casual" or "subjective" evaluation, its main emphasis is structured, systematic evaluation.

One writer defines evaluation as "a systematic process of determining the extent to which educational objectives are achieved by pupils."[2] There are at least two important principles implied in this definition.

1. *Evaluation is a systematic process.* It is not a casual, unplanned, unstructured endeavor; it is a process in which teachers and students learn about their respective achievements and about the possible need for change if growth is to take place.

2. *Evaluation is conducted within the context of the objectives identified for the program, course, unit or lesson.* The objectives may be for an individual, group or class. Only with clearly defined and stated objectives is it possible to judge the extent of progress. These objectives should be fully understood by students before teaching and evaluation take place.

THE CLOSE RELATIONSHIP BETWEEN TEACHING OBJECTIVES AND EVALUATION SHOULD BE FUNDAMENTAL TO ANY PROCESS OF STUDENT EVALUATION. One of the most common causes of faulty or ineffective evaluation is the absence of sound and clearly defined objectives.

Evaluation should not take place only in written form. Other forms of evaluation, such as observation or demonstration, are equally valid and could be more appropriate. A *balanced* evaluation program includes as many forms of evaluation as are possible and appropriate to the student's development and level of achievement.

Why We Evaluate Students

Although obtaining a comment, grade or mark for the report card is an important aspect of evaluation, other aspects may be at least as significant, or even more so.

The following points are not listed in order of importance but indicate a variety of reasons for evaluating students.

We evaluate students:

- To determine if the objectives were achieved;

- To find a basis for designing a program for the individual, group or class;

- To determine the knowledge and skills students have acquired and to observe the development of their attitudes and appreciation;

- To determine where the curriculum needs improvement:
  — Are the objectives being achieved?
  — What topics or activities should be expanded, reduced, added or eliminated?
  — What topics or activities need other forms of revision or modification?

- To determine how effective the teaching process or methodology has been:
  — Which teaching strategies have been successful?
  — Which teaching strategies or learning experiences need modification or improvement?

- To diagnose the level of understanding that students have of a topic or the level of skill development students have reached, before further instruction takes place;

- To gather information on the quality of the learning environment for specific kinds of learning:
  — Was there in the classroom a supporting atmosphere fostered by both teacher and students?
  — Was the classroom organized in such a manner that learning was facilitated?
  — Were there extenuating circumstances that affected the quality of learning in the classroom, for example, classroom temperature, previous activity, interruptions, holidays?

- To determine student response to aspects of the curriculum:
  — How well did students receive this topic or activity?
  — Did they enjoy this topic or activity?
  — How highly did they value this topic or activity?

- To assist the teacher to determine the direction of future study:
  — Based on the needs and interests of the students, what direction should the teacher take in the next activity, topic or unit?

- To determine how well students use their knowledge or perform their skills when asked to use them in a real-life or simulated experience;

- To summarize an activity, topic or unit of work:
  — Does the evaluation bring into focus the highlights of the activity, topic or unit and the important information, skills, and concepts studied?

- To provide a basis for extra help where needed:
  — Which students need assistance?
  — What lessons or remedial activities can be developed to assist them?
  — How can students be grouped to facilitate remedial work?

- To identify the most useful information to communicate to students or parents:
  — Did the evaluation specifically identify the strengths and weaknesses of individual students?
  — Can these strengths and weaknesses be communicated to students and parents in a comprehensive form with suggestions for assistance or proposals for extra help if required?

Significant Factors Affecting Student Evaluation

Significant Factors	Effect on Program	Effect on Student Evaluation
1. • Information explosion	• Greater emphasis on developing such skills as selecting, organizing, evaluating and applying information rather than on merely mastering content • Use of various media to teach and learn	• Need to develop and employ methods of evaluating students' skills in these processes
2. • Greater emphasis on the active involvement of the learner in the learning process	• Development of programs centered on the student so that he or she learns to inquire and discover	• Need to develop and employ evaluation methods and activities which measure: — what students are learning from the experience and the extent to which they can apply this knowledge or skill to new or different situations — students' ability to share in and profit from peer interactions

Significant Factors	Effect on Program	Effect on Student Evaluation
3. • Increased knowledge of the student's growth and development and how this relates to the learning process	• Development of programs based on accepted learning principles, such as the stages of development, and on students' knowledge and needs	• Need to develop and employ evaluation methods and activities which determine: — each student's stage of development — what each student already knows and can do
4. • Opportunities for students to make choices within a program or from a variety of programs or courses	• The same objectives can be achieved in different ways and with different activities or content • Students are provided with a variety of activities or different selections or material to develop skills or concepts	• Need to develop and employ ways to evaluate the achievement of stated objectives without tying the evaluation exclusively to specific content or activities
5. • Recognition of a wider variety of objectives in developing learning activities, courses and programs	• The objectives of learning activities, courses and programs have broadened to apply to: — content — academic skills — social skills — performance skills — values	• Need to develop and employ means to evaluate the full range of objectives
6. • Greater emphasis on development of cumulative skills in the subjects in which they apply	• Development of programs highlighting skills development and the cumulative building of these skills	• Need to develop and employ evaluation instruments which can determine the progress made in developing skills and indicate further work that may be necessary
7. • Less emphasis on rote learning	• Use of learning activities in which teachers and students employ facts and concrete experiences, not just as ends in themselves, but as means of developing an understanding of processes and generalizations	• Need to develop and employ evaluation methods that require the use and application of facts to demonstrate achievement in skill and process objectives

Significant Factors	Effect on Program	Effect on Student Evaluation
8. • Increasing stress on the accountability of school systems for the effective delivery of education	• Greater attention to identifying objectives and related learning experiences • Greater stress on communicating with students and parents regarding student progress, and with the entire community regarding school programs	• Need to develop and employ evaluation methods which demonstrate as clearly as possible the degree of achievement in reaching defined objectives • Need to gather more detailed information on each student's overall development • Need to communicate the results of evaluation to students and parents with as much clarity and precision as possible • Need to specify the relative weighting of objectives and to indicate the evaluation techniques by which the attainment of each objective will be determined
9. • Greater emphasis on meeting the needs of exceptional students	• Greater attention to the modification of programs for exceptional students	• Need to modify evaluation methods and procedures to meet the needs of exceptional students
10. • Greater emphasis on differentiating programs for students of differing levels of ability	• Greater attention to the development of activities or programs to address the needs of students of differing levels of ability	• Need to develop and employ evaluation methods and procedures to meet the needs of students of differing levels of ability in the same grade in elementary school and in the same course in secondary school

Characteristics of an Effective Evaluation Program

1. There must be a strong and obvious connection between objectives and evaluation.

   - The activity, test, or assignment must evaluate the students' success in meeting the objectives set for them. For example, does the activity evaluate only content recall when the course objectives emphasize the development of the ability to analyze, interpret and apply information?

2. There must be a strong and obvious connection between the learning process and the methods of evaluation.

   - The methods used to evaluate student performance and success often tell the students very clearly what and how they should prepare for tests.

   - More forcefully than anything else that is said or done in class, the evaluation approaches tell students what is really important about the course. For example, if the objectives stress acquisition of higher thinking skills, but the evaluation emphasizes only factual recall, students will conclude that the learning of facts is most important.

3. There must be a variety of evaluation approaches which take into account the student's strengths and weaknesses.

   - Learning is a complex process, and occurs in many ways and at many levels.

   - No single evaluation approach will enable the teacher or student to understand fully the extent of learning.

   - Evaluation should be comprehensive and take into account such factors as homework assignments, classroom presentations, daily work and effort, as well as tests, essays and examinations.

   - No single evaluation instrument or test can provide all the information teachers require to assess what and how their students are learning.

4. There must be informal, as well as formal, evaluation.

   - While there will be more emphasis on informal evaluation in the early years of elementary school, this practice is an important ingredient of any evaluation program.

5. There must be an evaluation plan for the whole school year. This plan must be made available to parents and communicated to students.

   - The evaluation plan should include diagnostic, formative and summative evaluation. (See pages 8-10.)

   - Where applicable, opportunities to evaluate students in the cognitive, affective and psychomotor domains should be included.

- Accurate and detailed records, including anecdotal comments, must be kept in such a way that they are meaningful to students and parents and not only to the teacher.

6. Evaluation activities must offer opportunities for higher level thinking while providing opportunities for students to learn as they are being evaluated.

   - These characteristics of an effective evaluation program may not be integral to every evaluation activity, but should occur frequently during the program.

   - In many situations, students should be asked to apply previously learned thinking skills to new content or situations.

7. Evaluation approaches should provide practical information to teachers and students.

   - The mark, grade or comment resulting from the activity, test or assignment must be readily understood by the students. These results must convey to them their relative grasp of the content or concepts, or the extent of their development of a particular skill or skills.

8. Evaluation procedures should suit both small groups and individuals.

   - The approaches used to evaluate student performance must take into account the growth and / or development of individual students so that the teacher can determine the suitability of the program and adjust it, if necessary.

Types of Student Evaluation

When planning the evaluation program for the whole school year, teachers should include the three types of student evaluation outlined below. All the various approaches to evaluation, such as observation, written tests and practical demonstrations, can be used for diagnostic, formative or summative evaluation.[3]

1. Diagnostic Evaluation

Diagnostic evaluation is often done at the beginning of a school year, semester, term or unit of study, or when there is evidence that an individual student is struggling. This type of evaluation should be done informally and continually. Although it may be used for anecdotal reporting, it should never be used as part of the student's mark.

Specific Purposes:

   (i) to assess the skills, interests, abilities, difficulties and level of achievement of an individual, group or class;

(ii) to determine the underlying causes of learning difficulties;

(iii) to make decisions about program modifications suitable or necessary for a particular individual, group or class.

2. Formative Evaluation

Formative evaluation is conducted continually throughout the course of instruction. *Its purpose is to improve instruction and learning, rather than merely to rank or grade students.* It keeps both students and teachers aware of the objectives to be achieved and the progress being made. The results of formative evaluation should be analyzed and used to redirect the efforts of the teacher and students.

Specific Purposes:

(a) Teacher-Conducted Evaluation:
   (i) to measure individual and class growth in skills, effort and attitudes;
   (ii) to provide information to the student, class and teacher on progress towards the objectives of the program, course or unit;
   (iii) to indicate which skills are at a satisfactory level and which need improvement;
   (iv) to evaluate the effectiveness of a program in terms of its content, methods, sequence and pace;
   (v) to provide records that will form part of a summative evaluation.

(b) Student Self-Evaluation:
   (i) to develop students' sense of responsibility for their own learning;
   (ii) to contribute to their awareness of the objectives of the course;
   (iii) to help students learn to evaluate their own work;
   (iv) to inform the teacher about student reactions to the program.

(c) Student Peer Evaluation:
   (i) to provide students with responses to their work other than those of the teacher;
   (ii) to create situations in which students can compare their work;
   (iii) to provide further records to be considered in summative evaluation.

3. Summative Evaluation

Summative evaluation occurs at the end of a unit, activity, course, term or program. It is used with formative evaluation to determine student achievement and program effectiveness. This combined assessment of a student's achievement can be used to evaluate students for the purposes of reporting and to ascertain the degree to which course objectives have been met. Summative evaluation should form only a part of the total mark or grade.

Specific Purposes:

(i) to measure student achievement;

(ii) to grant or withhold credit or promotion;

(iii) to report to parents, principal and students;

(iv) to monitor the overall performance of students;

(v) to measure the effectiveness of the program;

(vi) to measure the effects of program modifications or changes.

Is the Intended Evaluation Taking Place?

This section (pages 10-12) points out some of the pitfalls teachers and students may encounter during evaluation. Persons devising evaluation activities may believe them to be clear and effective. However, unperceived complexities may exist and unintended functions may supplant the desired focus of the evaluative exercise.

The points which follow are not listed in order of importance. They should not be construed as indications that certain activities should be avoided, but rather should remind the teacher to be aware of such pitfalls in devising the activity and assessing the results.

1. In evaluation activities requiring written expression, the intent may be to evaluate student's knowledge and ability to think, but the primary emphasis may fall on their ability to write.

   Students may know a considerable amount and be able to think at a relatively high level, yet not be able to put knowledge and thought on paper.

   THEREFORE, the evaluation is of students' ability to write, and not of their knowledge or ability to think.

2. It frequently happens that a student's failure to respond adequately to a question or solve a problem results from an inability to read and understand the instructions.

   For example, a student may be unable to demonstrate successfully achieved arithmetic skills when confronted by a "word problem" which assumes a certain level of reading skill.

   THEREFORE, the test has really evaluated reading ability, rather than mathematical ability. Such difficulties cannot be completely avoided, but they can be reduced by ensuring that instructions are straightforward and clear, and by providing an explanation of special terminology immediately prior to the evaluation activity.

3. Too frequently, undue emphasis is placed upon spelling, grammar, handwriting, format and computation, so that the student's comprehension and expression of ideas are given little or no credit.

   THEREFORE, in such cases, evaluation is of the student's ability to compute, spell, punctuate and write using acceptable grammar rather than the ability to perform the required task. In a written assignment, some marks should be given if there is evidence that the student has indicated a basic understanding of the issue, problem or task even though there may be numerous errors in format, spelling, grammar, punctuation or computation.

4. Many students find evaluation activities stressful. In stressful situations, mistakes are often made which would not be made in more relaxed circumstances. For example, in a test or examination in which the time allotted is barely sufficient to complete a difficult task, or in which the task may be too difficult, students will make errors and lose marks for errors which they would not make in a more relaxed activity.

    THEREFORE, students are losing marks because of the stress of the test rather than because they lack the required knowledge or skill.

5. Sometimes the level of abstraction of the evaluation activity is inappropriate. This problem has two dimensions.

    First, the content of the evaluation activity may be too abstract for the students' level of intellectual development.

    THEREFORE, the teacher may be evaluating the students' level of intellectual development rather than their knowledge and skills.

    Secondly, evaluation activities too frequently place excessive emphasis on factual recall and fundamental performance skills and ignore higher level thinking such as synthesizing and making judgments.

    THEREFORE, students may not have the opportunity to demonstrate higher levels of thinking and will be denied the chance to learn while being evaluated.

6. If students encounter, in an evaluation activity, a term or concept which they have not met in their broader cultural experience, then their inability to answer the question or do the activity may result from a difference of cultural background, rather than a lack of knowledge or inability to do the task.

    For example, if a class is given a problem which includes the term "bill of fare," many students may be incapable of completing the task. If a task or question involves the term "freeway" and several students do not respond, it may be that those students have recently come from a country where the term "freeway" is unknown.

    THEREFORE, an activity meant to measure acquired content or skill may err because it mistakenly assumes a common cultural background.

7. Students may be asked to demonstrate their ability with certain thinking skills. The teacher may conclude from positive results that the student possesses a particular skill. However, it may be that only memory has been evaluated because the student has merely memorized the content of the lesson without understanding it.

    THEREFORE, if a teacher has taught the skill of comparing, for example, using a specific body of content, and if the evaluation activity does not ask students to demonstrate that skill using different content, then the teacher cannot ascertain whether students have developed that skill or merely memorized the specific classroom example.

8. Instructions for evaluation activities may use terminology which confuses or misleads students. One teacher who asked a senior high school class to define the term "discuss" received the following interpretations:[4]

   (i) show or prove by explanation;

   (ii) discuss means to present analogies and comparisons and through their juxtaposition come to a conclusion based on evidence;

   (iii) discuss means to analyze, covering the question from every possible angle;

   (iv) discuss means to say everything you know about whatever is asked;

   (v) discuss means to present all the facts and express both sides of the argument and then give your personal opinion.

   THEREFORE, the focus of the evaluation may have become the students' ability to interpret the teacher's terminology rather than to demonstrate knowledge or skill.

Intended Evaluation and Students of Other Cultures, Languages and Dialects

Concern sometimes arises regarding the issue of "intended evaluation." As is emphasized throughout this document, it is imperative that evaluation procedures always achieve their intended function, which is to discover the degree of progress made by a student toward stated objectives. Some students may have trouble in some evaluation situations because the evaluation takes no account of possible difficulties caused by differences in culture, language or dialect. Students who do not perform as expected in an evaluation situation may have been unable to express what they know because of cultural or linguistic differences.

The following factors should be considered when evaluating the performance of these students:

1. The language students learn as young children, and use with their immediate family and closest friends, plays an important role in the development of their identity and view of the world. At whatever age they enter school, their first language or dialect has been, to that time, their principal tool for giving shape and meaning to their experience. Their first language has been an adequate and unquestioned means of communicating needs and interests and has enabled them to express both individuality and group membership.

   The students' confidence in the value of the first language must not be undermined.

2. Practices in educating children both at home and at school vary widely from country to country. It is to be expected that students who are unfamiliar with the community and its schools will find many of the new features of daily life confusing, or even threatening. The method of discipline used in the schools, the interaction between teachers and students, parental control over student behavior, peer-group interaction (particularly between the sexes), and the extent to which students are expected to direct their own learning may all be as challenging for some students as the new language itself. Failure to recognize the importance of such differences may well impede their progress in acquiring the new language.

3. In writing, reading and oral work, students may translate directly from their first language and produce constructions which appear or sound awkward.

4. When, because of cultural or language differences, a student feels inadequate standing in front of a class for an oral presentation or joining in a group discussion, alternate methods of presentation should be offered. One alternative is to allow a student the opportunity to tape a presentation and to play it to the class or group.

   For students who are reluctant to participate in group discussions while the teacher is nearby, the teacher may consider recording group interaction and assessing the student's participation later.

5. Many of these students have knowledge of the content of their courses, but have not acquired adequate writing skills to express that knowledge. In this situation, the teacher should evaluate the students orally and provide frequent assistance with their daily written work.

6. Many students from other cultures or countries may have had limited access to well-equipped school libraries and very little experience researching material. Incomplete, unsatisfactory projects may stem from a lack of research skills.

   Prior to making any assignment involving research skills, teachers need to undertake some diagnostic evaluation to ascertain what research skills these students have. If the students require training in research skills, the teacher should consider using a highly structured approach.

7. For some students, accuracy and penmanship were emphasized in their home countries. Time limits were not set. Therefore, it is essential to help these students to learn how to manage their time when writing tests and assignments.

Factors to Consider Before Using an Evaluation Procedure

Timing	Why am I evaluating at this particular time?
Purpose and Method	Why am I using this specific evaluation procedure?
Student Growth and Curriculum Effectiveness	What do I now know about each of my students, the class, and the effectiveness of the curriculum, and what do I expect to learn about them as a result of this evaluation procedure?
Student Learning Experience	What do I want my students to learn from this evaluation experience?
Objectives	How is this procedure related to the objectives? • In which objectives will progress be measured? • How much weight should I give to each objective I wish to measure? • Does this weighting correspond to the relative importance of this objective in the total program? • Will this evaluation procedure measure the degree to which the objective or objectives have been met?
Student Preparation	Have I prepared my students for the type of evaluation procedure to be used? Do my students clearly understand my marking procedures?
Time Allotment	Is the time allotment fair?
Assignment of Marks or Grades	Are the marks or grades appropriate to the difficulty of the task and the amount of time needed to complete it?
Different Levels of Ability	In devising the evaluation procedure, have I accounted for the varying levels of ability within the class?
Exceptionalities	In devising the evaluation procedure, have I taken into account exceptional students?
Reasonable Expectation	What will I consider a reasonable and acceptable response or performance?
Follow-up	Have I allocated time for follow-up activities after the evaluation?

Factors to Consider After Using an Evaluation Procedure

Clarity

Did the students understand what they were asked to do?

Time

Is there evidence that a number of students, including the exceptional students, had inadequate time to complete satisfactorily the evaluation activity?

Student Preparation

Is there evidence that a number of students were not adequately prepared for the evaluation activity?
- Was the lack of preparation the result of inadequate work or study on the part of the students?
- Was the material which was taught too abstract for the intellectual development of the students?
- Was the material presented clearly and in sufficient depth?
- Was the method of presentation of the material in class appropriate for the level of student ability?
- Was there sufficient time devoted to follow-up activities after presentation of the material in class and prior to the evaluation activity?
- Was the evaluation activity appropriate to the specific level of ability and stage of development of the students?

Unexpected Results

If actual marks or grades depart significantly from those expected, how will I use them?

Different Results from Different Classes

What can I learn from comparing my results with those of other teachers using the same evaluation procedure?

Exceptionalities

Did the results reflect adequately the provision I made for exceptional students?

Expectations and Results

How are the results related to what I taught and what I expected my students to have learned?
- Did the results indicate that the students are ready for the planned new activity or learning experience?
- Was there evidence that students enjoyed the learning process?

Future Use

- If I use this evaluation procedure again, what changes, if any, will I make in it?
- What other methods of evaluation might be more appropriate?

Now What Do I Do?

Once the teacher has studied the results of the evaluation procedure, he or she should consider the following activities.

Gather Student Reactions	Encourage students to express their reactions to the evaluation activity. If possible, this exercise should be done in writing.
Provide for Student-Teacher Discussion	Provide opportunities for individual student-teacher conferences for joint evaluation of difficulties and planning of future strategies.
Re-teach	Identify a group of students who require re-teaching, further study or assistance.
	Review or re-teach the particular material which was not understood and, if possible, use a different method of presentation.
Review Curriculum	Revise your classroom program by modifying, re-allocating or removing from the curriculum the inappropriate material, activities or objectives.
	Revise your classroom program by changing the pace of teaching and learning and by providing opportunities for repetition and reinforcement.
Review Study Techniques	Teach or review appropriate study techniques.
Re-evaluate	Re-evaluate, using a more appropriate activity or method.

No Surprises!

As teachers, we should be aware of what previous evaluation procedures our students have experienced. Otherwise we may use certain procedures on the assumption that students are familiar with them. This is of particular concern when students are moving from one grade or school to another, for example, from Kindergarten to Grade 1 or from elementary to secondary school.

1. It is important that whenever teachers are using any particular form of evaluation procedure they make sure that all students have had experience with the procedure to be used.

   THEREFORE, the teacher should be aware of the evaluation practices of previous years and should ensure that the students are capable of meeting the teacher's expectations in his or her proposed evaluation techniques.

2. Furthermore, if a teacher occasionally wishes to use a "surprise test" to find out what the students do or do not know, the practice can be beneficial for both students and teacher. However, this form of surprise test should be seen as diagnostic because it tells the teacher and students what is or is not known at that time *without preparation.*

   THEREFORE, any comment, grade or mark assigned to such a test should not be used in calculating the term or final mark for reporting purposes. The students also should be assured that this is an information-gathering exercise and not a formal evaluation. A surprise test must never be punitive or given to obtain an immediate mark to meet a reporting deadline.

3. Another form of "surprise test," and one which must be avoided, occurs when an evaluation has been announced for a particular time but is then re-scheduled at the last minute to a later date.

   THEREFORE, unless there are unavoidable circumstances which students understand, evaluations must occur as scheduled.

Developing a Program for Student Evaluation

The following questions should be considered when developing programs for student evaluation within a major unit, term, semester or school year. They may be considered by individual teachers, school staff or departments.

1. What are the objectives of the evaluation program?

2. Who should be involved in the evaluation?

3. What variety of evaluation techniques should be used?

4. Which alternative evaluation techniques should be used for certain students?

5. How will students be prepared for the proposed evaluation techniques?

6. When will students be informed of the evaluation techniques?

7. What information should be collected and recorded?

8. What information should students receive about the result of the evaluation and how should this be done?

9. When and how often should evaluation take place?

10. How should the results of the evaluation be used?

Developing a School Policy for Student Evaluation

Schools are encouraged to have available *in print* a school student evaluation policy. In developing this policy, schools should consider:

What is meant by student evaluation? (See page 2.)

What are the purposes of evaluating students? (See page 3.)

What types and methods of evaluation will be used?

What modifications will be made for certain individuals and groups, including exceptional students?

What provisions will be made to differentiate evaluation procedures for students at different levels of ability?

What methods of recording will be used (comments, grades, marks)?

What methods of reporting will be used (comments, grades, marks)?

Is the evaluation program fair and humane?
- How are students to be prepared for evaluation experiences?
- How will the conditions be set up to foster a positive evaluation experience for the students?
- How will a student's personal problems, anxieties and special circumstances be taken into account?
- How will administrative procedures be handled?
  - Will a particular evaluation activity, for instance, examinations, be used?
  - Will the evaluation activity be conducted on a cross-grade basis?
  - How frequently will a particular evaluation activity occur?
  - How many evaluation activities should a student experience on a given day?
  - What proportion of the mark or grade will be based on classroom activities, and what proportion on formal testing and examinations?

What use will be made of the results of standardized tests?

Developing an Evaluation Policy for a Grade, Subject or Department Within a School

Within the context of a school policy on student evaluation, teachers of particular grades or subjects or within particular departments, should develop a statement of policy and procedures.

Policy statements should begin with a philosophic base upon which the specific policies and procedures are developed. The following example, developed for music, can serve as a model for the design of a policy and procedures statement for student evaluation in most subjects or departments.

Example

Student Evaluation in Music

A. RATIONALE

As music educators, we agree with the tenet that evaluation is central to the teaching-learning process.

Because of the limitations of time, and the pressures to perform, there is an inherent danger that evaluation in music may become the sole responsibility of the teacher, rather than a participatory activity involving both teacher and student. Also, there is a possibility that the teacher may become the "conductor," a symbol of authority, rather than the educator, a catalyst for student growth.

In order to preclude these potential dangers, it is necessary to establish an overall philosophy regarding student evaluation in the music program.

Our rationale for music evaluation is based upon three principles:

1) While music is involved with aesthetics, there are certain qualities associated with sound and feelings which must be considered in the evaluation process;

2) Because music involves body, mind and emotions, the evaluation process must include a variety of techniques and procedures;

3) A most important "result" of music education is that students, *on their own*, grow in their ability to perform, listen and create. Therefore, self-evaluation is critical.

The following section is an expansion of the three principles listed above.

1) "Music Is Involved With Aesthetics"

In simple terms, music can be defined as "sound and feelings." Can these two components be evaluated and, if so, how?

Musical sounds have certain measurable elements such as pitch, duration, timbre and volume. When sounds are performed in the context of a piece of music, the acoustical result can be evaluated. Performance tests, for example, will examine such things as intonation, rhythmic accuracy, dynamic contrasts, appropriateness of tone and shaping of phrases.

While feelings cannot be measured quantitatively, their development through the teaching-learning process can be evaluated through a variety of methods which are described on the next pages in Section B. If the evaluation of the aesthetic is downplayed, there is the possibility that the "feeling side" of music may be overlooked by both teacher and student.

2) "Music Involves Body, Mind, and Emotions"

An ongoing, comprehensive evaluation of students in music must take into account the psychomotor, cognitive and affective domains. All these aspects must be looked at together.

In assessing a performance, for example, students should be encouraged to consider not only the "acoustical outcome" of the music, but also the physical techniques that were used and the effects of the music on the listener.

3) "Self-Evaluation Is Critical"

Students must be immersed in a learning environment where they are helped and encouraged to verbalize their feelings in order to make interpretive judgments.

So that students will be able to evaluate their progress in music, they must be helped to develop musical skills, vocabulary and knowledge. Initially, students may gain critical insight into developing these assessment skills by observing the teacher's evaluation techniques. Eventually, these techniques will become part of the student's own self-evaluation process.

We see three stages in the development of this self-evaluation process:

a) At first, evaluation is "teacher oriented," because students lack the necessary knowledge and skills to conduct the evaluation themselves.

b) Then, the teacher involves the student in an "evaluation partnership."

c) Finally, the student is encouraged to become a "self-evaluator."

B. OPPORTUNITIES FOR EVALUATION IN MUSIC

This section describes a variety of activities within the music program that provides opportunities for the evaluation of students. These activities include:

1. Rehearsal Strategies
2. Practicing
3. Observation
4. Demonstration
5. Creative Experiences
6. Projects
7. Performance Tests
8. Written Examinations
9. Public Performance

1. Rehearsal Strategies

The evaluation process is central to performance in music. As soon as the first note is sounded, evaluation begins.

The following points suggest ways in which the teacher can help students to evaluate the music performed during rehearsal.

a) Through skillful questioning, the teacher can involve students in self- and peer evaluation. For example, following the performance of a musical phrase, the teacher might ask students for specific ways of improving that phrase.

b) The "feeling" side of music is often expressed through tension and release, melodic "peaks and valleys" and dynamic contrasts. In order to help evaluate students' ability to recognize such features, they can be asked to "make visible" some of these feelings by translating them into graphs of such things as melodic contours.

c) Students can be asked to listen to their peers perform. Evaluative comments applying both to the concrete and abstract can then be shared.

d) Students can be asked to conduct their peers. The teacher and other students could observe. This observation may be followed by a discussion involving the teacher, the student conductor and the rest of the class. (This practice assumes that the teacher has given instruction in basic conducting techniques beforehand.)

e) The use of both audio and video recording can provide a worthwhile tool for self-evaluation.

2. Practicing

The evaluation process must be applied to the individual student's practice routine. The complexities of music-making are such that, unless the elements involved are clarified and simplified, the student will not be able to evaluate the result. This clarification and simplification process is essential because self-evaluation is a critical component of practice.

Listening is a key element of the music-making process. The brain perceives (through the eye) a musical symbol which must be translated into a musical sound. The brain then directs through the cortex the appropriate muscular actions for carrying out the command. The brain receives through the ear the acoustical result, causing an instant "evaluation" which leads to the necessary muscular adjustments.

The evaluation process will break down if, as a student becomes more manually proficient, communication between ear and brain is inadequate.

The following is an example of a practice method for string players which simplifies and clarifies the evaluation process.

a) The student identifies and plays the note pitches of the assigned music to the best of her or his ability.

b) While counting aloud the beats, the student claps the rhythm patterns involved.

c) In order to identify and evaluate the strengths and weaknesses of the right hand, the student plays with the right hand only the bowing patterns of the assigned music.

d) In order to identify and isolate the muscular co-ordination of the left hand and arm and thereby synthesize the pitch and rhythm elements, the student plays the assigned passage pizzicato.

e) The student practices the passage as written, to co-ordinate left and right hands.

f) Students who have achieved a measure of accuracy and co-ordination will be free to integrate the musical components and thereby evaluate the total musical experience.

By clarifying and simplifying the basic elements of music-making, students can identify a number of small, observable units through which they can readily evaluate their own performance.

3. Observation

In order to make as complete an evaluation of student progress as possible, an on-going evaluation of the student by the teacher is necessary. Observation should involve both concrete and abstract elements.

a) Evaluation must be built into the daily class routine. A music teacher can facilitate this process by moving about the class and observing closely, both aurally and visually, particular student's musical skills and progress. When the teacher is not "rooted to the podium," personal interaction and closer observation are improved.

b) Small ensembles provide a useful means of observing the individual's musical development and sensitivity.

c) Specific time during class can be set aside for a small group of students to perform. Some form of written evaluation by the teacher can then take place.

4. Demonstration

In the teaching of music, it is necessary to present exciting models for students to emulate. These models can be presented by teachers, peers and visiting artists, and through the use of film, tape and concerts. The students should be involved in verbalizing and synthesizing what they have seen and heard. Evaluating the performances of others should indicate to the students their own emerging skills. The teacher can then make evaluative judgments about the students' developing musical insights and perceptions.

5. Creative Experiences

The creative experience in music represents a continuous evaluation process. The teacher should, therefore, encourage students to evaluate the development of their unique musical skills and insights through a variety of creative techniques. The following is a partial list of such techniques:

a) Early in his or her school career, a student might be asked to suggest instrumental "colors" and rhythmic patterns to accompany a given song.

b) Later, a student could become involved in interpreting a piece of music by suggesting such elements as: dynamics, breathing places, tone color and articulation.

c) Still later, a student could share in creating a "soundscape."

d) Finally, a secondary school student may be challenged to arrange or compose music.

With all these examples, great care must be taken that the evaluation process is informal and does not discourage unique thought and divergent thinking. Ideas and insights given by a student should be positively received and heard, prior to shared evaluation among students, and between students and teacher; otherwise creativity may suffer.

6. Projects

In addition to the usual considerations regarding projects, the following points are of particular importance for music projects:

a) Projects in music should encourage a balance between the presentation of analytical data and the presentation of the individual's response to the given topic.

b) Title pages can, if not carefully planned, test ability in art rather than any musical perception.

c) The construction of a "homemade instrument" can be exciting if the project illustrates an acoustical principle.

d) Music composition can, even at a simple level, encourage analysis, synthesis and judgment.

e) The relevance of project assignments to students must be scrutinized.

f) A sufficient range of choices should be offered.

(For further information on assigning and evaluating projects, see the section on projects, pp. 95-108.)

7. Performance Tests

The formal performance test enables the teacher to see and hear a student and to give constructive criticism. Such tests are given on a one-to-one basis or with a small group of students.

Performance tests should examine such concrete elements as:

- accuracy;
- technique;
- posture and position;
- tone quality;
- sight-reading;
- articulation;
- dynamics.

Performance tests should reflect such abstract musical ideas as:

- imagination;
- musicianship;
- initiative, originality;
- appropriateness of tone, dynamics and articulation.

A formal performance test should take into account the ongoing work a student does in class. Consistency of effort is important in building a solid musical foundation.

8. Written Examinations

Written examinations in music should test factual information in such areas as history, theory and analysis. They should also include questions which enable students to react individually to the feelings created by the music.

An example of a question which refers to both the concrete and the abstract is:

> "Describe the mood of the last section of *Finlandia*. How do the musical elements (rhythm, melody, harmony, tone color, form, dynamics) contribute to this mood?"

9. Public Performance

Public performance provides a unique source of evaluation. Such an experience motivates students to consolidate their skills so that the "feeling aspect" of the music can be developed to the maximum and shared with an audience. The response of the audience becomes yet another evaluation criterion.

C. OBTAINING AND REPORTING A MARK OR GRADE

Because of the different levels of ability encountered in an elementary music class and the range of levels at which music may be offered in the secondary school, no single set of policy statements regarding obtaining and reporting marks or grades can be defined which would address fairly all groups of students. As a result, this example of a music policy does not attempt to provide a detailed policy on obtaining and reporting marks or grades. Individual schools, departments or teachers should develop this section based on their needs, the levels of ability of their students and the criteria outlined below.

Policy statements with regard to obtaining and reporting marks or grades should include at least the following:

- the percentage of the final report mark assigned to formal examinations (if any), and the percentage assigned to term work;

- a fair weighting among the various evaluation activities.

Learning Objectives
and Student Evaluation

Introduction

Student evaluation procedures are too often treated as an afterthought rather than as a central part of the teaching-learning process. This inattention to evaluation procedures leads to a lack of coherence between "learning objectives" and the procedures intended to measure their success.* When this happens, students usually will direct their efforts toward learning whatever they think the teacher is "testing for."

To do this, students will base their assumptions about learning objectives on what they can deduce about them from the evaluation procedures a teacher uses, rather than on any statements a teacher may explicitly make about them.

It should be understood in this context that, although attitudinal or aesthetic objectives are not easily evaluated, they should be included in a statement of objectives because they are an essential part of the educational experience.

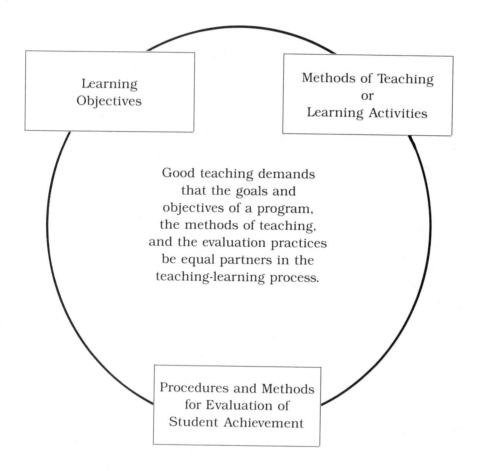

Learning Objectives

Methods of Teaching or Learning Activities

Good teaching demands that the goals and objectives of a program, the methods of teaching, and the evaluation practices be equal partners in the teaching-learning process.

Procedures and Methods for Evaluation of Student Achievement

---

* The term "learning objectives" as used in this document also refers, where applicable, to performance and attitudinal objectives.

To achieve the necessary partnership among learning objectives, teaching methods and evaluation practices, objectives must be clearly defined and stated, as frequently as possible, in measurable terms. As part of the teaching-learning activity, these objectives must be made known to the students in a manner appropriate to the students' grade level. Unless both teachers and students work towards the accomplishment of the full range of objectives, students will conclude that certain stated objectives are neither important nor real. Students discover what the teacher really regards as important by observing what and how the teacher evaluates. Therefore, the teacher's methods of presentation and evaluation must emphasize the particular attitudes, skills, concepts or content it is desired for the students to learn.

Because objectives are an essential part of any learning program, they must be carefully thought out and clearly stated before the classroom activities are developed.

Objectives and the Three Domains

Introduction

When developing objectives, it is essential that the teacher consider all three developmental domains: the cognitive, the affective and the psychomotor.

Cognitive Domain[5]	• knowledge
	• understanding
	• thinking
Affective Domain[6]	• feelings
	• interests
	• attitudes
	• appreciation
Psychomotor Domain[7]	• physical skills
	— handwriting
	— sculpting
	— typing or keyboarding
	— swimming

When objectives are being developed, most of them will usually involve more than one domain.

Each domain includes several major categories. These categories are classified in ascending order of difficulty. This classification is called a *taxonomy*. What follows is an abbreviated outline of a taxonomy for each domain, along with the verbs that could be used in writing learning objectives for each category.

A. Taxonomy for the Cognitive Domain

The categories in this taxonomy are presented in order, from basic (1.) to most complex (6.).

Categories	Examples of Verbs to Use When Developing Learning Objectives
1. Knowledge — remembering previously learned information	— describe, label, identify, name, state, locate, list, define, outline
2. Comprehension — understanding the meaning of information	— explain, give examples, summarize, rewrite, paraphrase, convert, distinguish, predict
3. Application — using learned information in relevant situations (putting knowledge and comprehension to work)	— infer, change, discover, operate, predict, relate, show, solve, use, manipulate, modify, demonstrate, compute
4. Analysis — breaking down information into component parts so that its structure can be understood	— analyze, break down, differentiate, discriminate, illustrate, identify, outline, point out, select, separate, sub-divide, categorize, classify, distinguish
5. Synthesis — putting component parts together to create a pattern or structure which could be new or different	— devise, compile, design, compose, explain, organize, re-arrange, plan, combine, categorize, show relationship, synthesize
6. Evaluation — judging the value of information or material based on personal or given criteria	— judge, compare, contrast, evaluate, criticize, justify, draw conclusions

B. Taxonomy for the Affective Domain

The categories in this taxonomy are presented in order, from basic (1.) to most complex (5.).

Categories	Examples of Verbs to Use When Developing Learning or Performance Objectives
1. Receiving — being willing to pay attention or receive information — being aware of the importance of learning — being sensitive (open-minded) to information, things, issues and points of view	— listen, observe, follow, question, show willingness, concentrate
2. Responding — complying with a request to perform a task — responding willingly to a request to perform a task — volunteering to perform a task without a request — enjoying the performance of a task	— comply, answer, ask, question, respond, assist, perform, practice, present, report, search out, volunteer, enjoy
3. Valuing (the worth or value attached to a particular object, phenomenon, or attitude) — recognizing the value of... — appreciating the value of... — expressing concern about the value of... — exercising commitment to the value of...	— recognize, accept, appreciate, differentiate, discern, justify, defend, select, share, express concern, demonstrate commitment
4. Organization — conceptualizing a value — bringing together different values — resolving conflicts between different values — building a personal and consistent value system	— compare, contrast, relate, arrange, alter, modify, combine, defend, explain, integrate, organize, synthesize
5. Characterization — possessing a value system that has controlled an individual's behavior long enough for that individual to have developed a characteristic lifestyle that is consistent and predictable	— act, display, practice, demonstrate

C. Taxonomy for the Psychomotor Domain

The categories in this taxonomy are presented in order, from basic (1.) to most complex (7.).

Categories	Examples of Verbs to Use When Developing Learning or Performance Objectives
1. Perception — using the senses to obtain cues to guide motor activities	— detect, differentiate, distinguish, identify, listen, observe, smell, isolate, taste, feel, touch
2. Set — being ready (mentally, physically, emotionally) to take a particular type of action	— proceed, react, respond, volunteer, show readiness
3. Guided Response — learning motor skills through imitation and trial and error	— repair, construct, dismantle, keyboard, assemble, dissect, throw, measure, sketch, display, type, print
4. Mechanism — performing motor skills consistently with some confidence and proficiency	— (same list as for "Guided Response" but at a higher level of proficiency, consistency and confidence)
5. Complex Overt Response — performing accurately, automatically, efficiently and without hesitation, motor skills which involve increasingly complex movement patterns	— (same list as for "Mechanism" but at an even higher level of proficiency, consistency and confidence)
6. Adaptation — modifying particular motor skills or movement patterns to meet a new or unexpected situation	— adapt, modify, change, alter, rearrange, revise, vary
7. Origination — creating a new skill or movement pattern to meet a new or unexpected situation	— originate, create, devise, compose, construct, design, arrange, combine

Suggestions on How to Write Objectives

Objectives must be carefully thought out and clearly stated and based upon the three domains. What follows are suggestions to assist teachers in developing and writing objectives.

1. Be very careful in the use of the terms "goals," "aims" and "objectives." They must not be used interchangeably.

   Goals: This term is most often used when referring to the goals of education as identified by provincial or state educational authorities.

   Aims: This term usually refers to general statements outlining broad intentions for school programs. They are usually developed at the provincial, state or local board level.

   Objectives: Objectives outline specific purposes within previously stated goals and aims. They may be found in current curriculum documents of a school board or may be developed by individual school staffs, departments or teachers.

   Objectives must be carefully thought out and clearly stated. Most importantly they should be constructed to address the appropriate stages of development regarding the three domains.

2. When writing objectives, teachers should refer to the appropriate current documents of their school board. Many of these documents will have well-defined objectives which may be used or adapted for classroom use.

3. Objectives should be stated in terms of what students should be able to do as a result of the classroom experience and not in terms of what the teacher intends to do with the students.

   Example:

   Acceptable: A student should be able to ...
   A student will be able to ...

   Unacceptable: The teacher will help the student learn to ...
   To show the student how to ...
   To help the student to ...

   The "unacceptable" examples above are unacceptable only because they cannot be used to measure student progress. However, it may be appropriate, in some instances, to state objectives in terms of the teacher's activities or intentions (for example, "to foster an appreciation of"). Objectives should be stated in this form *only* when the focus of the evaluation is meant to be on the effectiveness of the teacher's teaching rather than the student's learning.

4. Each objective should begin with the same part of speech. For example, if the first objective begins with an infinitive (for example, "to demonstrate proficiency in"; "to be able to"; "to show"), all subsequent objectives must follow the same format.

5. Ordinarily, it is not necessary for objectives to be listed in a hierarchy of importance or difficulty.

6. Measurable objectives should be stated as frequently as possible. To be measurable, they should be worded in such a way that what is to be evaluated is clearly and precisely defined. It should be understood in this context that, although attitudinal or aesthetic objectives are not easily evaluated, they should be included.

7. Teachers should be alert to the need to modify objectives that may not be appropriate for some of the individuals within a large group.

8. When developing programs for students of different levels of ability, it is essential that the objectives meet the needs of the particular students at each level of ability.

9. Objectives should never be "carved in stone." Be prepared to revise or adjust them as time and experience dictate.

10. Objectives should be written in language easily understandable by both students and parents. This will enable students to know what is expected of them and parents to know what and how their children are being taught. Objectives may sometimes be conveyed informally by indicating to students the purpose of an activity.

Stages of Cognitive Development From Junior Kindergarten to the End of Secondary School

Introduction

In evaluating students, it is essential to take into account their mental, physical and social development. For example, in their mental development:

1. A girl in Grade 3 may sound as if she knows what the term "prime meridian" means, but she probably will not have attained sufficient mental development to understand the concept. When evaluating, the teacher must be aware of the student's stage of development in order to determine whether the child understands the concept or is merely "word calling" by putting the right word in the right place at the right time.

2. A boy in Grade 10 may understand and apply the abstraction of the Pythagorean Theorem. However, he may not be at the stage of mental development required to cope with the abstraction of the nature and function of gerunds, participles and infinitives in a language program. That is, he can cope with a certain kind of abstraction in mathematics, but not with another kind in language.

The inability of the Grade 3 girl and the Grade 10 boy to understand and apply a particular abstraction may not result from a lack of trying or studying, or from ineffective teaching, or faulty testing. In both examples the problem may lie in the curriculum, because the individuals have been asked to cope with abstractions beyond their present capabilities. It would be unfair to evaluate them without considering their stages of development.

Although the four stages of development outlined in this section are linked to the age of the individual, these age references are not to be rigidly applied. The order in which human beings move through their developmental stages does not vary, but the age at which any person enters or leaves a given stage depends on a number of factors. In the following example Student A may be at Stage Two and Student B at Stage Three.

Example

<table>
<tr><td align="center">STUDENT A
(seven years old and at Stage Two)</td><td align="center">STUDENT B
(seven years old and at Stage Three)</td></tr>
<tr><td>

- physically immature for his age

- only child in a single parent family

- unhappy at home

- poor nutrition

- allowed to watch television until 11:00 p.m. each night

- poor medical and dental care

- rarely plays outside with other children

- very few toys at home

- not read to by parents

- no books or magazines at home

- few discussions of any length with peers or adults

- few or no family trips or excursions

- not allowed to plan or make decisions

</td><td>

- average physical maturity for his age

- one of several children in a two-parent family

- happy at home

- above average nutrition

- has ten hours sleep each night

- excellent medical and dental care

- frequently plays outside with other children

- a wide variety of toys at home

- read to frequently by parents and siblings

- many books and magazines which are read and talked about

- talks frequently with friends, siblings and adults

- frequent family trips and excursions
- discussions about trips and excursions before, while and after they occur

- encouraged to plan and make some decisions and be responsible for the consequences

- curiosity and questioning are encouraged

</td></tr>
</table>

Teachers should avoid labelling students as being at any given stage on the basis of their chronological age alone. In fact, any student may operate at one stage in some situations and at another stage in others. This holds true for adults as well as children and adolescents. For example, a person with a PhD in chemistry may show some Stage Two characteristics when learning to knit.

Teachers also should be aware that students may regress in any of the domains when they are placed in new, embarassing or otherwise stressful situations. Difficulties at home may have a similar effect. Evaluation procedures and techniques should be tailored to suit the occasion. Teachers who understand the stages of development will be able to evaluate more efficiently.

Teachers should observe a student's development within a stage, as well as from stage to stage. A simple example of this kind of development is the observation of a girl in Stage One. When she begins to crawl, she has moved a long way towards the ability to walk. In Stage Four, the observation that a student is not only able to recognize, but also to comprehend the nature and function of a metaphor tells the teacher that the student is moving towards the ability to distinguish and comprehend the differences between literary and psychological symbols and signs, and the ability to learn through analogy. Evaluation of development within a stage is just as important as the evaluation of a movement from one stage to another.

The Four Stages

The following outline of the four stages of cognitive development is based upon the work of Jean Piaget and his followers. An attempt has been made to eliminate confusing technical terminology so that teachers who have not studied child development may gain a clearer sense of how these stages are structured and what they involve.

Stage One (Sensori-motor)

During this stage, lasting from birth to about two years old, children approach their environment by means of non-verbal thought. Some of the ways in which they learn are outlined below.

Children at this stage show the following characteristics:

- The infant is interested in objects as things in themselves, not as things with a use.

- Objects exist only when present to the senses. When an object is out of sight, it is literally out of mind.

- The infant uses senses and physical movements to satisfy personal needs. He or she does not learn in a verbal way.

- Gradually, through experience, the child learns that the environment
  — has spatial relationships;
  — contains things having location and movement in space;
  — operates through cause and effect;
  — contains objects which are permanent.

- Children in this stage know about things, people and animals, but they cannot express their knowledge in words.

- They cannot cope with relatively complex directions.

Children in this stage need:

- many and varied opportunities to manipulate and feel things so they can build up a store of images of the world around them.

Stage Two (Pre-operational)

This stage is made up of two sub-stages; the first is from approximately ages two to four years, and the second from approximately ages four to seven years of age. For simplicity, this outline will treat the stage as a whole.

Children in this stage show the following characteristics:

- They are highly egocentric in thought and behavior.

- They grow and develop rapidly in their understanding and use of language, a fact which is particularly noticeable in their use of new vocabulary and their ability to formulate longer and more complex sentence structures.

- They do not think logically, and cannot generalize from particular instances.

- Because they consider only isolated parts of a whole situation, they remain unable to create a whole mental image of that situation. Therefore, they operate with distorted pictures of reality.

- They cannot reason that the quantity, weight or length of objects do not change when their positions or appearances have changed. For example, if a small ball of plasticine is formed into a long roll, they think the roll has more plasticine than the ball because it appears to take up more space.

- They cannot concentrate on two aspects of something at a time. Also, they are unable to relate objects in an order or series according to one or more criteria.

- They are able to recite numbers and appear able to count long before they have any concept of what the words or symbols mean. The concept of number will gradually be acquired through the children's experience with the classification of things. They recognize and classify things or sets of things by various properties, such as color, shape and texture. They learn the abstract concept of number by counting and matching numerals with the set being counted. When the children can match, for example, five blocks with the word "five" or the symbol "5," and can then scatter the same blocks over a wide area, and can still say and understand that there are five blocks, they have reached the stage of being able to understand conservation or invariance of number. Inherent in the process is the children's understanding and use of language. Language skills are the essential ingredient in developing mathematical thought. Also, when children are able to conserve number, most are able to learn to read and write.

- They are unable to understand that two classes of things may belong to a larger class of things. For example, if they have six red wooden beads and three green wooden beads, they cannot reason that they have more wooden beads than red beads.

- They lack the ability to understand and apply rules given to them by others.

- They know a great deal which they cannot put into words. However, they also can put into words many pieces of information which they do not really understand.

Children in this stage need:

- to experience, as frequently as possible, trips, music, literature, films, games and physical activities;

- to have many and varied concrete sensory experiences;

- to interact, solve problems, and create with many different materials and classes of things;

- to engage in a variety of social situations in order to learn to work with others, communicate with others and become less self-centered;

- to manipulate a variety of concrete materials in order to learn to discriminate, classify, quantify, measure, weigh and order;

- to have many and varied opportunities to communicate in both verbal and non-verbal ways;

- to have many opportunities for symbolic construction and fantasy play.

Stage Three (Concrete Operational)

At this stage (approximately seven to eleven years of age) the children are moving toward logical thought. However, they carry out only logical operations tied to direct personal experience and based upon materials which they manipulate themselves.

Children in this stage show the following characteristics:

- They are becoming less self-centred.

- They can play and work co-operatively using a high level of planning and of sharing the delegation of labor, authority and responsibility.

- They have begun to develop logical thinking.

- They have begun to appreciate the meaning of rules, to make them up and to apply them voluntarily and appropriately.

- They understand that things remain the same if nothing is added, even though there are changes in shapes, location or sizes of containers. For example, they understand that two half-litre containers of milk hold the same amount as a one-litre container does.

- They understand reversibility. For example, they know that $2+5=7$ is the same as $7=5+2$.

- They understand, through manipulating concrete articles, that two or more classes can combine into one class. For example, they understand that oranges and bananas are both fruit and that in a bowl of both kinds of fruit there are more pieces of fruit than of either oranges or bananas.

- They are able to understand some abstractions, associate meaning with two-directional forms and follow rules. Because of these abilities, most of the children will experience some degree of success in mathematics and reading instruction.

- They are often able to give systematic and logical descriptions and explanations about their actions.

- They are able to group objects in a series, refer to them according to ordinal positions and classify them according to several criteria, such as size, color, texture and function.

Children in this stage need:

- to experience all the activities listed for the children at Stage Two, but with greater variety and more social, linguistic and intellectual sophistication;

- to have sufficient time to play with a wide variety of materials and games;

- to have learning experiences based on concrete materials;

- to have frequent opportunities to link "doing" and "telling" through talking, reading and writing about present and past experiences;

- to be encouraged to persevere in activities;

- to be given opportunities to make connections between things, between people and between events;

- to be encouraged to draw conclusions and to make inferences.

Stage Four (Formal Operational)

From about twelve years old to maturity, pre-adolescents and adolescents increasingly approximate the way adults think and behave. However, as noted earlier, individuals may move back and forth between stages depending on their physical and emotional environment. So a person chronologically ready for Stage Four may sometimes display behaviors more appropriate to Stage Three.

Recent research, for instance, indicates that many college students, although in transition, still employ a number of Stage Three patterns to problem solve. Where their students lack previous experience in the more abstruse methods of mathematics, science or literary analysis, teachers may at first need to teach them by exploiting Stage Three reasoning strategies. For example, a mathematics teacher who is introducing three-dimensional vector geometry to a senior class may well use three metre sticks, placed mutually perpendicular, physically to illustrate length, width and height, so that students can visualize the X, Y, Z co-ordinate system concept.

Individuals in this stage show the following characteristics:

- They are able to consider others empathetically.

- They are able to think and act upon objects of thought which are themselves mental constructs and which may or may not refer to the world of physical objects.

- They often think in concepts in which possibility takes precedence over reality so that any element of a problem is seen as only one of a larger set of possible elements.

- They are able to comprehend and solve problems with several variables and to think in terms of combination, proportion, correlation and probability.

- They are able to understand symbolic structures and learn by analogy.

Individuals at this stage need:

- to be able to use strategies of the third stage when faced with new learning situations or when under emotional or mental stress;

- to be provided with many opportunities to talk, read and write about abstract concepts;

- to encounter many teaching-learning strategies which proceed from the concrete to the abstract.

Conclusion

There has been considerable research into the work of Jean Piaget, upon which this section has been based. The research has modified and extended his original work, but this simplified outline still has valid applications in the field of student evaluation. Teachers of all grades should be conscious of the implications of each stage of development while planning curriculum, and while teaching and evaluating students.

Study Skills
and Student Evaluation

Introduction

Success in learning is too frequently gauged by success in evaluation. Other than the influence of the teacher, students' success in evaluation is very closely related to their attitudes, their methods of learning, and their study skills. For many students, success in learning and in evaluation depends particularly upon how they study. Because studying is such an important skill for success in learning, it must be taught and practiced and re-taught. Teachers should not assume that study skills have been taught in previous years or in other subjects.

Suggestions for Teaching Study Skills

To teach study skills, the teacher should begin by helping students become aware of their present level of competence. The study skills inventories on the following three pages can be used to help students assess their present strengths and weaknesses.

The outline on pages 48-50, "Some Techniques for Improving Study Skills," is designed as a handout for students. The points in the outline should be discussed thoroughly with the students. *The sheets should not be distributed without discussion.*

As part of improving their study skills, many students will also require help with the management of their time. The calendars and charts on pages 51-53 could be adapted, where necessary, and handed out to students. The teacher should discuss with students various methods for scheduling their time.

Study Skills — Personal Work Habit Inventory

Read each sentence and decide how it applies to your work habits. Place a checkmark in the column that best describes your work habits. You need not share this inventory with your teacher or friends unless you wish.

DATE

	Very Seldom	Usually	Always
1. I plan my study time...			
2. I know exactly what the assignment is...			
3. I can find a good place to study...			
4. I keep my homework up to date...			
5. I keep my mind on my work...			
6. I keep my study equipment in order (pen, paper, notebook, etc.)...			
7. I listen attentively in the classroom...			
8. I can follow directions...			
9. I get my assignments in one time...			
10. I take part in class discussions...			
11. I ask questions when I am not sure of something...			
12. I review class notes as soon as possible after class...			
13. I begin preparing for a test several days in advance...			
14. I review lessons previously taught...			
15. I try to make the best grades I can...			

In order to improve your schoolwork, start working on the points you checked in the *Very Seldom* and *Usually* columns. Keep this inventory and re-do it at least once each term or semester.

Study Skills — Personal Study Inventory

Read each sentence and decide how it applies to your work habits. Place a checkmark in the column that best describes your study habits. You need not share this inventory with your teacher or friends unless you wish.

SECTION A: CLASSROOM WORK   DATE:

	Very Seldom	Usually	Always
1. I listen carefully to the teacher and to other students' response...			
2. I read ahead in the text...			
3. I make mental notes of important points...			
4. I check blackboard work against the text...			
5. I use the dictionary and reference material...			
6. I ask the teacher for clarification of difficulties...			
7. I check the timetable so that I am sure to bring the required materials to the lesson...			
8. I discuss with classmates what has been taught...			
9. I relate what has been taught to other subjects and to everyday experience...			
10. I make notes of key points...			

SECTION B: STUDYING AND HOMEWORK   DATE:

	Very Seldom	Usually	Always
1. I work in a quiet, well-lit study room whenever possible...			
2. I turn off or down distracting TV...			
3. I assemble required materials before I start...			
4. I work from a timetable to make sure that I will have time to study all subjects...			
5. I check the wording of each assignment carefully...			
6. I maintain a systematic review...			
7. I provide for short vocabulary drills in appropriate subjects...			
8. I set aside a regular study time each day...			

SECTION C: READING AND STUDYING A TEXTBOOK   DATE:

	Very Seldom	Usually	Always
1. I first skim quickly through the headings and sub-headings to get an overall sense of the chapter...			
2. I divide the chapter into sections and read them carefully...			
3. I use appropriate reading techniques for each section of the chapter, such as first skimming and then reading for detail...			
4. I look for relationships, connections, and important points...			
5. I ask myself questions about the content I have finished reading and try to answer them without reference to the text. Then I re-read the text as a check...			
6. I make a written outline or summary for each chapter...			
7. I re-read the whole chapter or section rapidly...			
8. I summarize the main points...			
9. I use a dictionary or glossary to understand essential words...			
10. I use the table of contents and index when searching for topics or answers to questions...			

Some Techniques for Improving Study Skills

TAKING NOTES

Good notes are essential whether you are a student in an elementary or a secondary school. Developing skills in taking notes will prove useful to you in your studies. Notes provide you with a record of work that has been covered. They assist you in completing homework, projects and essays. Notes are a major study aid for tests and examinations.

1. Organize your notes around points or outlines the teacher writes on the blackboard. Keep any handouts your teacher provides.

2. Keep your notes for each subject separate and in a safe place.

3. Make certain your notes are readable and accurate. Dating and numbering pages will assist you when reviewing for tests and may also indicate if any note is missing.

4. When making notes from texts and library books, use chapter headings and summaries to help you organize your points. Record material in your own words as much as possible so that your notes will be meaningful to you later.

5. Organize and review your notes the same day you write them rather than waiting for several days. Use titles, underlining, color coding, highlighting and marginal notes to emphasize important points.

6. Review your notes on a regular basis.

7. Look at the way you take notes and decide if you can improve your methods. Speak to your teacher or guidance counsellor if you require assistance.

MAKING A STUDY SCHEDULE

A study schedule is a calendar, chart or table which sets out specific tasks to be completed at specific times on specific dates.

1. Plan to use a regular and realistic amount of time each school night for home study.

2. Apportion time each evening to do the following:
   a) daily homework assignments;
   b) special class assignments such as projects and essays;
   c) review for tests and examinations.

3. Make certain you allow sufficient time to review each subject at least once a week.

4. Record the times and dates of *all* class assignments, tests and examinations. When absent, arrange for a reliable friend to do this for you.

5. Understand fully what is involved in completing assignments *before* you leave the classroom.

BEFORE BEGINNING TO STUDY

1. Select an uncluttered area with good lighting, comfortable seating and as few distractions as possible. If this is not possible at home, try the library.

2. Have all books, notebooks and writing materials available.

3. Establish a regular time to study and resist the temptation to do something else.

4. Keep a dictionary handy.

5. Make a daily list of assignments and due dates.

6. Keep all handouts in a notebook. Date each page and use the handouts like a textbook.

7. Set a work limit with short breaks.

8. Organize the various study tasks in the order you prefer.

9. Remember that study includes both review of class notes and completion of assignments.

STUDYING FOR TESTS AND EXAMINATIONS

1. At least two weeks before a major test or examination, draw up a study schedule. Divide the course material into sections and indicate on your schedule the nights you plan to review each section.

2. Know the scope of the test or examination. Find out exactly what material you are responsible for covering.

3. Find out what kinds of questions will be asked. Know how to answer each type of question, including essay-style, multiple-choice, matching and short-response.

4. Learn the meaning of key words in questions, including compare, discuss, describe, illustrate, define, summarize and criticize.

5. Listen carefully for hints the teacher may offer about the content of questions and sections that may be emphasized.

6. Develop possible questions. Old test and examination questions, if available, and questions at the end of chapters in textbooks may be of assistance. For essay-style questions, write out organized outlines of possible answers.

7. Have your textbook and notebook in front of you. Divide your task into short segments. Read the section in the textbook and then your notes on the same section. If there is an important point in the textbook that is not in your notebook, include it in your notes.

8. Make summaries and point form outlines, especially when you are covering a lot of material. Do not just read and re-read.

9. Make review sheets or cards for important points, definitions and names.

10. Use memory aids, including the following, to help you learn your notebook material:
    a) visual aids, such as color coding, underlining, highlighting, jotting keywords in margins;
    b) numbering points to be memorized;
    c) grouping, word associations, and idea associations;
    d) reading aloud key words. Express these in your own words. If possible, use a tape recorder.

11. Using your marginal notes as a prompt, cover the content to be learned and recite or write out the key words and ideas.

12. Re-do parts of previously assigned homework or classroom questions to see if you can still do them.

13. Re-read previously marked assignments, taking particular note of the teacher's comments.

14. Test your self after studying and reward yourself if you were successful in remembering.

15. Identify your trouble spots and spend extra time on those areas.

16. Request, as early as possible, assistance from the teacher on any difficulties you encounter.

17. Get a good night's sleep before the test or examination.

Homework and Assignment Chart

Subject	Assignment (Details)	Date Due	Done (Check)
Math	pp. 34, 35 questions 3, 5, 7, 9	Oct. 25	
English	Romeo & Juliet — read Act II	Oct. 25	
Geography	Complete map of Canada showing patterns of precipitation Refer to example in text p. 72	Oct. 25	

Weekly Study Schedule Chart

TIME TO BE SPENT ON:	Monday	Tuesday	Wednesday	Thursday	Friday	Saturday	Sunday
Daily Homework							
Weekly Review							
Test Preparation							
Project/Essays							

Calendar for Tests, Examinations and Special Class Assignments

Month _____, 19 ___

Monday	Tuesday	Wednesday	Thursday	Friday	Saturday	Sunday

A Variety of
Approaches to Evaluation

Introduction

This section of the document has two principal objectives:

1. to encourage use of the widest possible *variety* in the ways in which we evaluate our students;

2. to improve the *quality* of our *use* of each of the ways in which we evaluate our students.

It should be understood that not all of the ways of evaluating students examined in this section are appropriate for all grades. In evaluating young children, for example, teacher observation, informal testing, and cumulative records of children's work are most appropriate. Of course, these evaluation activities are appropriate for older students as well.

It is important to note that certain objectives of a program are easily assessed by some methods of evaluation while others require totally different approaches. For example, the evaluation of a student's ability to "develop insights" or "discuss with peers" may require the use of an essay or seminar presentation, whereas the assessment of a student's writing may best be accomplished by an examination of the student's writing folder, the use of checklists, and student self- and peer evaluation. Although there are no specific sections devoted to either self- or peer evaluation, suggestions regarding these important forms of evaluation recur frequently throughout this document.

When one considers the range of skills, interests, abilities and levels of achievement to be evaluated throughout the year, and the fact that all three domains must be taken into account, it is reasonable to conclude that no single procedure can possibly be used to evaluate everything. Teachers must make decisions about what should be evaluated and which strategies are appropriate. A variety of evaluation techniques should be used in every course or program to provide a balanced, flexible and effective plan for evaluating student achievement.

As decisions are reached about types of evaluation strategies, their purposes, and the frequency of evaluation, teachers should also consider the kinds of modifications necessary to meet the needs of exceptional students and the different approaches necessary to meet the needs of students with different levels of ability. Specific suggestions in this regard are given on pages 203-225 and 227-257.

This section discusses a number of approaches to student evaluation in some detail. These are:

> Observation
> Projects
> Tests and examinations
> Essay-style questions
> Essays
> Objective-style questions
> Diagnostic techniques

This is not an exhaustive survey of all the evaluation approaches a teacher can use. However, the list includes those procedures most commonly used by classroom teachers. There are other approaches, not dealt with in this document, which are suitable for classroom use. These include:

Oral presentations of various types
Pre-tests and post-tests
Dictations
Contracts
Field trips
Reports (film, book, business)

Although this document does not directly address these methods, it contains some useful material on them. For example, much of the material on essays could be suitable when considering and evaluating book, film and business reports.

Observation

Introduction

Observation is an integral part of an evaluation program for all students in all grades. It is the evaluation of a student's mental, physical or social activity while performing some educational activity. Observation is not only the evaluation of a finished product or a skill. Its most important aspect is the evaluation of the student's performance during the creation of the product or the performance of the skill. The emphasis should be on both the degree to which the activity is successfully completed and the identification of physical, psychological and social factors which help or hinder the acquisition of skill or appreciation. Observation should provide the teacher with clues for individual assistance and encouragement.

Teachers should avoid thinking in terms of skill alone when observing students. In addition to skills, they should place sufficient emphasis on the psychological, emotional and cultural factors which may be involved.

Up to Grade 3 or Grade 4, observation is the most important evaluation procedure; it remains an essential component in all subsequent grades.

Advantages and Disadvantages of Observation

Advantages	Disadvantages
• It helps the teacher to get to know the student as an individual person.	• It may become too imprecise and "subjective" if not carefully tied to specific criteria.
• It gives information other evaluation activities may not provide.	• It may be difficult to communicate the results of observation to the student and parents when the teacher is trying to be objective about an evaluation which is essentially subjective.
• It takes into account evaluation of certain aspects of student performance or behavior which cannot be measured using many other evaluation techniques, such as tests or examinations.	• It can be difficult to translate what was observed into a mark or grade.

Tips on Using Observation as a Method of Evaluation

- Base observation upon knowledge of the intellectual, physical, emotional and social development of the student. (See section on stages of development, pages 35-42.

- Develop a realistic plan which will concentrate on a small number of students for a given period of time.

- Have specific criteria in mind when using observation as an evaluation technique.

- Focus on one or two criteria and on a small number of students for a specific period of time.

- Where feasible, tape-record or videotape student activities.

- Make notes or keep informal records of what has been observed.

- Regularly discuss with the student those aspects of the student's performance which are observed and which will help the student develop or improve his or her performance or self-image.

- Develop a checklist to help you concentrate on the things you wish to observe.

Guideposts for the Construction of Observational Checklists

When evaluating students through observation, a record must be made, either while the observation is being conducted, or as soon as possible thereafter. The simplest and most effective means of recording these observations is the checklist.

There are various kinds of observational checklists. These include:

- a "yes-no" checklist, which records whether a specific action has been completed or a particular quality is present;

- a tally, in which the frequency of an action is observed and recorded;

- a numerical rating scale, in which a judgment is made on the degree or quality of an action or product;

- an anecdotal record in which a very brief comment is recorded to describe an observed action or characteristic.

When constructing observational checklists, the following points should be remembered.:

- The checklists should be based on the objectives for the course, unit or lesson.

- Each item should be clear and precise.

- Each item should avoid generalities and focus on specifics.

- Checklists should be designed so that they can be used as a basis for a discussion by the teacher with a student or parent. Therefore, they should be written in such a way that they can be readily understood by a student or parent.

- When checklists are developed in such a way that students can understand them, they may be used for self- and peer evaluation.

- Design a short checklist so that the observer can focus on a few specifics, or develop a longer checklist from which a few items can be selected for attention during a particular observation period.

- Checklists can be designed either for a single evaluation or a cumulative record.

Observational checklists can be used as the basis for diagnostic, formative and / or summative evaluation. One of the most important uses of observational checklists is as a basis for anecdotal comments.

Parents and students often cannot understand the purpose of anecdotal comments. The meaning of anecdotal comments should become more apparent if those comments are based on the teacher's interpretation of observations recorded in class on checklists.

Examples of Observation Techniques and of Methods of Recording Observations

Included in this section are some examples of observation techniques and recording methods which can be adapted or expanded by teachers for their personal use in evaluating student progress. These selected examples do not cover all subjects and grades other than those for which they were specifically designed. The examples are accompanied by an explanation of their intended use.

The following chart suggests the grades in which the observational activities described in this section could be used.

	K-GR.3	GR.4-6	GR.7-9	GR.10-12
Informal Print Experiences	X			
Dictated Material: Using the Child's Own Language	X			
Trade Books	X	X	X	
Record Sheet — Reading Strategies	X	X	X	
Assisted Reading	X			
Evaluation of Children at Play	X			
Individual Student Mathematics Record	X	X	X	
Evaluating Oral Language	X	X	X	X

(continued)

	K-GR.3	GR.4-6	GR.7-9	GR.10-12
Observation in Physical and Health Education	X	X	X	X
Observation in Dramatic Arts			X	X
Observational Checklist for Visual Arts		X	X	X
Observational Checklist for Evaluation of Affective Aspects of Job Performance in Technical Subjects				X
Observational Checklist for Evaluation in Service-Oriented Shops or Classrooms			X	X
Observational Checklist for Class or Small Group Discussions		X	X	X
Rating Scale for Evaluating Laboratory Work			X	X
Using Observational Checklists to Evaluate Practical Demonstrations			X	X

INFORMAL PRINT EXPERIENCES

Example 1

Informal print experiences are based upon real experiences and concrete material. These help students become aware of the meaningful purpose of print. Informal print experiences should be a large part of the Kindergarten reading program, and should continue to be included throughout Grades 1 and 2.

This chart can be used for the teacher's evaluation of activities occurring prior to the introduction of a formal reading program for the child. The information may be used for anecdotal comments or as a basis for interviews with parents.

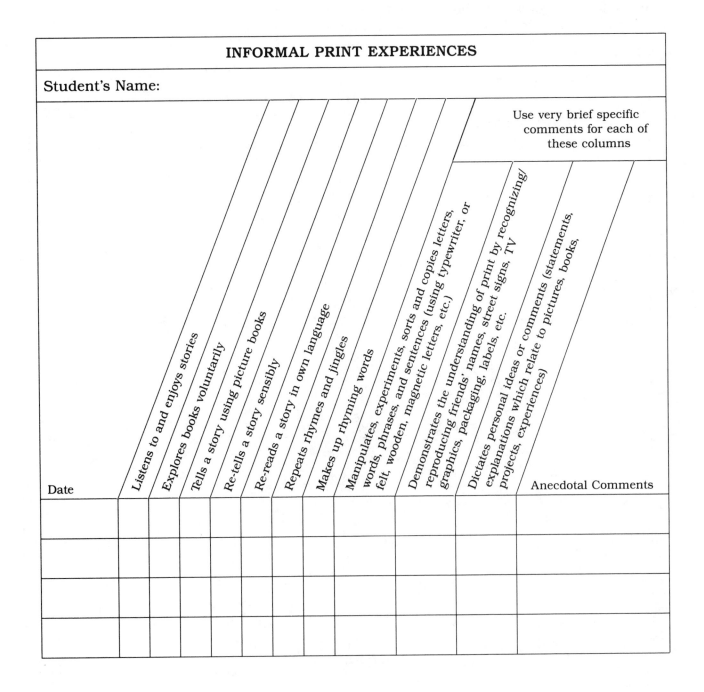

INFORMAL PRINT EXPERIENCES

Student's Name:

Use very brief specific comments for each of these columns

Columns (left to right):
- Listens to and enjoys stories
- Explores books voluntarily
- Tells a story using picture books
- Re-tells a story sensibly
- Re-reads a story in own language
- Repeats rhymes and jingles
- Makes up rhyming words
- Manipulates, experiments, sorts and copies letters, words, phrases, and sentences (using typewriter, or felt, wooden, magnetic letters, etc.)
- Demonstrates the understanding of print by recognizing/reproducing friends' names, street signs, TV graphics, packaging, labels, etc.
- Dictates personal ideas or comments (statements, explanations which relate to pictures, books, projects, experiences)
- Anecdotal Comments

Date

Example 2

DICTATED MATERIAL: USING THE CHILD'S OWN LANGUAGE

Some children learn to read informally through their many print experiences. Others need systematic reading instruction. There may be a few students in Kindergarten, most students some time in their Grade 1 year, and a few students in Grade 2, who will use dictated material and personal word banks for reading instruction. For those students who require systematic reading instruction in order to learn to read, the use of the child's own language is recommended.

This chart can be used to evaluate the child's progress in the early stages of the formal beginning reading program. This information may be used as the basis for anecdotal comments or for interviews with parents.

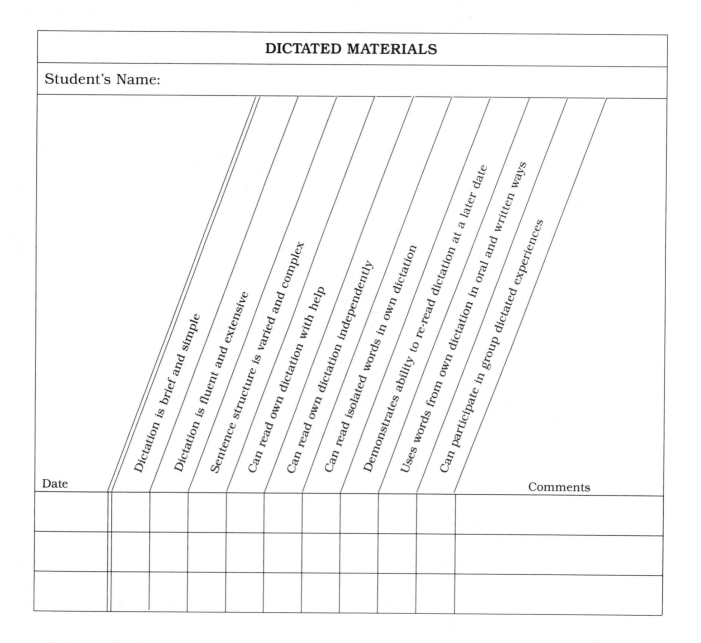

DICTATED MATERIALS

Student's Name:

Column headings (diagonal):
- Dictation is brief and simple
- Dictation is fluent and extensive
- Sentence structure is varied and complex
- Can read own dictation with help
- Can read own dictation independently
- Can read isolated words in own dictation
- Demonstrates ability to re-read dictation at a later date
- Uses words from own dictation in oral and written ways
- Can participate in group dictated experiences

Date | Comments

TRADE BOOKS

A "trade book" is any book which is not used as a textbook in a formal instructional manner. It could be a picture book, an anthology of verse, a children's classic, a storybook, or any book in which a child or small group of students read informally. (This definition does not preclude using the "trade books" for specific instructional purposes from time to time.)

Teachers can introduce children to trade books by reading aloud to them, or by showing them pictures individually, in small groups or as a class.

These records, originally designed for Grades 1, 2 and 3, may be adapted for use in the later grades. They are used as one part of the evaluation of student progress in reading. The information may be used for anecdotal comments or as a basis for interviews with parents.

Example 3a

TRADE BOOK RECORD

Student's Name: *Samantha Rego*

Date	Book	Comments	Signed
Sept. 29	*See Me*	Comment for the Student: *You read this book very well. Good for you, Sam!* Comment for the Teacher: *Helped her with some words: swings, climb, slide*	

Example 3b

THE TRADE BOOKS

Student's Name:

Date	Selects books with to look at simple repetitive language	Reads books with simple repetitive language	Selects picture books to look at with simple plots and characters	Reads picture books with simple plots and characters with understanding	Reads picture books with complex plots and characters with understanding	Selects books on a variety of subjects	Reads books on a variety of subjects with understanding	Chooses to read often	Shares books with others	Comments

Example 4

RECORD SHEET — READING STRATEGIES

This chart applies, with appropriate adaptations, to any subject in elementary or secondary school in which reading is a component of the program. It is an evaluation of the student's developing skills in reading. This information may be used for diagnostic, reporting or interview purposes.

		Word Comprehension							Word Recognition				
		Retells a story with sufficient detail	Able to predict	Able to set purposes	Can locate proof	Recalls ideas	Makes inferences	Able to justify thinking	Reads fluently	Self-corrects	Uses context clues	Uses phonic skills	Applies structural analysis skills
Date	Book												

RECORD SHEET — READING STRATEGIES

Student's Name: _____

Comments:

Example 5

ASSISTED READING

Assisted Reading is a technique used in Grades 1, 2 and 3. The following is a chart that teachers may use to record their observations of students with whom this technique is being used. Under each section, check marks can be used to indicate success, or anecdotal comments can be made. This information may be used for diagnostic, reporting or interview purposes.

RECORD CHART — ASSISTED READING							
Student's Name and Date	Can make logical predictions	Attends to print while teacher is reading	If requested, can point to words as teacher or child reads	Can locate some individual words in the stories	Uses context clues	Uses self-correction strategies	Has read the story to others several times
Bill Sept. 16	While being read to.	Most of the time	✓				
Nancy Sept 16	✓	✓	✓	Quite a few.			
John Sept 20	Some-times	If the story interests him	Some-times				

EVALUATION OF CHILDREN AT PLAY

The following charts provide samples teachers may use to record their observations of various aspects of play and children at play. Remember that these checklists are valid only if used several times for each student. These charts should be used only in conjunction with other records.

These charts can be used for diagnostic, reporting or interview purposes in Grades 1, 2 and 3.

Example 6a

RECORD CHART — CATEGORIES OF PLAY AND SOCIAL INTERACTION					
Student's Name _____ Birthdate _____					
Practice Play					
Symbolic Play					
Dramatic/ Fantasy Play					
Games with Rules Play					

RECORD CHART — FREQUENCY OF CHOICE OF PLAY

Week of _____	Frequency of Choice of Play		
Names of Students	Structured (Number of Times Observed)	Semi-Structured (Number of Times Observed)	Unstructured (Number of Times Observed)

RECORD CHART — CHOICE OF PLAY

Week of _____	Choices of Play																						
Names of Students	Home Center	Big Blocks	Small Blocks	Wet Sand	Dry Sand	Water Play	Handwork	Classroom Resource Center	Picture Book Story	Easy-to-Read Book	Record Player	Tape Recorder	Typewriter	Writing Center	Construction Toys	Puzzles	Stacking/Nesting Toys	Mathematics	Shape	Science	Music	Felt Board	Games	Other

Example 7

INDIVIDUAL STUDENT MATHEMATICS RECORD

The core objectives for a year's work in mathematics can be set forth as an observational checklist or record. Such a checklist or record could be used several times during the school year to assess student progress. The example below has been designed for Grade 2,[8] but similar checklists or records could be developed for any grade. The information collected can be used for diagnostic, reporting or interview purposes.

INDIVIDUAL STUDENT MATHEMATICS RECORD — GRADE 2

Problem Solving Assessment   *Comment and Date*

Perseverance
— Does the student "stick with it"?   _____

Confidence
— Is the student anxious or confident?   _____

Willingness
— Does the student accept new challenges?   _____

Breadth
— Has the student worked at a variety of problems utilizing different skills and
strategies?   _____

Depth
— Does the student show great insight?   _____

Creativity
— Is the student able to create new
problems?   _____

1. ARITHMETIC

(a) Counting
     By ones and by twos   _____
     By fives and by tens   _____
     By hundreds   _____
     By using the words "first" to "tenth"   _____

(b) Place Value
     Counting by tens starting
     at any number   _____
     Grouping a set into tens and ones   _____
     Arranging 2 or 3 two-digit
     numbers in order   _____

(continued)

(c) Addition and Subtraction

    Facts 5 + 5 and 10 − 5

    Concept of one more or one less than a two-digit number

    Facts to 9 + 9 and 18 − 9

    Using concrete materials to add or subtract 2 two-digit numbers *without* regrouping

    Using concrete materials to add or subtract 2 two-digit numbers *with* regrouping

    Addition of two or more addends in a column or row

(d) Multiplication and Division

    Concept of multiplication as an array or repeated addition

    Concept of division as sharing or as repeated subtraction

(e) Fractions and Decimals

    Concept of a fraction with a numerator of one including $1/10$

2. MEASUREMENT AND GRAPHING

(a) Using an appropriate vocabulary for different attributes

(b) Ability to conserve

    length

    mass

    capacity / volume

(c) Estimating and finding the number of non-standard units for

    length

    area

    capacity / volume

    mass

(d) Using an appropriate vocabulary of comparative terms

(e) Classifying data

(continued)

(f) Arranging 3 objects in order by
    length
    area
    capacity / volume
    mass

(g) Comparing the length of an object to a standard unit
    metre (m) / foot (ft)
    centimetre (cm) / inch (in)
    litre (L) / gallon (gal)
    kilogram (kg) / pound (lb)

(h) Using pictures to make a graph

(i) Estimating and measuring appropriate lengths
    in metres / feet
    in centimetres / inches

(j) Making relationships among the coins 1¢, 5¢, 10¢ and 25¢

(k) Making change from 25¢ or less

(l) Associating a time with different experiences

(m) Arranging events in order of time duration

(n) Understanding and telling time

3. GEOMETRY

(a) Sorting objects and explaining the rule

(b) Building with blocks, cubes and other solids

(c) Developing a vocabulary which describes and compares positions in space

(d) Making models of solids with appropriate materials

(continued)

(e) Identifying the real world objects which resemble geometric solids

_____

(f) Tracing faces of solids and identifying those faces which are the same

_____

(g) Making congruent figures

_____

(h) Identifying objects which are

the same size and shape

_____

the same shape but different size

_____

similar size but different shape

_____

(i) Making and continuing patterns

_____

(j) Tiling a surface with repetitions of a shape

_____

(k) Filling a space by stacking solids

_____

(l) Sorting and naming plane shapes

_____

Example 8

EVALUATING ORAL LANGUAGE — ALL GRADES

Introduction

Students in all grades and subjects need opportunities to use language in a variety of ways to encourage them to express ideas and feelings and to think more clearly. Teachers monitoring their students' oral language should take care not to mistake quantity for quality. Students who talk a lot are not necessarily communicating well.

The following language model was developed by Joan Tough to help teachers evaluate the purpose of students' language.[9] The model uses seven categories and is valuable for students from elementary through secondary school.

The categories are:

> Self-maintaining
> Directing
> Reporting on present and past experiences
> Logical reasoning
> Predicting
> Projecting
> Imagining

Most children begin school able to use language in ways falling under the first three categories, though many will not have had much occasion to develop an extensive capacity for "reporting past experiences." However, it is precisely these last four and one-half categories which will be the foundation for a student's school career. "Reporting past experiences," "logical reasoning," "predicting," "projecting" and "imagining" are all essential to reading and writing, to learning and appreciating literature, science, history, geography and mathematics. Students who cannot learn to use language effectively in ways described by all seven categories have little chance of educational success. If a child has not acquired some facility in all categories by the end of Grade 3, he or she will have serious difficulty ever developing the modes of thinking necessary to learning, thinking and appreciating.

Teachers, especially those who teach children in the first four or five years of school, should listen to children talking, either in informal settings such as play, or in teacher-directed situations such as a discussion of a story or picture. The teacher should concentrate on two or three students at a time and evaluate whether or not the students are using the seven categories. Observations of a particular child should be repeated at various times. When observing, teachers should be aware that just because a child predicts once or twice, it does not mean that the child has facility with prediction.

A Model of the Use of Oral Language

The following model, adapted from Ms Tough's monograph, identifies the seven categories of oral language. Within each category several criteria are listed so that the teacher may identify what kind of language the student is using.[10]

Self-Maintaining

This category allows an individual to maintain his or her own identity in society. It is typified by such statements as, "Watch me; watch what I can do," and "I'm hitting him because he spoiled my picture."

Statements in this category:

- Refer to physical and psychological needs and wants;
- Protect the self and self-interests;
- Justify behavior or claims;
- Criticize others;
- Threaten others.

Directing

This category has two aspects: the first is directing the actions of oneself; the second is directing the actions of others. An example of the first is, "I have to move the gearshift now." An example of the second is, "Take that box and put it over there."

Statements in this category:

- Monitor own actions;
- Direct the actions of the self;
- Direct the actions of others;
- Collaborate with action with others.

Reporting on Present and Past Experiences

This category also has two distinct functions: it reports on both present and past experiences. Most students can report on present experiences, but may have difficulty reporting past ones. This latter activity is necessary for success in most learning activities.

Statements in this category:

- Label the components of the scene;
- Refer to detail (for example, size, color and other attributes);
- Refer to incidents;
- Refer to the sequence of events;
- Make comparisons;
- Recognize related aspects;
- Make an analysis using several of the features above;
- Extract or recognize the central meaning;
- Reflect on the meaning of experiences, including own feelings.

Logical Reasoning

Up to about Grade 9, students will be moving toward the ability to reason logically. However, by the end of secondary school, students should be using logical reasoning for the most part.

Statements in this category:

- Explain a process;
- Recognize causal and dependent relationships;
- Recognize problems and their solutions;
- Justify judgments and actions;
- Reflect on events and draw conclusions;
- Recognize principles.

Predicting

Statements in this category:

- Anticipate and forecast events;
- Anticipate the detail of events;
- Anticipate a sequence of events;
- Anticipate problems and possible solutions;
- Anticipate and recognize alternative courses of action;
- Predict the consequences of actions or events.

Projecting

This category indicates the ability to sympathize or empathize with other people, situations or things.

Statements in this category:

- Project into the experience of others;
- Project into the feelings of others;
- Project into the reactions of others;
- Project into situations never experienced.

Imagining

This category can be an aspect of any of the other six categories as well as being one on its own.

Statements in this category:

- Develop an imaginary situation based on real life;
- Develop an imaginary situation based on fantasy;
- Develop an original story.

Record Chart — Observation of Oral Language

The preceding model of the use of oral language can be used to design an observational record chart to evaluate a student's development in the use of oral language. The following sample is an illustration of how the model can be used to construct such a record chart. The information collected on the record chart can be used for diagnostic, reporting or interview purposes. The teacher should be continually aware of all students' use of oral language, but only some students in the class may need detailed monitoring recorded on such a chart.

OBSERVATION RECORD CHART: ORAL LANGUAGE		
Student's Name: *Hilary Little*	Grade: *9 - General Level*	
Category	**Anecdotal Comment**	**Date**
Self-Maintaining	*Continually threatens others*	*Sept 26*
	Fewer threats.	*Dec 4*
Directing	*Always directing others*	*Sept 26*
	Beginning to collaborate	*Feb 16*
Imagining		

Example 9

OBSERVATION IN PHYSICAL AND HEALTH EDUCATION

Observation is a significant approach to evaluation in Physical and Health Education. Teachers in all grades have an obligation to record and communicate their observations to students and parents in a concise and meaningful way. It is important that teachers understand, when evaluating skills in the psychomotor domain, that a student can learn to perform a movement in a continuum from basic to progressively complex patterns. Thus, a teacher should be aware of the range of possibilities within a particular movement skill. Such a range of possibilities is outlined below in the example of bouncing a ball where the movement progresses from the simple to the complex. This range of possibilities does not refer to the social and intellectual learnings that would be developing simultaneously while the student is doing this activity. A similar range of possibilities exists for other movement skills such as running, jumping and kicking.

The example which follows illustrates a continuum of bouncing activities based on objective criteria for observing and reporting the student's progress related to the skill of bouncing. It is not intended that the teacher comment on each criterion, but rather report on the student's progress within a range of the continuum. For example, a student could attain some success within each of the divisions of the continuum without attaining true competence in the more complicated activities within one or more of the divisions.

Evaluation Through Observation of the Development of a Physical Skill — Bouncing a Ball

Note: The structure of this chart is not intended to convey any particular grade expectations.

When observing any physical activity, the teacher should begin by observing individual experimentation in order to determine where the student is at in the continuum.

— bounce and catch freely

— bounce and catch:
  • with one hand
  • with other hand
  • with alternate hands

— bounce continuously

— do all of the above on the spot (personal space)

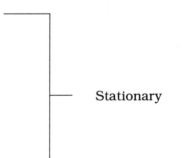

Stationary

— do all of the above on the move (general space)

— bounce the ball:
  - with the body in different positions, for example, kneeling, assuming different positions of balance
  - at different speeds on the spot (personal space)
  - at different speeds on the move (general space)
  - at varying levels
  - in different directions
  - around / through / over body parts
  - with different body parts

  - making a sequence *based* on *one* of the above, for example, students bounce the ball in different directions — forward ⟶ sideways ⟶ backward

  - making a sequence *involving more* than one of the above, for example, directions and speeds
  - combined with other ball-handling skills of throwing, catching, rolling
  - combined with other locomotor activities, for example, hopping, jumping, running
  - with a partner
  - with a small group
  - with a piece of equipment, for example, a paddleball racquet
  - in / at / through / over a target

— create a game using the skill of bouncing (Working with a partner or small group and creating a game may occur anywhere along the continuum, but creating a complex game is a high level skill.)

In Motion

In Combinations

Example 10

OBSERVATION IN DRAMATIC ARTS

The following suggested categories can be used by teachers to develop a checklist or anecdotal record to use while observing and evaluating a dramatic presentation. The information collected from these observations can be used for diagnostic, reporting or interview purposes.

Student's Name _____

Student's Grade _____

Date _____

Dramatic Presentation _____

Vocal Performance
— projected with character nuances
— projected with characterization
— audible
— moments of inaudibility
— inaudible

Physical Performance
— natural assumption of character movement
— believable and thoughtful work
— some believable attempts at physical character
— audience too aware of the actor working
— no attempt to find physical reality

Characterization
— moving performance
— convincing performance
— solid performance
— awareness of actor
— unbelievable

Communication With Other Actors
— intimate communication — listens with sensitivity
— a good positive relationship
— co-operative attempt
— not an honest attempt or too strong an individual effort
— a disruptive influence on the group

Degree of Performance Responsibilities
— assumed more than required responsibilities
— added a positive energy to group effort
— fulfilled required responsibilities
— occasionally let the group down

Example 11

OBSERVATION IN VISUAL ARTS

Observation is one of the most effective techniques for evaluating student progress in visual arts. In addition to evaluating the product, the teacher can also record the student's attitude and awareness as they are demonstrated throughout the process of creation.

The following criteria, along with others indicated by a specific guideline or course of study, can form the basis for an anecdotal evaluation for students beyond Grade 3.

Attitude
— shows originality
— respects own work
— is easily motivated
— enjoys using a wide range of materials and techniques
— concentrates on the project at hand
— completes projects within a reasonable time
— works well with others
— accepts suggestions and evaluates whether or not they will be put into use
— possesses confidence in own ability
— is willing to share work and opinions with others
— respects the work and opinions of others

Awareness
— is visually aware
— is developing an awareness of the elements and principles of design in the natural environment
— is critically aware of the designed environment
— is respectful of environments whether natural or made by people
— understands and accepts the individual's role and responsibility in an environment

Process
— regards unsuccessful attempts as a learning experience
— shows initiative in finding and implementing ideas
— evaluates own work constructively
— applies new learning to the project at hand
— draws on previous learning and applies it to the present project
— works with concentration
— is capable of accepting the unforseen as part of the expressive act
— strives for a higher level of achievement
— works in a methodical manner
— shows originality and imagination
— takes the assigned project and develops it into a personal expression
— uses the elements and principles of design in an effective manner
— is aware when the project is complete

Product

— produces an art form which is of a quality equal to his or her best ability

— incorporates the new skills that have been taught

— respects own work and can discuss it critically and honestly

— regards the work as a springboard to the next part of a sequence of learning

— is proud to share work with others

— sees work as part of the total classroom experience

— sees the study of the work of others as an opportunity to extend knowledge

Example 12

OBSERVATIONAL CHECKLIST FOR EVALUATION OF AFFECTIVE ASPECTS OF JOB PERFORMANCE IN TECHNICAL SUBJECTS

Cognitive skills and psychomotor skills are often much easier to evaluate than skills in the affective domain. However, students should know about their development in the affective domain as well as in the other two domains. For example, it is important for teachers and / or employers of students preparing for the workforce to convey to these students their perceptions of the students' attitudes and values.

In many shops and classrooms, students are assigned jobs where they either work by themselves or as part of a group, and which require that they be evaluated in the affective domain. The following observational checklist is a sample form for such an evaluation.

Evaluation of Affective Aspects of Job Performance	Good	Average	Needs Improvement
Job Attitude			
• is enthusiastic			
• is willing to work and co-operate			
• desires to improve			
• is a good team worker			
• is concerned with the safety of others			
Initiative			
• is able to work without supervision			
• is aware of jobs to be done and does them without being told			
Dependability			
• is trustworthy			
• follows directions			
• is prompt			
• is consistent in attendance			
• meets obligations			

(continued)

Evaluation of Affective Aspects of Job Performance	Good	Average	Needs Improvement
Accepts Suggestions			
• is eager to improve			
• seeks assistance			
• follows through			
Adaptability			
• learns routines quickly			
• can move to, and adapt to, a new task easily			
• follows detailed instructions well			
Ability to Get Along			
• is co-operative			
• is well-mannered			
• is even-tempered			
• gets along well with others			

Example 13

OBSERVATIONAL CHECKLIST FOR EVALUATION IN SERVICE-ORIENTED SHOPS OR CLASSROOMS

In some service-oriented shops or classroom situations (for example, food preparation, hairdressing, cosmetology, repair shop) tasks are frequently assigned for which observational checklists may be used.

Although the following is a specific example of a checklist for a Grade 9 or 10 food preparation class, it may be adapted for any other service-oriented shop or class. The first column lists the tasks the student is expected to perform in a given period of time. The other columns provide the teacher with an opportunity to evaluate the process and product, provide the student with immediate feedback and provide the teacher with an anecdotal record which will be part of the student's mark or grade.

FOOD PREPARATION — GRADE 9 OR 10

Student Name _____

Evaluation Period From _____ To _____

Assigned Tasks	Understands the Task			Quality of Work			Efficiency			Comments or Suggestions for Improvement
	Yes	?	No	Fair	Good	Ex-cel-lent	Fair	Good	Ex-cel-lent	
Make the sauce for lasagna										
Clean the pots and pans										
Serve three tables in the dining room										

Example 14

OBSERVATIONAL CHECKLIST FOR CLASS OR SMALL GROUP DISCUSSIONS

The following checklist provides the teacher with a suggested method of recording his or her observations of students in a small group or class discussion. The information collected can be used for diagnostic, reporting or interview purposes.

OBSERVATIONAL CHECKLIST FOR CLASS OR SMALL GROUP DISCUSSIONS									

Code:
  A = Always
  B = Sometimes
  N = Never
 	
Date _____
 	
Student's Name
	Volunteers information or ideas	Contributes information or ideas when called upon to do so	Shows willingness to have ideas questioned	Questions the ideas of others	Modifies views when faced with new or conflicting evidence	Considers facts before reaching conclusions	Shows respect for ideas of others	Supports ideas and observations with facts or details	Listens to others' views without interrupting

Example 15

RATING SCALE FOR EVALUATING LABORATORY WORK

Rating scales are similar to checklists except that they also include a measure of the *quality* of the performance. The scale below could be used when observing and rating a student's performance in a laboratory setting. Consideration should be given to students' finished experiments, projects or laboratory reports, as well as to the performance. The information collected can be used for diagnostic, reporting or interview purposes.

RATING SCALE FOR EVALUATING LABORATORY WORK

Student Name _____

Date _____

	Poor				Excellent
A. Demonstrates understanding of the problem to be investigated	1	2	3	4	5
B. Follows directions carefully (or adequately designs steps to follow)	1	2	3	4	5
C. Uses appropriate equipment and materials	1	2	3	4	5
D. Uses equipment efficiently and accurately	1	2	3	4	5
E. Observes adequate safety precautions	1	2	3	4	5
F. Records data systematically	1	2	3	4	5
G. Formulates conclusions based on data	1	2	3	4	5
H. Cites limitations and/or assumptions involved in the experiment	1	2	3	4	5
I. Follows proper clean-up procedures	1	2	3	4	5

USING OBSERVATIONAL CHECKLISTS TO EVALUATE PRACTICAL DEMONSTRATIONS

One of the situations in which observation is of utmost importance is in practical demonstrations. Practical demonstrations are frequently used as a teaching technique. For example, after a demonstration by the teacher, a student or group of students can be asked to demonstrate a procedure, technique or skill. The intent is to help the rest of the students learn how to perform the particular skill. However, practical demonstrations can also be used for evaluation purposes in a variety of subjects. Examples include:

- bell ringer tests in the science laboratory;

- sculpting in the art class;

- demonstration of the correct sequence of steps for a particular skill in a technical subject;

- a "study" in theatre arts;

- a routine in physical education;

- a performance test in music;

- a dialogue presentation in French.

In each case it is likely that the method of evaluation will be based on observation using a checklist. The following are samples of the development of observational checklists for evaluating a student's practical demonstration of a performance skill in technical subjects. This evaluation procedure is used most effectively when the skill to be demonstrated can be divided into a series of clearly defined, specific, observable steps or actions.

In developing this kind of checklist, the following procedure should be employed:

1. Determine and clearly indicate each specific step or action expected in the performance of the task;

2. Include in the checklist mistakes commonly made by students, provided they are helpful to the evaluation and not too numerous;

3. List the actions or steps, including the mistakes, if appropriate, in the expected sequence.

ELECTRICITY — GRADE 11 OR 12

Checklist for a house-wiring project involving one light fixture controlled by two 3-way switches using non-metallic sheathed cable.

Directions
A check in the appropriate box indicates that the student has met the objectives involved in this project.

	YES	NO
1. All switch boxes are mounted at the correct height.	☐	☐
2. The correct length of conductor is left in each outlet box.	☐	☐
3. All terminal screw connections meet code specifications.	☐	☐
4. Cables are properly mounted on studs and joists.	☐	☐
5. All solderless connectors used to join conductors are secure and of the correct type.	☐	☐
6. The neutral conductors are connected to observe correct polarity on light fixtures.	☐	☐
7. The correct color code has been observed in making connections.	☐	☐
8. Proper grounding procedures have been used.	☐	☐
9. All cables are fastened with approved straps according to code specifications.	☐	☐
10. The project, when connected to the power supply, operates satisfactorily.	☐	☐

ELECTRONICS — GRADE 11 OR 12

In the following example, the teacher is evaluating a printed circuit board amplifier containing an integrated circuit. The board has been made by the "photo-etch" method.

CONSTRUCTION OF A PRINTED CIRCUIT BOARD INTERCOM SYSTEM

	YES	NO
1. Has the negative been placed in a straight position on the board?	☐	☐
2. Are the conductors parallel to the edges of the board?	☐	☐
3. Has the etching process been done correctly?	☐	☐
4. Is there "undercutting" indicating too much etching?	☐	☐
5. Has the correct size of drill bit been used for component leads?	☐	☐
6. Have component leads been bent at 90° angles prior to being mounted on the board?	☐	☐
7. Are components in their correct locations on the board?	☐	☐
8. For components needing correct polarity, has this requirement been observed?	☐	☐
9. Have component leads been trimmed to the correct length on the underside of the board?	☐	☐
10. Has soldering been done correctly:		
• Have any conductors lifted due to overheating?	☐	☐
• Are there any "cold solder" joints indicating inadequate heating?	☐	☐
• Has too much solder been used?	☐	☐
11. When the amplifier is connected for testing, does it work?	☐	☐

DRAFTING — GRADES 9-12

EVALUATION OF A DRAWING IN A DRAFTING CLASS

STUDENT NAME _____

DRAWING _____

DATE _____

Rating Scale
1 — poor
2 — fair
3 — good
4 — very good
5 — excellent

	1	2	3	4	5
Clean finished drawing	☐	☐	☐	☐	☐
Line work quality	☐	☐	☐	☐	☐
Accuracy	☐	☐	☐	☐	☐
Completion on schedule	☐	☐	☐	☐	☐
Dimensioning	☐	☐	☐	☐	☐
Lettering	☐	☐	☐	☐	☐

Projects

Introduction

A project is a formal assignment given to a student or small group of students on a topic related to the curriculum and perhaps involving some out-of-class research and development. It is generally inappropriate to assign a *formal* project to children in Kindergarten through Grade 3. In Grades 4, 5 and 6, projects should be developed and completed within the classroom, so that the teacher may assist the students. A distinction is made here between projects and essay-style assignments. For more information, see the section "Essays."

A project may include constructing models and / or preparing written reports with or without diagrams, pictures, tables and graphs. It could also include producing sound or videotapes, films, collages, collections of photographs, plays and mime.

The project is primarily a learning activity, not primarily an evaluation activity.

Advantages of the Project Assignment

The project assignment:

A. provides students with an opportunity to formulate their own questions and find answers to them;

B. provides students with an opportunity to demonstrate individual or group initiative;

C. provides students with an opportunity to use concrete materials to express their ideas and talents;

D. permits the teacher to assess a student who is using other skills than those involved in written or oral tests;

E. makes it possible for the teacher to assign projects at different levels of difficulty to account for individual differences within the class;

F. provides choice, allowing students to pursue individual interests and possibly demonstrate otherwise hidden talents;

G. can be highly motivating to students;

H. can become a powerful teaching tool when completed projects are used for classroom instruction or presented by students;

I. provides an opportunity for students to talk together and exchange ideas while creating their project in the classroom;

J. provides an opportunity for students to talk about something which is both concrete and their own;

K. may raise the self-esteem of some students;

L. provides an alternative for those students who have difficulty writing.

Disadvantages of the Project Assignment

The project assignment:

A. may create a situation in which certain students, because of their background and home environment, have an advantage or a disadvantage with respect to other students in the class. If a member of a family "takes over" a project so that a student has minimal involvement in its completion, then little or no learning has occurred for the student. If, however, a member of a family, by consultation, advice or demonstration, assists the student to a limited degree, then the student may have had a valuable learning experience.

B. raises important questions regarding the evaluation of the project, not all of which can be easily answered.
   — Will the teacher be able to determine that the project is entirely the student's own work?
   — Will the teacher be able to establish and apply objective criteria for marking the project?
   — Will it be possible to mark the full range of projects using the same evaluative criteria?
   — Will the teacher be able to separate the physical attractiveness of the project from its content and/or skill?
   — Will the teacher be able to explain clearly to the students how their projects were marked?

C. requires a considerable amount of time for the teacher to organize, plan and mark;

D. may require the student to spend too much time and effort completing the project for a very small proportion of the total term mark, year mark or final grade;

E. demands that the teacher devote a substantial amount of thought and time to providing guidance to the students before and during work on the project;

F. requires the teacher to be aware that assignments demanding out-of-school time create difficulties for some students;

G. may place unreasonable demands on the resource center of the school, the school office and the public library;

H. because of its visual nature, may increase peer comparisons harmful to the self-esteem of some students.

Guideposts for Assigning and Marking Projects

A. *Ensure that students understand what a project is and how they are to go about doing it.* Students must be directly taught how to do a project *before* it is assigned.

B. Ensure that students have ample opportunity to discuss various aspects of a general topic and to select a manageable smaller aspect of that topic for their own project. For example, the topic "The Inuit" would be too broad, but "Inuit Methods of Hunting" would be manageable for most students.

C. Ensure that the project is within students' capabilities so that they can derive personal satisfaction from completing it.

D. Provide students with opportunities to practice the skills of project preparation in the classroom, especially in Grades 4 to 10.

E. Ensure that students know precisely and in advance the teacher's expectations regarding the project.

F. Provide students with a written outline of the assignment, including the following information:
   — the objectives of the project;
   — the specific terms of the assignment;
   — the due date or, where appropriate, a deadline for each phase of the project;
   — the criteria on which the project will be evaluated, including the marking scheme.

   Suggestions could also be included in the outline regarding sources and / or location of sources. In order to avoid confusion and delay at home, students in Grades 4 to 10 should be encouraged to show the written outline of the assignment to their family as soon as possible after it has been distributed.

G. Prepare the project assignment in close consultation with the resource center teacher. Ensure that sufficient resources, including non-print materials, are available for each project and in sufficient quantity for all students. If other teachers will be involved or affected, also consult with them.

H. Maintain continuous consultation with individual students on their plans and progress. This will ensure that projects will not be inappropriate, unmanageable or unrealistic in either time or scope.

I. Ensure that exactly the same project topics are not assigned in one or more succeeding grades.

J. Provide, where applicable, each student with a written evaluation based on the criteria announced when the project was assigned. Be prepared to spend time discussing the written evaluation with individual students.

K. Provide the marks or comments regarding the student's completed project on a sheet of paper separate from the project. Do *not* place marks, grades or comments on the student's completed project. This practice will allow projects to be displayed in the classroom, school or community, if deemed appropriate and agreed to by the student. A child's work should never be exhibited against his or her will or for purposes of comparison or competition. The manner in which a child's work is displayed reflects the teacher's respect for individuality and effort.

L. Use the completed projects, where feasible, as part of the teaching and learning program.

M. Provide opportunities for students to generate their own topics for project assignments and to suggest how they could be developed and evaluated.

N. Provide opportunities for some students, at some times, to choose a project, rather than another type of assignment, such as a major essay.

O. Consider providing an opportunity for a small group of students to *volunteer* to work together to complete a project, with the understanding that each member of the group will receive the same mark, grade or comment.

Sample Outline of a Project Assignment Sheet

Whatever the project assignment may be, it is assumed that the guideposts for assigning and marking projects provided on pages 98-99 have been taken into account.

The following sample outline of a project assignment sheet provides a framework of headings for five essential components of a good project. Each heading is followed by suggestions regarding the information to include under each heading.

The outline containing the detailed information for a specific project should be given to each student when a project is assigned. There should be an appropriate amount of time devoted to discussing with the students the five essential components of the project assignment sheet.

PROJECT ASSIGNMENT SHEET

Topic Choice(s):

Assign a specific topic, provide a group of topics from which students can select, or allow students to propose their own topics within the general subject area.

Objectives:

Provide a short list of specific objectives, for both the project and student learning related to the project. These objectives should be stated in student terms.

The Task:

Include in the task description what the students may do, how they might do it, where the work will be done and what form the completed project might take.

Due Dates:

Preliminary Dates:

Indicate several dates for each teacher / student consultation, peer discussion and consultation, and progress report.

Final Submission Date:

Criteria for Evaluation:

Include the specific criteria directly related to the stated objectives upon which the projects will be evaluated. (See pages 101-102 for a discussion of the criteria to consider when evaluating projects.)

Suggested Evaluation Criteria for Projects

The following points may guide teachers in developing specific criteria for the evaluation of projects. Whatever criteria are selected, they must be included on the "project assignment sheet" given to the students.

The following points are divided into two sections. The first section deals with the *process*, or the activities, leading to the completed project. The second deals with the *product*, or the completed project, itself.

A. EVALUATION OF THE PROCESS OR ACTIVITIES LEADING TO THE COMPLETED PROJECT

1. Did the student understand the task assigned?

2. Was the student's attitude towards the task positive?

3. Did the student show a willingness to be involved in the work?

4. Was the student prepared to engage in a number of approaches to the task?

5. Was the student willing to undertake any extra work?

6. Did the student assume personal responsibility for the work?

7. Was the student open to suggestions from his or her peers and from the teacher?

8. In teacher-student consultations, peer discussion groups and progress reports:

   • Was the student always aware of the purpose of the assignment?

   • Did the student constantly encourage the others in the group to work towards the purpose of the assignment?

   • Did the student keep the group on topic?

   • Was the student sensitive and attentive to the needs and contributions of the others in the group?

The information gathered by considering the above questions will assist the teacher to help students in their social development, as well as in their work habits, and study and research skills. This information should be used as a basis for anecdotal comments to be used for diagnosis, reporting and interviewing purposes. It should *not* be transferred into marks or grades. Perhaps the most important use of this kind of evaluation can occur in a student-teacher conference in which life skills, such as those outlined above, can be emphasized.

B. EVALUATION OF THE PRODUCT OR THE COMPLETED PROJECT

1. Did the completed product indicate that the student understood the task?

2. Were all the required elements incorporated?
   - Were they complete?
   - Were they relevant?
   - Were they accurate?

3. Did the project display:
   - unity of elements?
   - logical organization and sequence?
   - appropriate emphasis?
   - use of support materials?
   - originality of ideas and presentation?
   - positive visual impact?

Examples of Project Assignment Sheets

On the following pages are three examples of project assignment sheets which could be used with the appropriate students:

Example 1 — Physical and Health Education — Grades 7 and / or 8

> *Note:* For suggestions on how to differentiate this assignment for students of different levels of ability, see pages 238-243.

Example 2 — Mathematics — Grades 7 to 10

> *Note:* This specific example is one of a group of topics that would be prepared for a class. Every student in the class would not receive the same assignment sheet.

Example 3 — History — Grade 7

Example 1

Physical and Health Education — Grades 7 and/or 8

Topic *The development of a personal fitness plan using the range of available programs in the school.*

Objectives 1. To determine the range of programs available in the school related to physical activity.

2. To develop a personal fitness plan based on the programs available in the school and the components of physical fitness which you have learned about in your various classes.

The Task *What you should consider including in your project:*

1. Activities and programs that you think are appropriate for learning about and developing your physical fitness. Give reasons for your choices.

2. A realistic long-term plan or program for you to follow in order to develop your own physical fitness.

3. A personal weekly schedule of physical activities that you might follow.

4. Direct reference to the fitness kit. When making these references, include:
   — the *name* of each instrument;
   — what physical fitness *component* each instrument measures;
   — *how* each instrument measures the fitness component.

5. A pre-test schedule and form.

6. A post-test schedule and form.

7. A list of references (people, books, magazines, visuals) that you used.

———————————

Your personal feelings about this project. (Written on a separate page attached to the project.) ———————————

Your project assignment, including any schedules, forms, charts, graphs or diagrams, should be submitted according to the dates stated.

(continued)

(Example 1 continued)

Due Dates   *Preliminary Dates:*

        A) Classroom work and group discussion   _____

        B) 1st Student/Teacher Consultation   _____

        C) 2nd Student/Teacher Consultation   _____

        D) Draft Submission   _____

Final Submission Date: _____

It is suggested that you allot the following amounts of time to completing this project:

    in class   _____   periods

    out of class   _____   hours

How Your Project Will Be Marked

Marks will be awarded for:

30%	— developing a personal fitness plan which is balanced, reflects the appropriate activities and programs available in the school and includes references to the fitness kit, and an example of a pre-test and a post-test;
20%	— information that is complete, on topic, and accurate for each aspect of your project;
10%	— ideas that are developed in an organized manner;
15%	— including materials such as charts, graphs, pictures, schedules, models, photographs, and drawings to support or illustrate the information in your project;
10%	— indications that you have done research and that you have presented the information from this research in a manner that is easy to read, brief, and to the point;
10%	— originality of content and method of presentation;
5%	— attractiveness, neatness and visual impact.

Example 2

Mathematics — Grades 7 to 10 Project Assignment Sheet

Topic   *Golden Section or Golden Ratio*

Objectives   1. To understand and explain the meaning, the mathematical development and the application of the Golden Section or Golden Ratio.

2. To be able to identify and locate the Golden Section or Golden Ratio in art and architecture.

3. To express in written form the understanding of this mathematical concept.

4. To be able to research a mathematical concept as it applies to art and architecture.

The Task   From sources such as the *Life Science Library: (Mathematics)*, encyclopedias and other resource books on drawing and painting, locate and record all facts, diagrams and calculations needed to complete your assignment. Your final report should include a title, an explanation or definition of the Golden Section, diagrams and calculations showing how the ratio is developed, a brief history of its application in works of art, two or three examples, and a written summary in which you briefly explain why you think this ratio is so often selected by artists and architects.

Some class time will be provided to do the project. However, you should expect to do most of the work out of class. Your final report, including the title page, should be no more than four pages.

Due Dates   Project assigned Nov. 1

A) Rough copy to show to, and discuss with, your teacher   <u>Nov. 12</u>

B) Final submission date   <u>Nov. 20</u>

(continued)

(Example 2 continued)

Criteria for Marking

25%   *Originality:*
Are the diagrams, comments and written work and the structure of the presentation your own work?

30%   *Mathematical Thought and Application to Art and Architecture:*
Is there a clear indication of your understanding of the mathematics of the topic and its application to art and architecture?
Is there evidence that you have researched the topic?

20%   *Appearance and Workmanship:*
Is your presentation attractive and neat?

25%   *Clarity:*
Would the concepts, as you have explained them, be understood by readers?
Are the diagrams, pictures and explanatory notes orderly and relatively simple?

Note: This project will be worth _____ per cent of your term mark.

Note: This specific example is one of a group of topics that would be prepared for a class. Every student in the class need not receive the same assignment sheet.

Example 3

History Project — Grade 7

General Topic

The Inuit and their environment

Topic Choices

Select one of the following topics:

1. Inuit Transportation

2. Inuit Homes

3. Inuit Food

4. Inuit Family Life

5. A topic of your choice which has been approved by the teacher

Objectives

1. To show through your specific topic, your understanding of the important effect of the environment upon the Inuit;

2. To show your ability to research, organize and present your information in a clear, informative and attractive way.

The Task

1. From sources such as the various texts and picture sets in the classroom, books and visual materials in resource centers, and libraries, and any other sources you can find, locate and record all information you need to complete your project.

2. Decide the best way to present the information you have collected. Your final project could be a written report, a collage or a model. A written report could include some or all of pictures, drawings, charts or maps. A collage or model should have a written explanation with it.

3. You will be given _____ periods to work on your project in class. You should plan to spend no more than _____ hours outside of class working on your project.

(continued)

(Example 3 continued)

Dates   A. Project Assigned   _____

                   B. Student/Teacher Consultation(s)   _____

                   C. Progress Report or Teacher Review of Draft Copy   _____

                   D. Project Handed In   _____

How Your Project Will Be Marked

Marks will be awarded for:

— specific evidence or examples related to your topic, which clearly and accurately demonstrate the effect of the environment on the Inuit;

— indications that you have done some outside research on this topic;

— the presentation of the information from your research in a manner which is well-organized, easy to understand, interesting and attractive.

Tests and Examinations: Written and Oral

Introduction

In this document, the term "testing" is a generic term. "Testing" refers to any kind of school activity which results in a mark or comment being entered in a record book, or on a sheet, checklist or anecdotal list. In other words, observation, the writing of an essay, a short quiz, a classroom test or a cross-grade examination can all be referred to as "testing." Alternatively, the term "test" is used to denote the structured, formal, oral or written evaluation of student achievement.

In this document, the word "test" frequently refers to both tests and examinations. Examinations are tests which are school scheduled rather than classroom scheduled. Traditionally, they tend to cover more of the curriculum and be assigned a greater percentage of the student's mark than any individual classroom test or assignment.

In this section, diagnosis is not a major focus; rather, the main emphasis is upon written and oral tests, the outcomes of which are recorded as part of a term, semester or year mark. Other forms of evaluation are dealt with elsewhere in the book.

For the most part, tests and examinations are not appropriate from Kindergarten to Grade 3. Teachers of these grades should refer to the section titled "Observation."

Planning Evaluation

Teachers planning a course of study or classroom program should make their evaluation component clear to their students as soon as possible. Testing is an integral part of the teaching-learning process and should receive as much emphasis in planning as other course components. To plan their programs, teachers should decide in advance when they are going to give a pre-test to find out what the students know and do not know. Pre-testing will often save valuable classroom time, because if the class or group already has adequate knowledge or skill, the teacher may proceed to a new topic or activity.

Sometimes tests are constructed too quickly under the pressure of competing demands. Testing, however, is so important that a re-allocation of scarce teacher time is necessary to assure that planning for evaluation takes place. One important aspect of this planning is to establish the necessary balance and integration of testing components with the rest of the curriculum.

Balance and Integration

BALANCE

A good program has neither so many tests that it becomes a testing program rather than a learning situation, nor so few tests that students and teachers have no consistent indication of progress.

A well-balanced program also requires the careful consideration of the amount of classroom time to be devoted to formal testing. Teachers should decide what proportion of classroom time should be devoted to testing. This probably will vary considerably; some aspects of a subject may require only ten minutes in a predetermined number of days for adequate testing, while others may require longer tests and longer intervals between them.

INTEGRATION

Tests should be an integral part of the teaching-learning process and should not be separated from the ongoing daily classroom teaching. For most of the time in the classroom, the student's mind-set is a feeling of rapport with peers and the teacher. In an unstructured testing program, the mind-set can shift so that the student sees the teacher as an adversary, rather than as a partner in the learning process. This change of role reinforces the lack of integration between learning and testing.

The student should see testing as part of the learning process and, as much as possible, not be threatened by it. One way to achieve this productive atmosphere is to ensure that there is a constant, powerful connection among teaching-learning objectives, classroom activities and testing activities. When testing is perceived as a learning process, students have an opportunity to display what they have learned and identify topics for further study or investigation. When teachers and students view testing in this way, it is no longer merely a process of acquiring a mark for a report card.

A fully integrated teaching-testing component of a program should provide test situations only when there is a logical and obvious completion of a theme, section or unit of study. Therefore, it becomes almost impossible to follow the practice recommended above and also require that every Thursday afternoon there will be a test. Some aspects of some subjects, however, such as vocabulary study in a foreign language, lend themselves to a fixed pattern. For example, in studying vocabulary, a class may be pre-tested on Monday, study from Tuesday to Thursday, and be given a post-test on Friday. This pattern is based on logical units of study.

88 Key Questions to Ask About Tests and Examinations

At first glance, 88 questions about tests and examinations may seem outrageous. However, it is not necessary that every question be considered each time a testing program is planned or a test is prepared and marked. Nevertheless, the questions raise issues fundamental to all aspects of the testing program. At various points in the test planning process, teachers should consider the issues raised by these questions.

QUESTIONS TO ASK ONESELF WHEN PLANNING THE YEAR'S TEST

- In my school's calendar, are there specific items set aside for formal tests or examinations?

  If so, what are they?

  How can I plan the rest of my evaluation program around these dates?

- At what points in my program should there be a test?

  How many tests will this plan produce?

  Are there too many, just enough, or too few tests?

  If there are too many tests, which units can I combine for testing purposes?

  If there are too few, where are the logical points within a unit where I may test?

- Have I considered my schedule of tests in the context of the student's total school program?

  Will this schedule be fair to the students, or will they be over-burdened?

- How can I provide variety in my proposed evaluation program?

  Have I provided a number of different evaluation procedures other than tests, such as observation, oral presentations and projects?

- Within my test schedule, have I provided a variety of test techniques, such as objective-style questions, essay-style questions, sight passages and open-book tests?

- Have I provided adequate time for marking the tests of my students?

  Will this time permit me to give personal attention to each student's tests?

- What proportion of marks for reporting purposes will be based on tests?

  What proportion will be based on other evaluation components, such as observation, projects and participation?

  Is this proportion fair and equitable for the particular students I am teaching?

- Is there a school policy regarding missed tests?

  If not, do *I* have a policy?

- Is my evaluation program integrated with the objectives of my course or program?

- What possible modifications for testing and my testing schedule must I make for students with exceptionalities?

QUESTIONS TO ASK ONESELF BEFORE BUILDING A PARTICULAR TEST

- Why am I giving this test?

- What do I now know, and what do I hope to learn from this test, about each of my students, the class and the curriculum?

- What do I want my students to learn from this test?

- What is the most appropriate type of test to find out this information?

- How is this test related to the course objectives?
  Which of the course or unit objectives will be measured in this test?

- How much weight should I give to each objective that I wish to measure?
  Does the weight assigned correspond appropriately to the relative importance of this objective in the total course?

- Which questions will I relate to which objectives?

- Have I prepared my students for the method of evaluation and styles of questions I am proposing to use?

- Do my students have a clear understanding of my evaluation techniques and marking procedures?

- Have I provided enough time for each question? Is the time allotted for the text sufficient for the student to answer the questions, re-read their work and revise where necessary?

- Is the proportion of marks for each question congruent with the difficulty of the question and the amount of time needed to answer it?

- Will the distribution of the difficulty of the questions take into account the varying levels of ability within the class?

- In my marking scheme for each question, what will I consider a reasonable and acceptable answer?

- What are my expectations regarding overall student performance on this test?

- Have I allocated time for follow-up activities after marking the test?

- In constructing and marking this test, have I made provisions for any students with exceptionalities?

QUESTIONS TO ASK ONESELF WHILE BUILDING THE TEST

- Are the questions clear and concise?

- Am I asking for too much information in the time available?

- Have the questions been asked using vocabulary the students will understand?

- Is there a suitable distribution of difficult and less difficult questions?

- Did I try out the questions on an informed colleague, if possible?

- Have I been able to work through and answer the questions in a third to half the time given the students?

- Is the amount of time required to answer the test question commensurate with the amount of time required to read the material? For example, are the marks for answers worth the time and effort required to read a difficult sight passage?

- If there are choices or alternate questions, are they of equal difficulty and worth?

- Are the instructions for guiding students' choices among questions or sections clearly stated?

- Have I considered the effect on the students of the format and general appearance (for example, legibility) of the test?

- Have I asked questions which require higher levels of thinking as well as factual recall?

- Have I prepared a detailed marking scheme for the whole test?

- Does the test indicate the mark distribution and suggested time allocation for answering?

- Have I avoided phraseology that will allow students to give a ridiculous answer which I will be forced to accept?

    Example: Who do you think killed Julius Caesar?
    Student Answer: Calpurnia.

(Full marks should be given because the question asks, "Who do you think....")

QUESTIONS TO ASK ONESELF ABOUT GIVING THE TEST

- Have I checked to see whether the same students have other tests scheduled for the same day?

- Have I avoided scheduling the test at inappropriate times during the week?

- Have the students been given sufficient advance notice in order to prepare adequately for the test?

- Have the students been informed about:
    - the date of the test?
    - what is to be covered by the test?
    - the length of the test?
    - kinds of questions to be used (for example, objective or essay-style, or both, or open-book)?

- Have the students been taught how to answer the type of question to be used on the test? (The test experience should never be the first experience of any type of question.)

- Have the students been taught how to study for a particular type of question?

- Have students been taught how to deal with key directing words and phrases in questions, such as *compare, identify, state the importance of*?

- Have I ensured that the students know the meaning of all the words used to ask the questions?

- Have I considered appropriate modifications for students with exceptionalities?

- Have I allowed time for students to ask me clarifying questions during the day or so leading up to the test?

- Have I informed the students of the materials, instruments or printed matter they will need to bring with them to the test?
  Are the students aware of the routines (e.g., consequences or procedures) which will likely follow if they fail to bring the appropriate materials to the test?

- Is all the material I need for conducting the test present in the classroom?

- Is the room in which the test is to be given suitable?

For a further discussion of preparing the students for tests and examinations, see also the section on this topic in the "Guideposts for Essay-Style Questions," pages 123-126.

QUESTIONS TO ASK ONESELF WHILE MARKING AND AFTER MARKING THE TEST

- Were the questions or problems clearly stated?

- Is there evidence that a number of students, including the exceptional students, had inadequate time to complete satisfactorily particular questions or the whole test?

- Is there evidence that a number of students were ill-prepared to answer a particular question?
    - Was the lack of preparation the result of inadequate study on the part of the students?
    - Was the material taught too abstract for the intellectual development of the students?
    - Was the method of presenting the material in class clear and sufficiently extensive?
    - Was the method of presenting the material in class appropriate to the level of student ability?
    - Was sufficient time devoted to follow-up activities after presenting the material in class and prior to the test?
    - Were the questions appropriate to the specific level of ability of the students?

- Is there evidence that I should adjust my marking scheme and re-score tests already marked?

- Am I alert to unexpected, acceptable responses which differ from those listed in the marking scheme?

- If the number of students obtaining a low mark or a high mark is above expectations, how am I going to use the marks?

- If the level of achievement on the test was very low, what changes should I make in my methods of classroom presentation and follow-up?

- If the results of other teachers' classes using the same test differ greatly from mine, what could be the cause of this discrepancy?

- What other methods of evaluation might have been more useful?

- Did the test results adequately reflect the provisions I made for students with exceptionalities when I prepared the test?

- Were the questions which required higher level thinking too easy, adequate or too difficult?

- Should I use this test again?

Now What Do I Do?

Once you have assessed the results and suitability of the test, some of the following suggested activities may be carried out, where necessary:

- Identify students who may require re-teaching, further study or assistance, and re-testing;

- Provide opportunities for individual student-teacher conferences for joint evaluation and planning;

- Encourage students, from time to time, to write reaction papers regarding their perceptions of the test;

- Re-test with a more appropriate instrument or method;

- Teach or review appropriate study techniques;

- Review or re-teach the necessary part of section using a different method of presentation;

- Revise your classroom program by modifying, re-allocating or removing the inappropriate material or activity.

No Surprises!

1. It is important that, whenever teachers are using tests and examinations, they should make sure that all students have had experience with all types of questions to be used.

    THEREFORE, the teacher should be aware of the evaluation practices of previous years and should ensure that the students are capable of meeting the teacher's expectations in his or her proposed evaluation techniques.

2. If a teacher occasionally wishes to use a "surprise test" to find out what the students do or do not know, the practice can be beneficial for both students and teacher. However, this form of surprise test should be seen as *diagnostic* because it tells the teacher and students what is or is not known at that time *without preparation*.

    THEREFORE, any comment, grade or mark assigned to such a test should not be used in calculating the term or final mark for reporting purposes. The students also should be assured that this is an information-gathering exercise and not a formal evaluation. *A surprise test must never be punitive nor be given to obtain an immediate mark to meet a reporting deadline.*

3. Another form of "surprise test," and one which must be avoided, occurs when an evaluation has been announced for a particular time, but then is re-scheduled at the last minute to a later date.

    THEREFORE, unless there are unavoidable circumstances which students understand, *tests and examinations must occur as scheduled.*

Essay-Style Questions

Introduction

An essay-style question is a question on a test or examination which requires a written response in sentence and paragraph form. Below Grade 7, this type of question should be used infrequently.

Advantages and Disadvantages of Essay-Style Questions

Advantages	Disadvantages
Higher Level Thinking The major advantage of the essay-style question is that it can encourage higher level thinking such as synthesis and evaluation.	**No Marks Assigned for Higher Level Thinking** Marks are too often given for factual content and style, and not for displays of higher level thinking.
Freedom for the Student The essay-style question permits more flexibility than objective-style questions. Students have more freedom to select information, organize the material in different ways and interpret or express information in their own styles. Given a choice of essay-style questions, students can answer those which best allow them to demonstrate their strengths.	**Pitfalls of Freedom** A student may feel comfortable with the content aspect of the answer, but be uncertain how to organize the material. If the student has a choice of essay-style questions to answer, there is an inherent danger. Choice implies that the student is able to select the answer which will best demonstrate his or her strengths. It also assumes that the student understands the criteria for marking the various questions and that all questions have the same degree of difficulty. In short, the teacher may be pre-supposing selection skills that a student does not have.
Versatility and Scope Essay-style questions offer greater latitude. Topics can be examined in considerable detail or several topics can be compared. The student can establish and defend a position on an issue or evaluate or synthesize other statements on that issue.	**Lack of Breadth** An essay-style question involves the consideration in depth of a particular topic. The danger is that breadth is sacrificed for depth. A student may be rewarded or unfairly penalized because he or she has a wealth of information about a particular area of study.

(continued)

Advantages	Disadvantages
Application of Learned Skills In an essay-style question, the process (as well as the content) remains an important consideration. The ability of a student to organize and synthesize information and express it in a coherent and logical pattern is one of the keys to a successful essay-style answer. Skills and concepts useful to the student beyond the classroom can be tested in this format.	**Reward for Content** It is easier to recognize and use specific facts related to the question than to apply required skills and concepts. Hence, answers sometimes become a recital of memorized information. In this type of answer the objective content becomes the focus of the student's response, not the use of higher skills and concepts.
Emphasis on the Development and Demonstration of Writing Ability The essay-style question provides the student with an opportunity to practice skills necessary to answer questions requiring specialized writing skills, for example, comparison questions.	**Emphasis on the Development and Demonstration of Writing Ability** The student who knows the content but is unable to write effectively may be unduly penalized. Sometimes an essay-style answer may be given a high mark because all or most of the content points are present and no attention was given to form and style by the marker. In other cases, an essay-style answer may be given a failing mark, though there are sufficient content points, because its form and style are very weak.
Writing and Learning Writing is a valuable means of learning. When a question demands that an answer deal with material which has not been previously covered in class, for example, by comparing two disparate things, the student can learn by answering the question.	**Writing...Not Enough Time** Time, or a lack of it, can be a major source of stress in an exam or test situation. This stress can block students' ability to learn from the exercise.

(continued)

Advantages	Disadvantages
Apparent Ease of Construction For many teachers, the attractiveness of the essay-style question lies in such practical considerations as their preparation time. For example, it seems to take much less time and effort to prepare one essay-style question worth twenty marks than it does to prepare twenty multiple-choice questions worth one mark each.	**Apparent Ease of Construction** The attractiveness of setting essay-style questions is, to a large extent, based on an illusion. It can appear to be a simple, straightforward enterprise, but in reality it is very difficult to do well. The following factors make the setting of an essay-style question onerous: — the question must be based on the objectives of the topic or unit to be evaluated; — the wording of the question must be specific and clear; — the time allotted to answer the question must reflect its difficulty and its importance with respect to the rest of the test or examination; — when the question is constructed, a detailed marking scheme must be prepared which accounts for the widest possible range of acceptable responses; — the marks allotted must reflect the difficulty of the question and the time required to respond.
Flexibility in Marking Teachers have greater scope in marking essay-style answers than in marking objective-style answers. The subjective dimension allows more room for interpretation on the part of the marker and permits the teacher to credit intangible, but worthy, factors such as creativity, originality, and other indications of higher level thinking.	**The Subjective Factor** Flexibility in marking is obviously a disadvantage as well as an advantage. Research studies demonstrate that different teachers grade the same paper in dramatically different ways. Moreover, the same teacher may well grade the same paper differently on different days. Among the features of a successful test are its reliability and its validity. The crucial role of the teacher in determining the final mark for the student and the wide disagreement among teachers as to what constitutes a "good" answer are serous limitations.

Note: While there are limitations to the essay-style questions, it remains an important method of evaluation for the teacher of students from Grade 7 onward. A number of disadvantages of essay-style questions, especially those which place undue emphasis upon writing and which include a limited time factor, can be of particular concern for some exceptional students.

Suggestions for dealing with these concerns will be found in the guideposts for essay-style questions in this section and in the sections dealing with modification and differentiation.

The following guideposts can be used to ensure that essay-style questions are a worthwhile experience for students and teachers.

Guideposts for Essay-Style Questions

FIVE STEPS IN THE CONSTRUCTION AND USE OF ESSAY-STYLE QUESTIONS

1. Preparing the students.

2. Planning the use of essay-style questions.

3. Constructing essay-style questions.

4. Marking essay-style questions.

5. Using information obtained from marking essay-style questions.

1. Preparing the Students

A. Ensure that the essay-style question is an extension of, or logical follow-up to, what is going on in the classroom. There should be a powerful connection among learning objectives, classroom practices and evaluation activities.

B. Teach the students how particular types of questions are to be answered. These questions typically begin:

> Compare....
> Discuss the....
> Describe the causes of...and effects of....
> Read the quotation and discuss....
> Describe the technique....
> Describe the procedure....
> Illustrate....
> State the....

C. Do not assume that students are able to transfer skills and techniques learned in one subject to problems or assignments in another. In all subjects where essay-style answers are required, teachers should teach or review paragraph and essay construction with their students. This teaching or review is especially important in Grades 7 to 10 when the students begin to develop these skills.

D. Diagnose students' degrees of ability to complete various kinds of assignments in written form during daily classroom activity. These diagnoses should not occur only in the context of preparing for a test.

E. Help students to improve their study skills. The section "Study Skills and Student Evaluation" (on pages 43-53) could be used to assist students in developing these skills.

F. Inform the students of all topics for which they will be responsible, though not all of these topics may be tested.

G. Indicate to students how marks will be apportioned for aspects of an answer. For example, if a question asks for three concepts or facts and the total number of marks is twelve, students should understand that each concept should be developed for a total of four marks apiece. If marks are to be awarded for organization and style, students should understand that the three concepts are worth three marks each, and that an additional three marks are awarded for the organization and style of the whole answer.

H. Teach the students to look for indications of whether or not they will be able to choose among several questions. For example, teach them to circle such words as OR between questions.

I. Teach students practical techniques for answering essay-style questions. The outline, "Some Techniques for Improving Performance on Essay-Style Questions in Tests or Examinations" (pages 125-126), is designed as a handout for students. Use sample questions to illustrate the points in the outline. Hand out the outline only *after* the techniques have been taught.

Consider using the checklist on page 132, "Answering an Essay-Style Question: A Student Checklist," as a part of the preparation for writing essay-style answers. This checklist may also be included with the test or examination paper in order to assist students.

(Guideposts for Essay-Style Questions continued on page 127)

SOME TECHNIQUES FOR IMPROVING PERFORMANCE ON ESSAY-STYLE QUESTIONS IN TESTS OR EXAMINATIONS

Before Beginning to Answer Your Questions:

1. Check to make sure you have all the question pages.

2. Check the back of the question pages to see if there are questions there.

3. Read *all* test or examination instructions and questions.

4. In the instructions, underline or circle all key words or phrases, such as *and, or, answer three of the following....*

5. Within each question, underline or circle all key words or phrases, such as *discuss, list, explain, compare, three causes of....*

6. Note the numerical value of each question and the total time allowed for the test or examination. Then convert the numerical value to the appropriate number of minutes per question. Remember to deduct five minutes for preparation and at least ten minutes for reading, correcting and revising the test or examination paper. The proofreading and revision will be made easier if questions are answered on every other line.

7. Note which questions or sections are compulsory, optional or allow for choice.

8. Make certain you know the number of questions you are required to answer.

9. Choose the question you wish to do first. The question you answer first should be the one with which you feel most confident. Spend only the appropriate amount of time, or less, on this question. The order in which you answer the questions need not be the order in which you finally arrange your answers before you hand in your paper.

While Answering Your Questions:

10. For each question, jot down on a separate piece of paper (rough work), the key ideas or facts pertaining to that question.

11. Take into account the marks allotted for each question or sub-question, and decide how much emphasis should be placed on each idea or fact. If a question asks for three concepts or facts, and the total number of marks is twelve, assume that each fact or concept should be developed and that marks may also be assigned for organization and style.

(continued)

12. Decide which ideas or facts to include in your answer, based on what is required in the question. For example, if the question asks for three facts or concepts, choose from your list of key ideas or facts the three most important facts which you can expand upon.

13. Decide on the format of the answer. Will you discuss each concept in a paragraph of its own, or will you compare concepts within a paragraph?

14. Compose the introduction of your answer so that it includes the key words or phrases in the question. The introduction should also indicate the direction the answer will take and suggest, but not state, the conclusion you hope to reach.

15. Develop the body of your answer so that it includes the points you have chosen to present. Make sure you write your answer in the format you have chosen. Stay with this format throughout your answer.

16. Compose a final paragraph in which the conclusion that you suggested in the introductory paragraph is now clearly stated.

17. Leave space at the end of each answer. This space will allow you to add further information if you recall something important and you have time at the end of the test or examination.

18. Go immediately to the next question of your choice. Start each answer on a new page.

After Answering All Your Questions:

19. When you have completed all the answers, organize them in your preferred order or in the order required by the instructions of the test or examination.

20. Make certain you have answered the required number of questions. Number each page and arrange all pages in order.

21. Read all your answers carefully and correct or revise where necessary.

22. Identify your paper as instructed, including subject, your full name, the teacher's name and your grade or class.

2. Planning for Essay-Style Questions

A. *Know Your Course Objectives*

- Know the general objectives of the course. Keep them in mind while setting the essay-style question.

- Refer to the objectives of the unit or topic. Choose clear and precise and, where possible, measurable objectives.

- Know what it is that you hope to achieve in the particular topic for which you are preparing an essay-style question.

B. *Know Your Students*

- Know the diverse levels of development and abilities of the students to be tested.

- Determine the appropriate modifications for your exceptional students in the class.

- Decide whether essay-style questions are the most appropriate format for assessing students' achievement of the specific objectives being addressed.

- Know specifically what you expect in the answer to the question. These expectations should be the basis of the marking scheme.

C. *Know the Purpose of the Essay-Style Questions*

- Provide opportunities in the test that will allow for higher level thinking, demonstration of skills and disciplined expression, as well as for knowledge of content.

- Plan to allow class time subsequent to the test as a basis for further instruction and learning.

3. Constructing Essay-Style Questions

A. *Preliminary Considerations*

- Decide on the portion of the test which will be essay-style questions, the approximate time required to answer these questions and the proportion of marks to be allotted.

- Decide if there is to be a choice of questions. If there is choice, don't overwhelm the students with too many choices.

- Relate any essay-style questions to an important objective of the topic or unit. There should be a correlation between the number of marks for the essay-style question and the amount of class time spent on the topic.

- With each essay-style question, provide suggestions for the students to guide their responses. These suggestions could include such things as:
  - overall time allotment;
  - time allotment for the whole question;
  - time allotment for parts within the question;
  - mark allotment;
  - mark allotment for parts within the question;
  - criteria on which the answer will be evaluated. (See page 129 for examples.)

- In deciding on the time allotment for the question, remember that students need time to think, as well as to write.

B. Wording the Essay-Style Question

- Be precise in the selection of words and phrases. Define the task in clear terms. For example, "Discuss" can be very general and ambiguous and can fail to suggest to the student any specific framework or organization. (See pages 135-136.)

- Develop questions that encourage selection, organization and application, rather than mere recall.

- Distinguish between terms that ask for recall and those that ask for higher level thinking. Terms such as "List" and "Outline" encourage the student simply to recall memorized information, while expressions such as "Compare" or "Explain" require the student to select, organize and apply information.

- Word the question as briefly as possible.

For a more detailed discussion and examples, see pages 135-139, "The Use of 'Directing' Words in Formulating Essay-Style Questions."

C. Developing and Providing Evaluation Criteria

Provide students with an outline of the criteria to be used in marking the question. This outline should be included with the essay-style question. These criteria should be developed as the question is being prepared.

This practice has a number of significant advantages:

- It provides students with a close link between some of the program, course or unit objectives, and the question asked.

- It tends to produce a clearer and more explicit wording of the question because it forces the teacher to indicate clearly in the question the components expected in an answer.

- It states the basis of the evaluation in an open and fair manner. This approach diminishes the chance for student frustration due to hidden agendas and the unwanted adversarial relationship between the teacher and the students.

- It helps weaker students to organize material and aids stronger students in focusing their abundance of information on the topic at hand. In this manner students are helped to learn how to write more effectively.

- It helps the teacher to clarify in advance what is expected in an acceptable response and thus to prepare a marking scheme which will provide a standard for consistent evaluation.

Two examples follow which illustrate many of the points mentioned above.

The following is an example of an essay-style question suitable for a Grade 11 and 12 Canadian History course.

Is Louis Riel best understood in Canadian history as a villain or a martyr?

Take a position on this question and, in your answer, support your point of view with specific evidence from the time period.

(15 marks)
Suggested Time Allotment: 30 minutes
Evaluation Criteria:

The teacher will evaluate your answer with the following criteria in mind:
- Did you clearly state both viewpoints?
- Did you establish your specific points of view on the issue?
- Did you use supporting evidence to prove your point of view?
- Did you indicate why other points of view are less satisfactory?
- Did you organize your answer in a clear, logical, convincing manner?

The following example is suitable for a Grade 7 or 8 Science course in which the teacher might use an essay-style question.

---

1. "A tree is a living thing; a rock is not."
   Using paragraph form, explain the above statement.

(15 Marks)
Marks will be given for:

(5 marks) i) the organization of the answer. A good opening sentence, a sensible development of your answer and a reasonable conclusion are expected.

(10 marks) ii) indicating a maximum of 5 major characteristics of things. (Characteristics such as respiration should be briefly explained.)

D. Designing the Marking Scheme

- Formulate the "model" answer you would hope for from students. Prepare a marking scheme for this answer while you are devising it.

- Ensure that marks allotted for the question are sufficient to distinguish among weak, mediocre, good and excellent answers.

- Ensure that the proportion of marks allocated to the question reflects fairly the time and effort required to answer the question. (For example, a question requiring a half-hour, one and one-half pages, 12 content points and considerable organization in order to answer, should be worth more than 15 marks on a 100-mark test.)

- Consider the ratio of marks to be assigned for content and for organization and presentation.

- Consider, in some instances, postponing the assignment of the exact number of marks to the question until the model answer has been completed. The total number of marks for a test or examination need not be a multiple of ten.

- Attempt to find a balance between a marking scheme that is too loose or too rigid.

- Be prepared to re-draft the initial marking scheme based on a sample set of responses, and to inform the students of the reasons for the changes.

- Consider reducing the stress upon deducting marks for spelling in a timed test or examination situation.

4. Marking Essay-Style Questions

- Read without grading, a selected sample of three or four answers to the same question in order to decide to what degree students have met your expectations.

- Take steps to ensure as much objectivity and fairness as is possible in assessing each student's response.

- To ensure consistency, allow enough time towards the end of your marking to re-mark some of the first answers marked.

- If feasible, have another teacher mark one or two of your papers to compare results.

- While marking, look for indications of:
  — topics that may need re-teaching;
  — topics which were too difficult for many students to comprehend and which may suggest the need for revision of curriculum or teaching activities;
  — flaws in the design or wording of the question.

- While marking, identify any students who may need extra help.

SUGGESTIONS ON THE MARKING OF ESSAY-STYLE QUESTIONS

The following checklist for teachers is a sample of an approach to marking the answer to an essay-style question. Part A deals with the components of an essay-style answer. Part B deals with the criteria for establishing the approximate mark or grade. The following checklist shows how this approach may be implemented.

TEACHER CHECKLIST FOR MARKING ESSAY-STYLE QUESTIONS	Yes	Partially	No
A. General Components Does the essay-style answer exhibit:			
1. a clearly stated point of view, theme or thesis?			
2. an orderly and logical development of the point of view, theme or thesis?			
3. coherent organization of arguments?			
4. specific examples and evidence to support point of view, theme or thesis?			
5. proper essay format?			
6. relationship of information to the requirements of the essay?			

B. Criteria for Establishing Mark or Grade Range

Above Average Answer	√	Average Answer	√	Below Average Answer	√
• draws explicit overall conclusion based on a summary of the facts		• contains enough facts to answer the question satisfactorily		• contains insufficient facts to answer the question satisfactorily	
• contains information appropriate to the central thesis or idea		• demonstrates an understanding of the facts involved in the issues but builds only an adequate relationship between the facts and the central thesis or idea		• does not establish a point of view and consistently support it	
• displays evidence to reinforce specific point of view that student is attempting to prove				• catalogues the facts rather than organizing and presenting a point of view supported by the facts	
• where applicable, deals with more than one side of a problem in order to illustrate why one interpretation is superior to the other		• attempts with a fair degree of success to establish a point of view and to relate evidence to that point of view			
• demonstrates strong evidence of maturity of style and clarity of organization and presentation					

ANSWERING AN ESSAY-STYLE QUESTION: A STUDENT CHECKLIST

		✔
Pre-Writing	Did I read the question carefully?	
	Did I underline key words or phrases?	
	Did I prepare a rough outline that included the key words and the main ideas?	
Writing the Essay Answer Introduction	Did I clearly state the topic in the introduction?	
	Did I state my point of view, theme or thesis clearly?	
Body	Does every paragraph in the body relate directly back to my introduction?	
	Is each point in the introduction developed adequately in the body?	
	Is there specific evidence to support my arguments?	
Conclusion	Does the concluding paragraph reinforce what I previously stated?	
	Was I careful to avoid introducing new evidence not previously stated?	
Post-Writing	Did I re-read the final product for possible revisions and corrections of such things as spelling and grammar?	

5. Using Information Obtained From Marking Essay-Style Questions

A. *Implications for Teaching, Curriculum and Future Evaluation*

- Was the question clearly stated?

- Did the students, including the exceptional students, have adequate time to answer the question satisfactorily?

- Were the students well prepared to answer the question?

- Did the students know exactly what topics or content were to be included on the test, or did the responses indicate that the students were confused about what they were to study?

- Were poor responses the result of inadequate study, or lack of study skills?

- Was the question too abstract for the students' cognitive development?

- Do the results indicate inappropriate curriculum content?

- Could the method of presentation in class have been made clearer and more extensive?

- Should this question be used again? If so, are there any changes that should be made?

- Would another method of evaluation have been more effective in this instance?

- Did the results reflect adequately the provisions made for exceptional students?

- Did the question require higher level thinking? If so, was it too easy, adequate, or too difficult?

- If a large number of students were unsuccessful in answering the question, what should be done with the marks for the question?

B. *"Taking Up" the Essay-Style Question*

Evaluation is a learning activity. The teacher should, therefore, use the procedures outlined below.

- Maintain the students' self-esteem by giving them their results as anonymously as possible. It must be the students' decision to share the marks with others.

- Take great care when using student answers as samples in follow-up instruction.

- Provide individual consultation for students regarding their answers.

- Decide how much class time to devote to "taking up" the answers as part of the learning experience.

- Discuss with the students a teacher-prepared model answer so that the students will understand what was expected. During this discussion, students should be encouraged to analyze their strengths and weaknesses with respect to this type of question.

- Identify topics in need of additional instruction. This identification could lead to re-teaching, helping individual students, explaining again the techniques in answering essay-style questions, and reviewing study habits.

The Use of "Directing" Words in Formulating Essay-Style Questions

One of the most prevalent difficulties encountered by students attempting to answer an essay-style question is the interpretation of the important "directing" word or words. A "directing" word is a verb such as *compare*, *explain* or *prove*, which indicates to students what they are to do in answering the question. Such "directing" words can create problems concerning ambiguity and levels of thinking.

AMBIGUOUS DIRECTING WORDS

Introduction

Directing words can be so ambiguous that a student does not know exactly what the teacher's expectations are regarding the quantity of information to be provided, the breadth of the issue to be considered and the format or structure in which the answer is to be presented.

Students may be either confused or misdirected:

- if they have no previous experience with questions containing the directing word;

- if they have been prepared to interpret a directing word in one way, but a cross-grade examination or test demands it be used in another way;

- if the remainder of the question does not clarify the directing word or provide more specific direction.

As a result, students may produce answers which are inadequate or incomplete. Students may also produce answers which *they* consider to be thorough and well done, but to which the teacher assigns a reduced mark because they are "off topic."

The Ambiguity of "Discuss"

Perhaps the most frequent ambiguity arises from the use of *discuss* as a directing word. The flexibility or openness of this word can create serious problems. Unless the rest of the question clearly focuses the topic and indicates the direction the student should take in answering the question, *discuss* will often be interpreted to mean *tell all you know about....*

The ambiguity of *discuss* as the directing word in questions is exemplified by the following list of responses from senior high school students to the question, "What does *discuss* as the 'directing' word in a question mean to you?"[11]

STUDENT INTERPRETATIONS OF THE WORD "DISCUSS"

- Show or prove by explanation.

- Discuss means explain in my own words using an introduction and conclusion to the statement. In the body I would put in a few points and relate them to the story to prove or disprove the statement.

- Discuss means to analyze in depth.

- Discuss means to present analogies and comparisons and through their juxtaposition come to a conclusion based on evidence.

- Discuss means to explain fully what is meant by the statement.

- Discuss means to tell all you know and use proofs.

- Discuss means to talk about, to show how different events are related.

- Discuss means to put down facts with evidence that supports them.

- Discuss means to talk about the importance of character, plot, etc.

- Discuss means to analyze, covering the question from every possible angle.

- Discuss means to write as much as you can about something, using examples to illustrate.

- Discuss means to present all the facts and express both sides of the argument and then give your personal opinion.

- Discuss means to say everything you know about whatever is asked.

It is obvious from the list above that more explicit directions are needed when the word *discuss* is used as a directing word. The questions below, taken from actual examinations, indicate both ineffective and effective uses of *discuss*.

Ineffective

(6 marks)   **Fully discuss the function of the Common Man in all his roles in the play *A Man for All Seasons*, both as a dramatic technique and as a personality within the play.**

[Senior level English]

This question is ineffective because *discuss* is not the correct word; there is little argument or debate involved in an account of dramatic function. Moreover, the rest of the question does not indicate clearly to the student the extent of the answer required, especially when the terms *fully* and *all* are also included in the question. The six marks allotted for the question in a 75-mark, two-hour examination, do not reflect the amount of time, thought and writing required to answer the question adequately.

Ineffective

Discuss the involvement and contributions of the United States in World War I, both in Europe and on the home front.

[Grade 10 History]

The above question was one part of a two-part question of a one-hour examination consisting of five questions.

This question is ineffective because the student is given no guidance other than the word *discuss*. *Discuss* as it is used here, really means *tell all you know about*. The potential breadth of information that could be included in an answer to this question is enormous. The difficulty is aggravated by the lack of any direction as to the length of the response, or the amount of time to be spent in writing that response. Another important factor is that students in Grade 10 usually need help in selecting the information required and organizing their responses. This question provides no such help.

Effective

Discuss is a suitable directing word only when its meaning for each teacher on a school staff is clearly understood by all students. For example, the question:

Discuss the use of pesticides in controlling mosquitoes.

[Grade 10 Science]

is appropriate only if the students have been taught that *discuss* means *consider from various points of view, present different sides of*, etc.

Avoiding Ambiguity with Other Directing Words

Students must clearly understand the meanings of other frequently used directing words. It is important that students understand what *each* of their teachers means by these directing words. Some other directing words and the usual meaning for each are listed below.[12]

- **Contrast**
    — Bring out the points of difference.

    Example: Contrast Jane Austen's *Pride and Prejudice* with William Thackeray's *Vanity Fair.*

- **Compare**
    — Bring out the points of similarity *AND* points of difference.

    Example: Compare the games of basketball and lacrosse.

- **Criticize**
    — State your opinion of the correctness or merits of an item or issue. (*Criticize* may involve approval, disapproval or both.)

    Example: Criticize the use of nuclear power as a means of generating electricity.

- **Define**
    — Give the meaning of a word or concept by placing it in the class to which it belongs and setting it off from other items in the same class.

    Example: Define the term "archetype."

- **Describe**
    — Give an account of; tell about; give a word picture of.

    Example: Describe the Pyramids of Giza.

- **Enumerate**
    — Name or list in some order and in concise form.

    Example: Enumerate the great Dutch painters of the seventeenth century studied this term.

- **Evaluate**
    — Give the good points and the bad ones; appraise; give an opinion regarding the value of; explore the advantages and disadvantages of.

    Examples: Evaluate the use of teaching machines in classroom learning.

- **Explain**
    — Make clear; interpret; make plain; tell "how" to do; tell the meaning of.

    Example: Explain how scientists can, at times, trigger a rainstorm.

- **_Illustrate_**
    - — Use a picture, diagram, chart or concrete example to clarify a point; using words, make clear by using examples. (The wording of a question using the directing word _illustrate_ must make clear to the student whether or not a sketch or diagram should be used to answer the question.)

        Example: **Illustrate, through sketches, the use of catapults in medieval warfare.**

        Illustrate, by giving three examples from _To Kill a Mockingbird_, how Atticus Finch was a good father.

- **_Interpret_**
    - — Make plain; give the meaning of; give your thinking about the meaning of.

        Example: **Interpret the line "He jests at scars who never felt a wound," and relate it to....**

- **_Justify/Show How_**
    - — Show good reasons for, or give evidence and present facts to support your position.

        Example: **Justify the American entry into World War II.**

- **_Outline_**
    - — Give, in order, the main points of; sketch, in general terms.

        Example: **Outline Neville Chamberlain's argument for trying to appease Hitler in the late 1930s.**

- **_Prove_**
    - — Establish the truth of something by giving factual evidence or logical reasons.

        Example: **Prove the reflector property of the parabola and relate it to use of dish antennae.**

- **_Summarize_**
    - — Briefly give or review the main points.

        Example: **Summarize the ways in which food can be preserved.**

- **_Trace_**
    - — Follow the course of; give a description of the development of.

        Example: **Trace the development of counting machines from the abacus to the microcomputer.**

Directing Words and Levels of Thinking

INTRODUCTION

Directing words may require students to operate at a level of thinking beyond their present abilities, or beyond the level actually intended by the teacher. The level of thinking required to answer a question depends on several factors.

If the material asked for by a question has already been taught in class in the same way as expected in the answer to the question, then the level of thinking can be no higher than recall of knowledge.

> *Example:* **Judge the importance of the Fenian raids, compared to the other factors which brought about the Confederation of Canada in 1867.**

If this "judgment" has been directly taught in class, the question is a content recall question. However, if the students have been taught the content related to the Fenian raids but not their *relative* significance in bringing about Confederation, then the question demands a much higher level of thinking than mere factual recall.

If a new situation or element is introduced in the question, then a higher level of thinking is required. For example, if two poems on the same theme have been studied in detail in class, but have *not* been compared and the question asks for a comparison, then a higher level of thinking is demanded. If the comparison has been taught, then the question may appear to require a higher level of thinking, but remains a factual recall question.

ISSUES

What follows is a discussion of three issues concerning the use of directing words as they relate to levels of thinking.

1. An example of a directing word that can fail to indicate the level of thinking at which the student is expected to operate is *explain*. This could be taken to mean several different things:
   — Describe in either written or diagrammatic form... [recall of knowledge];
   — Demonstrate comprehension of the intricacies of an operation... [comprehension];
   — Outline what would happen if... [application];
   — Indicate the relationships among... [analysis];
   — Defend the point of view taken... [evaluation];

   In other words, caution must be taken when using directing words.

2. When using the same content base for a question, the directing word or words will determine the level of thinking demanded for an answer.

   Examples:
   - **State five causes of the rebellion in Upper Canada in 1837.**
     [factual recall]
   - **Analyze, from Lord Durham's point of view, the causes of the rebellion in 1837 in Upper Canada.**
     [mainly analysis]
   - **"Historians will argue that there is rarely a single cause behind any historical event." Judge the accuracy of this statement with regard to the rebellion in Upper Canada in 1837.**
     [evaluation]

   The directing word or words ask that students operate at one or more of the levels of thinking. As a result, careful thought must be given to the selection of directing words to ensure that students are being asked to operate at a level of thinking appropriate to the teacher's expectations.

Examples of the Use of Directing Words Appropriate to the Different Levels of Thinking

This ladder lists some directing words and the levels of thinking they generally call for. Steps may easily overlap; "application" must include factual recall and may also require some analysis, synthesis and evaluation. Moreover, some directing words may lead to thinking at varying levels, depending on the rest of the question.

Example:

Identify five parts of a flower.

Identify the similarities and differences between flowers which self-pollinate and those which cross-pollinate.

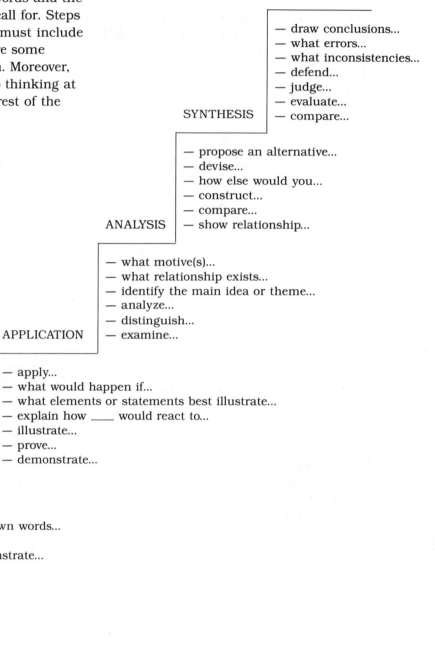

EVALUATION

— draw conclusions...
— what errors...
— what inconsistencies...
— defend...
— judge...
— evaluate...
— compare...

SYNTHESIS

— propose an alternative...
— devise...
— how else would you...
— construct...
— compare...
— show relationship...

ANALYSIS

— what motive(s)...
— what relationship exists...
— identify the main idea or theme...
— analyze...
— distinguish...
— examine...

APPLICATION

— apply...
— what would happen if...
— what elements or statements best illustrate...
— explain how ____ would react to...
— illustrate...
— prove...
— demonstrate...

COMPREHENSION

— why...
— how...
— state in your own words...
— condense...
— show or demonstrate...
— paraphrase...
— re-tell...
— interpret...
— summarize...

KNOWLEDGE

— what...
— where...
— when...
— who...
— define...
— outline...
— state...
— list...
— describe...

Essays

Introduction

An essay is usually a formal assignment given to an individual student on a topic related to the curriculum; it may involve some out-of-class research and development. Generally, it is inappropriate to assign a *formal* essay to students below Grade 6. For the purpose of this document, a "formal essay" is an expository or descriptive writing assignment.

The issues related to evaluation of essays are so numerous and varied that they warrant a book on their own. Therefore, this document concentrates on a few of the most important issues. These are:

1. the development of specific and appropriate objectives for the essay based on the overall objectives of the course;

2. the development of specific criteria for evaluating the essay based upon the objectives of the course;

3. the stating of objectives and evaluation criteria based upon the level of ability of the student;

4. the practice of frequently assigning short, and sometimes personal, essays throughout the year or semester, rather than assigning one or two long, major, critical essays;

5. the practice of marking some but not all of the student's work;

6. the need for clear and detailed instructions in an essay assignment to establish such aspects as purpose, audience, format;

7. the "first draft syndrome" or the "rough draft, good draft" syndrome;

8. the marking of the essay;

9. the role of peer and self-evaluation;

10. the different purposes, objectives and criteria for evaluation of different types of essays.

1. Essay Assignments and Objectives

Each essay assignment should be a learning experience and, therefore, must be firmly tied to the objectives for the course or program. The particular objectives for a particular essay should be clearly stated in terms students will easily understand. Teachers should avoid assigning an essay only for the purpose of obtaining a mark. For a further discussion of the role of objectives in assignments, see the material in "Learning Objectives and Student Evaluation," pages 27-34, and "Projects," pages 95-102.

2. Objectives and Evaluation Criteria

It is important that the criteria on which the essay will be evaluated are established at the time the assignment is developed. It is even more important that these criteria be given to the student as part of the assignment.

This practice has a number of significant advantages:

— It provides the students with a close link between the essay assigned and some of the program, course or unit objectives.

— It tends to produce a clearer and more explicit wording of the assignment by forcing the teacher to ensure that the components expected in the essay are clearly indicated in the assignment.

— It states the basis of the evaluation in an open and fair manner. This approach diminishes the chance for student frustration because of hidden agendas and the unwanted adversarial relationship between the teacher and the student.

— It helps weaker students to organize material and stronger students to focus their abundance of information on the topic at hand. In this manner students are helped to learn how to write more effectively.

— It helps the teacher to clarify in advance what is expected in an acceptable essay and thus provides a standard for consistent evaluation.

3. Objectives, Evaluation Criteria and Levels of Ability

It is important that essay assignments be appropriately differentiated for students of differing levels of ability. Such differentiation concerns all elements of the assignment, including evaluation. For further information on objectives, evaluation criteria and levels of ability, see the section "Differentiating Evaluation for Different Levels of Ability," pages 227-257.

4. Frequent Short Essays

It is preferable to assign many short essays in a given year or semester rather than one or two long essays. These shorter assignments should include personal, formal, informal and critical essays. Short essays should, for the most part, be written within class time. Benefits are that students learn how to write in a more efficient manner. Teachers' comments and criticisms are more frequent and immediate and, therefore, students have more opportunity to improve, and improve more quickly. In all subjects, students should be encouraged to write about topics of personal interest from their own experience. Also, teachers of all subjects should emphasize other aspects of writing in addition to content and surface features.

It should be noted that the practice of assigning frequent short essays applies to students from Grade 6 to the end of secondary school.

5. Selective Evaluation

If students write only as much as the teacher can evaluate, then they are not writing enough. Because students should be given the opportunity to write many short pieces in a given subject, they should also be given the opportunity to choose which one of three or four finished pieces will be handed in for the teacher's formal evaluation. Through this practice, the students are encouraged to evaluate their own work and make a decision which is important. This practice does not, however, preclude the teacher's identification of certain pieces to be evaluated.

6. Need for Clear and Detailed Instructions

It is essential in any essay assignment to provide clear and detailed instructions regarding its purpose, audience and format.

• PURPOSE

With regard to essays, the word "purpose" is used here to describe two components:

- deciding on the reason for writing;
- choosing the appropriate form for the writing.

The purpose for an essay assignment can be determined in a number of ways:

- each student freely identifies his or her own purpose;
- each student selects a purpose from a teacher-prepared list;
- the teacher assigns one specific purpose.

The way which is selected will depend on the student's ability and experience in writing for different purposes and to different audiences.

When a student sets the purpose for writing, rather than writing something for a purpose assigned by the teacher, the student has more sense of "ownership" and probably will produce a more interesting and better written essay. While it is preferable for students to set their own purposes for writing, the teacher sometimes may need to set a purpose, such as writing an article for a well-known magazine, a column for a newspaper, a letter to the editor, an editorial, a film or book review or an explanation for younger students.

• AUDIENCE

It is important for students to learn how to write for different audiences. If students set their own purposes for writing, or are provided with purposes other than merely something for the teacher to mark, they must tailor the writing for a specific audience other than the teacher. This opportunity will encourage students to learn how to adapt style to suit the audience.

• FORMAT

If the purpose and audience have been clearly identified, then the appropriate format choice will be suggested or determined. Purpose will often determine the form and length, while the audience often determines the style.

There are both benefits and dangers inherent in assigning a definite length to an essay. Teachers should carefully consider the advantages and disadvantages. One advantage is that it eases the students' uncertainty about the length of the assignment. However, an assignment which specifies a minimum of 1500 words may lead a student who has written an effective essay in 1000 words to diminish the quality of a good essay by adding 500 additional, and perhaps unnecessary, words.

Example of an Effective Essay Assignment:

Merely asking students to write an essay of a specified length on the topic of "Acid Rain" would provide ineffective and inadequate instructions to the students. If, however, objectives are clearly established for the students and the purpose, audience and format of the essay are clearly understood by them, then the essay assignment will be much more effective.

The following example, designed for students in Grades 11 and 12, illustrates clear and detailed instructions for an essay assignment in which the teacher has established the purpose, audience and format.

GRADE 11 OR 12 ESSAY ASSIGNMENT: ACID RAIN

You are a journalist who writes a daily column for one of the major national newspapers we recently studied. Choose and identify the newspaper for which you are writing.

Your editor has asked you to write a column on acid rain. In the column, you are to write about *at least two* of the following aspects of the problem: the costs to the economy, the moral obligations of industry and individuals, the ecological consequences for the future, the possible deterioration of Canadian-American relations. If you are interested in an aspect of the acid rain issue other than those listed, you may include it as part of your discussion.

Your essay will be evaluated for the following:

- accuracy of information;
- organization of information;
- style suitable for the chosen audience;
- suitable length for a newspaper column;
- clarity and effectiveness;
- correctness of grammar and spelling.

Note:

This assignment assumes that the students have studied the different types of columns found in at least three national newspapers and are familiar with the style and format of column writing in each of these newspapers.

An assignment of this type provides a clear-cut purpose, suggests an audience and requires the student to make decisions regarding style, format and length.

7. "The First Draft Syndrome"

Professional writers rarely submit their work for publication without first revising carefully and proof-reading it. Students, however, often submit for evaluation what is, in effect, their first draft, with the merely cosmetic improvements offered by better handwriting or typing.

It is better for all concerned if students are encouraged to submit essays only after completing the following process:

- discussing the topic with the teacher and / or with one or two other students prior to writing;

- if necessary, discussing the topic briefly and informally with the teacher and / or one or two other students while the first draft is being written;
- briefly consulting with one or two students or a teacher after they have read the completed first draft;
- re-writing the first draft as a result of the brief, informal conferences;
- after the revision process, having either peer or teacher aid, or both, in proof-reading for grammar and spelling errors.

It is good practice to allow a student to select one of three or four essays written in this fashion for formal evaluation by the teacher. Students given the opportunity to follow this writing process tend to become more discerning about the quality of their own writing. This is an important component in evaluating one's own writing.

8. Marking the Essay

It is helpful to both teachers and students if a "criteria for marking" sheet is used to evaluate and discuss an essay. *(See Example 1 on page 149.)*

When marking essays, teachers should confine their comments to previously established criteria related to the techniques of effective writing. These comments should refer to both the presentation of content and the effectiveness of the discussion or argument. It is understood that these aspects of essay writing will have been explored and practiced in previous lessons. In the evaluation of essays derived from units in which the teaching emphasis is placed on the development of a particular concept or skill, teachers should evaluate only that one aspect of the student's writing. The aspect of the student's writing to be evaluated should be clearly stated in both the objectives for the assignment and the criteria for marking it.

With certain kinds of essay assignments, it may be desirable to focus on such aspects as the student's skill in presenting and developing a point of view, or the development of a personal writing style. If the emphasis is to be placed on a particular aspect, then the distribution of marks on the "criteria for marking" sheet should be adjusted accordingly. The teacher's written and oral comments should reflect the aspect being emphasized. If, for example, the focus is on point of view, comments on spelling and grammar should be kept to a minimum.

After the essay is marked, a brief oral discussion offers an efficient and personal way of communicating criticism and suggestions to the student. The discussion should be based upon the "criteria for marking" sheet and may lead to a follow-up assignment which should be specific, and directly related to identified weaknesses in the student's writing or analysis.

The following are examples of:

- a sheet for marking short expository essays *(Example 1)*;
- an actual essay marked by a teacher *(Example 2)*;
- a completed marking sheet *(Example 3)*.

Example 1, the blank marking sheet, can be adapted for use by the teacher. The adapted sheet can be photocopied in quantity to be completed and attached to essays prior to returning the essay to the student. Each student should keep a file folder of the marked assignments. A copy of the adapted blank marking sheet could be given to each student at the time the essay is assigned.[13]

EXAMPLE 1

SUGGESTED CRITERIA FOR MARKING A SHORT EXPOSITORY ESSAY

Student's Name _____ Title of Essay _____ Date _____

Main Merit(s)

Criteria	Possible Marks	Student's Mark	Comments
Content: convincing, pertinent, imaginative, specific, perceptive	20		
Point of View: clear, consistent, appropriate in mood and emphasis to purpose and approach	10		
Essay Organization: logical, coherent, unified, suitable to purpose, developed in an orderly way building to an effect or conclusion	10		
Paragraph Organization: precise statement of topic, effective development, varied paragraph structures	10		
Style: flavor, interest, flair, imagination, freshness; expression suited to content, flow, dominant effect	10		
Sentence Structure: skillful use of a variety of sentence patterns such as parallelism, contrast, balance, repetition and exclamation	10		
Diction: vocabulary and tone appropriate for topic and projected personality of the writer; specific, imaginative, vivid, precise	10		
Use of Language Conventions: correctness in punctuation, spelling, and grammar; avoidance of awkward, disjointed, fragmented, run-on sentences	20		
TOTAL	100		

Additional Comments: (Use reverse side of this page)

an interesting opening paragraph

EXAMPLE 2

ON DINING OUT*

I can remember it all very clearly now; it comes rushing out from the back of my mind like a flood, though it was some years ago. Yes, it was my paternal grandmother's third wedding. After a talk given by a minister, there was to be a dinner at one of the dining rooms at the Voyager Motor Hotel. Since my uncle Don works there, we could get the room [with a certain percentage of the price off.] *awkward*

Dining out usually means dressing in one's best evening garb. For me, at the time, this consisted of a two-piece suit, the best one I had. After about two hours, I was washed, dressed and ready to go.

Once we were there, the older folks engaged in conversation, while we of the younger generation, [put ourselves to games which utilized the   *ambiguous* mind.] Well, by the time everyone was there, we were (ravinous) with *sp* hunger, (especially me, for all I had for lunch was a glass of water, and a toothpick!). The announcement was made that we could begin to serve ourselves *omit* (it was a (smorgisborg), and so there was a line made at once. *sp*

Another thing about dining out *omit* is that one is on one's best behavior, and using the best of manners. Therefore, us younger ones were placed near the rear of the line, and immediately there was a fight as to who was closest to the front. Me being the oldest, and maturest of all the younger ones, I didn't put up much of a fight, and so found myself at the very back of the line. By the time I got [to the table the food was on,] I was so hungry, I *awkward* filled my plate quite generously. .

As I mentioned before, one *was* on one's best behavior when dining out, and this is helped by the fact that one doesn't want to get one's clothes dirty. So eating must be done in a careful manner, so as to keep the food off *omit* (of) one's clothes, and transfer one's food from the plate to one's mouth in a graceful way. First of all, one opens one's napkin, and places it on one's knees, [which I accomplish after a while.] After this was done, I managed to   *Highlight* consume some of my food. Good manners also (intails) eating all of the food *sp* *the humour* on one's plate. This I did, having to force the last bite down, and skip *here by* dessert. Afterward, I had the worst case of indigestion in my life! *using different* *punctuation.*

In conclusion, all I have to say is that dining out is all/right if not done *two words* too often. This I have learned from personal experience.

Mark assigned: 66

*This essay was written by a student in Grade 12 and marked by a teacher.

150

EXAMPLE 3

SUGGESTED CRITERIA FOR MARKING A SHORT INFORMAL EXPOSITORY ESSAY

Student's Name *Ron Logan* Title of Essay *On Dining Out* Date *Oct. 31/84*

Main Merit(s) *A personal and honest essay in a lively and entertaining style. Your frankness and humour in the essay are refreshing.*

Criteria	Possible Marks	Student's Mark	Comments
Content: convincing, pertinent, imaginative, specific, perceptive	20	16	*Your introduction is effective. Your ironic and humorous handling of the incident is set up effectively by the first two sentences.*
Point of View: clear, consistent, appropriate in mood and emphasis to purpose and approach	10	7	
Essay Organization: logical, coherent, unified, suitable to purpose, developed in an orderly way building to an effect or conclusion	10	6	*Try to develop more of the possibilities for humour in your essay. Most of the humorous touches are subtle. You may want to*
Paragraph Organization: precise statement of topic, effective development, varied paragraph structures	10	6	*highlight some of them. Perhaps the incident of finding*
Style: flavor, interest, flair, imagination, freshness; expression suited to content, flow, dominant effect	10	7	*yourself at the end of the line could be exaggerated slightly.*
Sentence Structure: skillful use of a variety of sentence patterns such as parallelism, contrast, balance, repetition and exclamation	10	6	*I assumed that you were being deliberately colloquial and*
Diction: vocabulary and tone appropriate for topic and projected personality of the writer; specific, imaginative, vivid, precise	10	6	*ungrammatical for effect, and so I didn't indicate*
Use of Language Conventions: correctness in punctuation, spelling, and grammar; avoidance of awkward, disjointed, fragmented, run-on sentences	20	12	*all "errors".*
TOTAL	100	66	

Additional Comments: (Use reverse side of this page)   *See over*

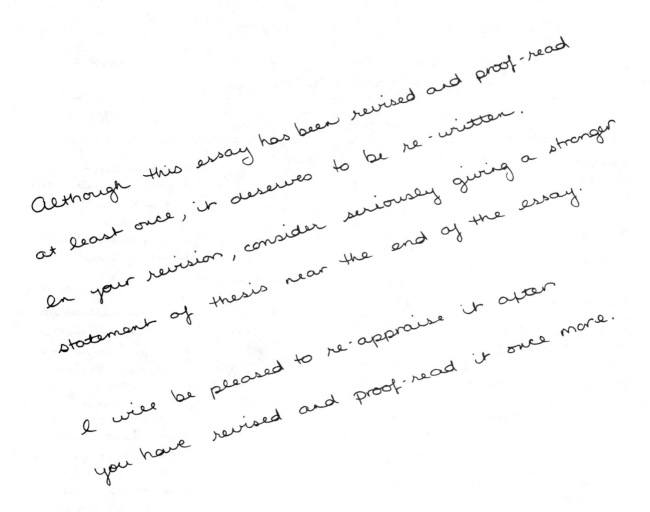

Although this essay has been revised and proof-read at least once, it deserves to be re-written. In your revision, consider seriously giving a stronger statement of thesis near the end of the essay.

I will be pleased to re-appraise it after you have revised and proof-read it once more.

9. Peer Evaluation of Essays

Wherever essays are an important part of both the learning and evaluation processes, it is useful for students to practice writing for an audience other than "just the teacher." Sharing their writing with a peer audience can allow students to benefit from a wider range of opinions offered more frequently than possible when only a teacher sees the assignments. Peer evaluation cannot, of course, replace marking by the teacher.

Teachers should feel no obligation to use peer evaluation to determine student marks, but they should recognize that the comments of classmates are often of great value in helping students to improve their writing. Moreover, because students have the right to accept or reject part or all of their peers' evaluations, the original writers tend to become more critical of their own writing.

There can sometimes be difficulties in the use of peer evaluation if the procedure is not handled carefully. Teachers should be sensitive to the self-worth of students and, in some situations, try to avoid pairing a gifted writer with a writer who is encountering difficulties. While this type of pairing can be beneficial, it sometimes can be damaging. In addition, many students find it difficult to evaluate the more sophisticated aspects of essay writing.[14]

Basically, there are five ways by which students may help each other to write better essays:

1. **reading** (as audience)
   Students help each other to develop an awareness of a wider and more varied audience.

2. **reacting** (as critics)
   Students provide feedback on how clearly or effectively peers have communicated their ideas and feelings.

3. **advising** (as editors)
   Students can suggest ways of expressing ideas more vividly and clearly.

4. **encouraging**
   Positive comments from peers motivate more and better writing.

5. **evaluating**
   Peer evaluation permits more writing to be examined critically.

10. Different Types of Essays

Different types of essays serve different purposes and objectives and require different criteria for evaluation. In all subjects, consideration should be given to assigning such types of essays as short descriptive essays, familiar essays, short responses to classroom experiences and reaction papers. Individual objectives and criteria for evaluation must be established and provided for students in every case. Some short essays, such as reaction papers, should not be evaluated for a mark or grade.

Objective-Style Questions

Introduction

Objective-style questions include the following:

- multiple-choice questions;

- true-false questions;

- matching questions;

- short-response items.

The distinguishing characteristic of objective-style questions is that they have highly specific, pre-determined answers requiring a very brief response.

Evaluation should be a learning experience for both the student and the teacher. However, objective-style testing is frequently ineffective as a learning experience for either the student or the teacher because objective-style questions too often require only the recall of facts and do not allow the student to display thinking processes or the teacher to observe them. Considerable effort needs to be made to develop and use objective-style questions in a more versatile manner, so as to include questions which demand higher level thinking.

A good evaluation program should not be composed exclusively of objective-style tests, nor does it *have* to include objective-style questions. However, if objective-style questioning is included, then it should be balanced by other modes of evaluation.

The following factors should be kept in mind when developing and using objective-style questions:

- Objective-style questions are often used for the wrong reasons; that is, they are faster and easier to mark than other types of evaluation.

- Objective-style questions are often used to test only factual recall.

- Objective-style questions, when they are well-designed, can quickly and efficiently evaluate a wide variety of skills and deal with a large amount of subject matter.

- The most effective use of well designed objective-style questions involves the evaluation of students' ability to use a wide variety of skills, including skills at higher levels of thinking.

- When objective-style questions evaluate higher level thinking skills, sufficient time must be allotted in the test situation for students to think through their responses.

- Objective-style questions are often an inappropriate method of evaluation; for example, in mathematics the teacher will wish to know *how* the student arrived at the answer.

- When evaluation is prepared by the teacher, she or he should be aware that objective-style testing may be inappropriate in certain situations for example, in Grades 1 to 4, objective-style testing is inappropriate because the level of abstraction and the level of reading comprehension required to answer the questions are beyond the ability of many of the children.

- It is often assumed that objective-style questions are more appropriate for students who are having difficulty with the program or with other types of evaluation. However, some styles of objective questions often require complex reading and thinking skills not readily apparent in the wording of questions; therefore, the questions may be more difficult than the teacher intends.

Advantages of Objective Types of Evaluation

- A well-developed objective test can quickly and efficiently evaluate a wide variety of skills and deal with a large amount of subject matter.

- Objective-style questions present tasks for which the solutions are predetermined and presented among pairs or groups of responses. The intent of the questions cannot be avoided or "written around."

- In objective-style questions which do not require students to write out the answers, their writing skills, including grammar and spelling, do not influence the grade students receive. The neatness or appearance of the answer also has no bearing on the evaluation.

- The results of the test can be analyzed to enable a teacher to look at the response pattern to the individual question, groups of questions and the test as a whole. This analysis can be used to determine:
    - suitability and clarity of the questions;
    - topics which require further teaching using a different approach;
    - content or skills which proved too demanding for the students.

- The marking of the answers is unbiased. A teacher's opinion or preconception of a student's work will not be a factor.

- Objective-style questions avoid the discrepancies often found in evaluations of essay-style answers.

- The questions may be used effectively for diagnostic tests or pre-test purposes for individuals and groups.

- Objective questions are effective for testing large groups, especially in cases where the teacher's marking time is limited.

Disadvantages of Objective Types of Evaluation

- Frequently, an objective-style test requires only the recall of facts.

- Over-emphasis upon objective-style tests will not allow students to practice and demonstrate writing skills.

- Sometimes objective-style questions evaluate something other than what is intended. For example, a question intended to evaluate factual knowledge may in fact evaluate students' ability to understand cause and effect relationships.

- Objective-style tests often require a disproportionate amount of reading time. Although the amount of writing expected is minimal, the amount of time required for reading and thinking can be exceptional. Therefore, some objective-style tests can be reading tests rather than tests of knowledge and skill.

- Objective-style questions are inappropriate for students in Grades 1 to 4 because the complex format of many objective-style questions, with the possible exception of short-response items, is confusing to young children.

- The problems presented in print often require more advanced skills than those currently possessed by the students.

- Because a specific, pre-determined answer is expected, great care must be taken in composing these questions and their expected responses.

- Preparation of effective objective-style questions is very time-consuming.

- Because it takes so long to develop a good objective-style test, there may be a temptation to use the same test unchanged year after year. This practice fails to take into account the differing needs of individuals and groups in each class. However, banking of effective questions or items for possible use for new tests is an acceptable procedure.

- Objective-style questions often promote uneducated guessing.

- Many students may be able to select the correct answer without really understanding the response.

- Because most types of objective-style questions do not measure language acquisition or development as effectively as other forms of evaluation outlined in this document, they should be used only rarely to evaluate students' language skills.

- Some types of objective-style questions fail to provide clues to the thinking processes of individual students.

Types of Objective-Style Questions

The following sections deal with several specific types of objective-style questions. These include:

1. The Multiple-Choice Question
2. The True-False Question
3. The Matching Question
4. The Short-Response Item

In each case, the type of question is defined, its advantages and disadvantages are outlined, guideposts for its construction provided and samples given.

When preparing an objective-style test, it is advisable to provide on the test paper a completed example of each type of test item. It is also helpful to work through two or three examples with the whole class immediately prior to the test.

1. THE MULTIPLE-CHOICE QUESTION

Introduction

As illustrated in the sample below, a multiple-choice question involves the selection of the appropriate response to a specific direct question. These direct questions should not be restricted to mere factual recall. For example, because responses (a), (b), and (c) are all correct, (d) is the best response.

Place a check mark on the line beside the best response.

What important educational objectives can multiple-choice questions measure?

_____ (a) knowledge

_____ (b) understanding and judgment

_____ (c) problem solving ability

_____ (d) all of the above

If a multiple-choice test is to evaluate knowledge, understanding, judgment and problem solving ability, then the designer of the test must come to grips with the objectives for testing. Each question must focus on some legitimate, specific, course-related idea, and be directed at a particular skill.

Advantages and Disadvantages of Multiple-Choice Questions

Advantages	Disadvantages
• Multiple-choice questions have a directness which some other types of questions lack.	• The indiscriminate re-use of complete multiple-choice tests reduces their relevance and validity.
• The form of a multiple-choice question, in which the question is followed by a number of responses (at least one of which is correct), may help students determine the appropriate response.	• It takes considerable time to construct good questions, especially those that test higher level thinking.
• Multiple-choice questions can be marked quickly.	• Multiple-choice questions could be testing a student's reading ability more than any other skill.
• In a properly designed test, the response to an individual question can be analyzed quickly and easily.	• Wording a multiple-choice question clearly is a demanding task.

Guideposts for Constructing Multiple-Choice Questions

Note: 1. Although these guideposts are presented as "do" and "do not," they are not intended to be rigid rules. Rather, they are intended to show what is preferable practice.

2. The statement-question part of the multiple-choice item is called the "stem"; the potential answers, the "responses." Among the responses, the incorrect ones are referred to as "distractors."

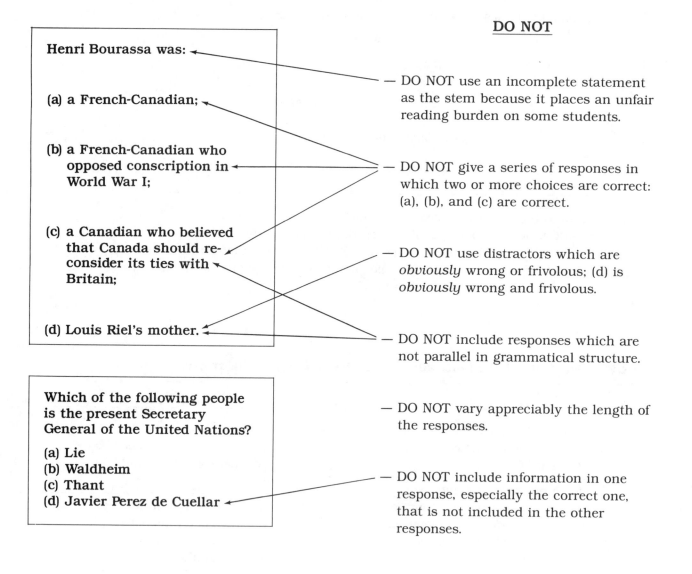

DO NOT

Henri Bourassa was:

(a) a French-Canadian;

(b) a French-Canadian who opposed conscription in World War I;

(c) a Canadian who believed that Canada should reconsider its ties with Britain;

(d) Louis Riel's mother.

— DO NOT use an incomplete statement as the stem because it places an unfair reading burden on some students.

— DO NOT give a series of responses in which two or more choices are correct: (a), (b), and (c) are correct.

— DO NOT use distractors which are *obviously* wrong or frivolous; (d) is *obviously* wrong and frivolous.

— DO NOT include responses which are not parallel in grammatical structure.

Which of the following people is the present Secretary General of the United Nations?

(a) Lie
(b) Waldheim
(c) Thant
(d) Javier Perez de Cuellar

— DO NOT vary appreciably the length of the responses.

— DO NOT include information in one response, especially the correct one, that is not included in the other responses.

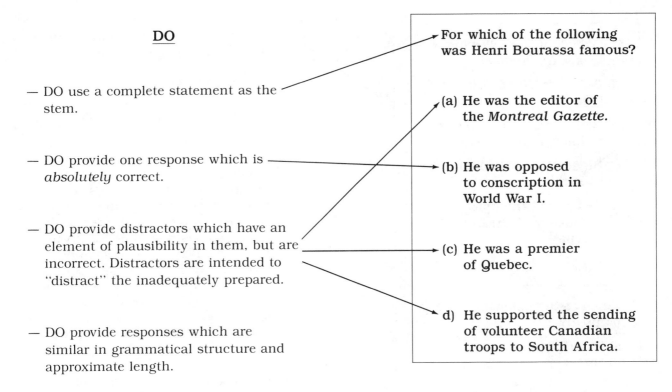

DO

— DO use a complete statement as the stem.

— DO provide one response which is *absolutely* correct.

— DO provide distractors which have an element of plausibility in them, but are incorrect. Distractors are intended to "distract" the inadequately prepared.

— DO provide responses which are similar in grammatical structure and approximate length.

For which of the following was Henri Bourassa famous?

(a) He was the editor of the *Montreal Gazette.*

(b) He was opposed to conscription in World War I.

(c) He was a premier of Quebec.

d) He supported the sending of volunteer Canadian troops to South Africa.

(Guideposts for Constructing Multiple-Choice Questions continued next page)

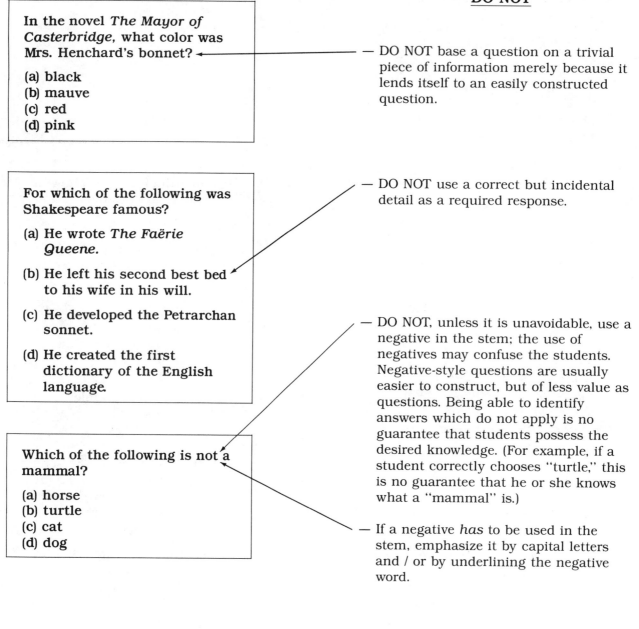

DO NOT

In the novel *The Mayor of Casterbridge*, what color was Mrs. Henchard's bonnet?

(a) black
(b) mauve
(c) red
(d) pink

— DO NOT base a question on a trivial piece of information merely because it lends itself to an easily constructed question.

For which of the following was Shakespeare famous?

(a) He wrote *The Faërie Queene.*

(b) He left his second best bed to his wife in his will.

(c) He developed the Petrarchan sonnet.

(d) He created the first dictionary of the English language.

— DO NOT use a correct but incidental detail as a required response.

Which of the following is not a mammal?

(a) horse
(b) turtle
(c) cat
(d) dog

— DO NOT, unless it is unavoidable, use a negative in the stem; the use of negatives may confuse the students. Negative-style questions are usually easier to construct, but of less value as questions. Being able to identify answers which do not apply is no guarantee that students possess the desired knowledge. (For example, if a student correctly chooses "turtle," this is no guarantee that he or she knows what a "mammal" is.)

— If a negative *has* to be used in the stem, emphasize it by capital letters and / or by underlining the negative word.

DO

— DO use a positively phrased stem because this kind of stem tends to measure more important learning than do negative stems.

Which of the following is a mammal?

(a) fish
(b) snake
(c) turtle
(d) cow

Additional Guideposts for the Construction of Multiple-Choice Questions

1. Put as much of the pertinent information in the stem as possible in order to clarify the problem and reduce the reading time for the choices.

2. Be aware that questions which ask students to select the *best* from among four correct responses require higher level thinking and demand that the teacher be able to explain and defend the required response.

3. When marking, always be prepared for unforeseen but valid student interpretations of questions and responses. Very frequently negative stem questions lead to this kind of difficulty. For example:

Which of the following does *NOT* belong?

(a) Giotto
(b) Raphael
(c) Dante
(d) Rembrandt

The teacher may have expected the students to choose (c) because Dante was a writer, not a painter. Some students, on the other hand, may have selected (d) because Rembrandt was Dutch while the other three were Italian. The teacher would have to accept that (c) and (d) are both correct in this situation.

4. Avoid repetition of key words in the stem and in the correct response.

5. Avoid giving away the correct response by building too obvious a connection between the stem and the correct response. If, for example, a plural is called for in the stem, make all the responses plural.

6. Multiple-choice questions usually include either four or five choices. Five choices will reduce the possibility of correct guessing. However, it is often difficult to devise four *plausible* but incorrect choices. Adding an obviously wrong answer weakens the question.

7. Information in one question should not give away the answer to another question.

8. Do not use "all of the above" or "none of the above" as throw-away distractors, only to get a fourth or fifth possible choice. All choices must be plausible to the uninformed.

9. Be sure there is no recognizable pattern in the order of correct responses.

10. Before administering the test to students, try out questions on an informed colleague to ascertain if they are clear, accurate and fair.

11. By composing a few questions after each lesson or two, teachers can reduce the time spent putting the test together when it is required, and can facilitate the construction of good questions because the material is fresh.

12. Avoid the use of terms such as "may be," "should," "could be" and "sometimes." The use of these imprecise or conditional terms unfairly confuses the students.

13. A good check on the clarity and completeness of the stem is to cover the responses and judge whether the question could be answered without the choices.

14. Avoid designing questions containing complicated "choices within choices." Such questions usually increase the level of reading difficulty, cause confusion, require an unjustifiable amount of time and rarely are worth more than other, simpler questions. Therefore, avoid questions such as the following:

The choice of being tried by a judge alone or by judge and jury is offered in:

(a) Provincial Court

(b) County Court

(c) Supreme Court of Ontario

(d) Supreme Court of Canada

(e) both (b) and (c)

(f) both (a) and (c)

(g) both (a) and (b)

(h) all of (b), (c) and (d)

(Reprinted from a test in a
Law Course in a secondary school)

---

15. Consider adapting the wording or phrasing of questions, the choice of vocabulary, and the concept load to students of different levels of ability.

Multiple-Choice Questions and Higher Level Thinking Skills

In using multiple-choice questions, teachers should make every effort to include questions which test higher level thinking skills. Frequently, multiple-choice tests are used exclusively to evaluate students' factual recall. While there are occasions when testing factual recall is appropriate, the use of multiple-choice questions in a manner that includes questions demanding higher level thinking can lead to a more balanced testing situation.

Notes:

1. **Do not confuse the difficulty of the question with the demand for higher level thinking. The term "higher level thinking" refers to the upper levels of the taxonomy for the cognitive domain found on page 30. "Difficulty" and "higher level thinking" are not necessarily synonymous terms.**

2. With multiple-choice questions, it is always possible to guess the correct answer. Therefore, the teacher cannot be certain that higher level thinking has taken place unless the student has been asked to defend the choice in another part of the question.

Example 1

> **General Cable was offering cable TV to all of the residents in a new subdivision. The company sent a letter to Mr. Jones stating that if it did not hear from him in one week it would consider that he wanted the service. Jones ignored the letter and went on a holiday. While he was away, the housekeeper let the company connect the cable.**
>
> **(a) Jones must pay for the service since it is connected to his TV.**
> **(b) Jones did not reply; therefore, he implied that he accepted the service.**
> **(c) Jones can order the service removed and not pay any charges.**
> **(d) Jones must pay the installation cost because the housekeeper did allow the company in and the company was acting in good faith.**
>
> (Reprinted from a test in a
> Law Course in a secondary school)

The above question is an example of one which demands higher level thinking skills, but it is still possible to guess the correct answer. To assure that students use higher level thinking skills, they should be asked to defend their choice by giving three reasons stated in sentence form. This format allows the teacher to allot more marks for the question, to evaluate the knowledge and skill of the student and to make the multiple-choice question approach the depth of an essay-style question. Sufficient time must be allowed, however, for reading, thinking and writing.

Example 2

It is possible to extend a multiple-choice question into a multiple-choice/multiple-answer question in order to test higher level thinking at least to the level of analysis. Although the example shown is from Senior Algebra, the form of the question could be used for other subjects.

The following is a list of adjectives which are used to describe linear systems.

(A) CONSISTENT   (B) INCONSISTENT   (C) DEPENDENT
(D) INDEPENDENT   (E) HOMOGENEOUS

Below are ten augmented matrices. For each system, circle all the capitalized letters (representing the adjectives) that apply to it.

Marks will be awarded for each letter which is circled and should be. Marks will be deducted for letters which are circled but should not be, and for letters which are not circled but should be.

(a) $\begin{bmatrix} 2 & -1 & 3 & 0 \\ 1 & 1 & -2 & 0 \\ 4 & 3 & 1 & 0 \end{bmatrix}$ 　　(a) 　A 　B 　C 　D 　E

(b) $\begin{bmatrix} -1 & 2 & -3 & 0 \\ 4 & -3 & 12 & 0 \\ 2 & -4 & 6 & -1 \end{bmatrix}$ 　　(b) 　A 　B 　C 　D 　E

(c) $\begin{bmatrix} 3 & 4 & 1 & -2 \\ -2 & -1 & 0 & 0 \\ 2 & 3 & 1 & -1 \end{bmatrix}$ 　　(c) 　A 　B 　C 　D 　E

(d) $\begin{bmatrix} 1 & -1 & 2 & -2 \\ 2 & -2 & 1 & -1 \\ 3 & -3 & 6 & 6 \end{bmatrix}$ 　　(d) 　A 　B 　C 　D 　E

(e) $\begin{bmatrix} 4 & -2 & -6 & -8 \\ 6 & -3 & -9 & -12 \\ -2 & 1 & 3 & 4 \end{bmatrix}$ 　　(e) 　A 　B 　C 　D 　E

(f) $\begin{bmatrix} 2 & -1 & 3 & 0 \\ 4 & 5 & -2 & 0 \\ -6 & -4 & -1 & 0 \end{bmatrix}$ 　　(f) 　A 　B 　C 　D 　E

(g) $\begin{bmatrix} 2 & 3 & -1 & 4 \\ -1 & -2 & 3 & 1 \\ -1 & 0 & -7 & -11 \end{bmatrix}$ 　　(g) 　A 　B 　C 　D 　E

(h) $\begin{bmatrix} 4 & -2 & 8 & -6 \\ 5 & -1 & 7 & 0 \\ -6 & 3 & -12 & 9 \end{bmatrix}$ 　　(h) 　A 　B 　C 　D 　E

(i) $\begin{bmatrix} 1 & -2 & -1 & 4 \\ -1 & 2 & 1 & 4 \\ -3 & 6 & 3 & 9 \end{bmatrix}$ 　　(i) 　A 　B 　C 　D 　E

(j) $\begin{bmatrix} 1 & 2 & -1 & 4 \\ 2 & -1 & 0 & 1 \\ 5 & -5 & 1 & 2 \end{bmatrix}$ 　　(j) 　A 　B 　C 　D 　E

2. THE TRUE-FALSE QUESTION

Introduction

The true-false question requires the student to decide whether or not an individual statement is correct. In some cases, questions may be designed to be answered "right" or "wrong," or "yes" or "no," instead of "true" or "false." This document will consider all such questions as true-false questions.

There are at least three major criticisms of true-false questions:

First: They tend to test almost exclusively the ability to memorize rather than to apply more complex thinking skills.

Second: The results may be unreliable, because an uninformed student with weak skills or a lack of knowledge has a 50/50 chance of guessing the correct responses.

Third: Statements that are absolutely true (or false), with no qualifications or exceptions, are difficult to design. Too frequently, the better-informed students will be confused by such statements because they see that the statements should be qualified and, therefore, suspect a trick or a trap. Although this problem is common with objective-style questions in general, it is especially acute with true-false questions.

Example:

T   F   Water freezes at 0°C.

The better-informed student may challenge this statement for a number of reasons, such as the failure to indicate whether the water is salt water or fresh water, or whether the water is at sea level or a higher altitude.

Advantages and Disadvantages of True-False Questions

Advantages	Disadvantages
1. There is an apparent ease of construction.	1. The apparent ease of construction is based on the frequent practice of lifting statements from the text and changing some of them to false statements. The correct statements, and those that have been made incorrect statements, then become the test items. Such a practice can have two results: • the test items are often so obvious that everyone gets them right; • the items are so ambiguous that they become a reading test. This ambiguity promotes guessing even by the best students. While it is easy to construct weak true-false items, an extremely high degree of skill is required to construct unambiguous items which measure significant learning.
2. There appears to be considerable breadth of course material that can be tested in a true-false test.	2. In all subjects, there are large areas which cannot be phrased in absolutely true or false statements. In most cases, only the most trivial statements can be reduced to absolute terms.
3. Two thinking skills lend themselves to the use of true-false questions: • distinguishing between fact and opinion; • identifying cause and effect relationships.	3. For the most part, this type of question tests only simple knowledge recall. Even distinguishing between fact and opinion and identifying cause and effect relationships can be measured more effectively by other means.
4. A perceived advantage is that the use of this type of question is a way of modifying and differentiating evaluation for some students.	4. What may be a well-intentioned attempt at making evaluation less onerous for some students may, in reality, create problems for the students. These problems arise because: • the test creates a more stressful atmosphere for the already insecure students because it concentrates on very specific items; • the way the items are worded makes this more of a reading test than a test of knowledge. There are other ways of modifying or differentiating evaluation procedures for these students.

Advantages	Disadvantages
5. True-false questions can be scored quickly and objectively.	5. Although they can be scored quickly, they do not provide diagnostic information. They may be answered correctly on the basis of misinformation or answered incorrectly as a result of the student misreading or misinterpreting them.
	6. This form of questioning promotes random guessing. (See "The Guessing Factor" below.)

The Guessing Factor

The guessing factor is a major disadvantage when using true-false questions.

"With only two alternatives, a pupil has a 50-50 opportunity of selecting the correct answer on the basis of chance alone. Because of the difficulty of constructing items that do not contain clues to the answer, the pupil's chances of guessing correctly are usually much greater than 50 per cent. With a typical 100-item true-false test, it is not unusual to have the lowest score somewhere above 80. Although an indeterminate amount of knowledge is reflected in such a score, many of the correct answers, beyond chance, can be accounted for by correct guesses guided by various clues that have been overlooked in constructing the items. A scoring formula utilizing a correction for guessing is frequently suggested as a solution for this problem. This formula takes into account only chance guesses, however, and does not include those guided by clues. In addition, such a scoring formula favors the aggressive individual willing to take a chance. When warned that there will be a penalty for guessing, he will continue to guess, using any clues available, and will do better than chance. The cautious student, on the other hand, will mark only those answers he is certain are correct and will omit many of the items he could mark correctly on the basis of clues and partial information. Thus, the scores tend to reflect personality differences as well as knowledge of the subject.

"The high likelihood of successful guessing on the alternative-response item has a number of deleterious effects. (1) The reliability of each item is low, making it necessary to include a large number of items to obtain a reliable measure of achievement. (2) The diagnostic value of such a test is practically nil, since analyzing a pupil's response to each item is meaningless. (3) The validity of pupils' responses is questionable because of response sets... [that is, the] consistent tendency to follow a certain pattern in responding to test items. In taking a true-false test, for example, some pupils will consistently mark them "false." Thus, any given test will favor one response set over another and introduce an element into the test score which is irrelevant to the purpose of the test."[15]

Based upon the comment quoted above and the views of other experts in student evaluation, we conclude that true-false questions are of questionable value and should have limited use.

Guideposts for Constructing True-False Questions

Note: The construction of true-false questions which are free from ambiguity and misleading clues is an extremely difficult task. The time commitment necessary to develop them may not warrant their use.

1. Word the statements simply and clearly. Vague or ambiguous wording may confuse the student.

2. Avoid over-generalizing. Generalizations are seldom unqualifiedly true.

   Example:

Poor	T	F	Heavy smoking causes lung cancer.
Better	T	F	Heavy smoking often causes lung cancer.

3. Avoid trick questions. They promote mistrust and resentment.

   Example:

	T	F	General Wolseley led Canadian troops to Manitoba in 1870.

   (This statement contains three 'tricks." Wolseley was a colonel, not a general; the troops he led were British, not Canadian; and Manitoba was not yet the name of the area.)

4. Do not use trivial statements in order to "pad out" the number of questions and marks to arrive at a predetermined total.

5. Do not take exact statements from texts or notes. Statements should be reworded or, preferably, put into a new context. This will help to discourage memorizing information instead of comprehending it.

6. Statements should be entirely true or entirely false.

   Example:

Unacceptable	T	F	In the play *King Lear*, Regan ordered Gloucester's eyes to be plucked out and Gloucester died when he jumped off the cliff at Dover.

   (This statement has two parts, the first of which is correct and the second of which is incorrect.)

Acceptable	T	F	In the play *King Lear*, Regan ordered Gloucester's eyes to be plucked out.
			OR
	T	F	In the play *King Lear*, Gloucester died when he jumped off the Cliff at Dover.

7. Avoid including universal descriptors such as "never," "none," "always" and "all." Perceptive students will realize that the statement is probably false because few things are in reality that definite.

8. Avoid negative words because they are often overlooked by students. Double negatives often increase confusion and really test logic rather than knowledge.

   Example:
Poor	T	F	**It was not unheard of for Henry VIII to close monasteries in England.**
Better	T	F	**Henry VIII closed some monasteries in England.**

9. Do not use long, complicated sentences or unnecessarily difficult words.

   Example:
Poor	T	F	**The competent author endeavors to eschew obfuscation so that the reader is able to glean semantic information as readily as possible.**
Better	T	F	**The competent author writes clearly so that the reader obtains information easily.**

10. Do not include two ideas in one statement unless you are evaluating students' understanding of cause and effect relationships.

    Example:
Poor	T	F	**Porpoises are able to communicate because they are mammals.**
Better	T	F	**Porpoises are mammals.**
			OR
	T	F	**Porpoises are able to communicate.**

11. Provide a "T" and an "F" beside each statement and ask the students to circle the one they consider to be correct. This practice avoids the problem of students writing illegible letters.

Other Varieties of True-False Questions

A number of variations on the traditional true-false question may be used.

Questions can be designed, perhaps using a map or chart, which require interpretation in order to determine whether the statement is true or false.

Example 1[16]

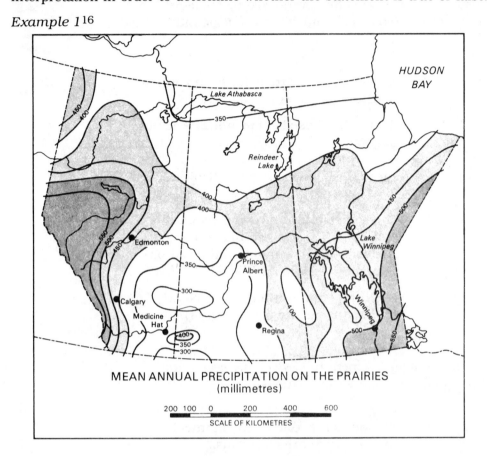

MEAN ANNUAL PRECIPITATION ON THE PRAIRIES
(millimetres)

200 100 0 200 400 600
SCALE OF KILOMETRES

For each of the following statements, indicate whether the information given

A. is TRUE, based on evidence given on the map;

B. is FALSE, based on evidence given on the map;

C. CANNOT BE DETERMINED from evidence given on the map.

In each case, print the letter indicating your choice in the space to the left of the statement.

_____ Medicine Hat receives more precipitation on the average than does Calgary.

_____ Areas to the north and west generally receive more precipitation than does the south central area.

_____ Regina receives on the average more precipitation in winter than in summer.

_____ Winnipeg receives more precipitation on the average than does Edmonton.

_____ Throughout the area, precipitation in winter falls mainly as snow.

172

Example 2

> **T   F**   **Adolf Hitler told his military leaders in 1937 that Germany's greatest enemies were France and Russia.**

Students can be asked not only to indicate whether a statement is true or false, but also to correct by changing words, phrases or clauses in them, any statements they consider to be false. This practice has several benefits:

- It reduces the guessing factor.

- It provides the teacher with diagnostic information about an individual student or about the effectiveness of the program.

- It allows the teacher to see clearly that information should be re-taught where significant numbers of students change statements which are correct.

In alloting marks, the usual marking scheme for a regular true-false question will apply, but false statements which students correct will be allotted additional marks.

> **T   F**   **Adolf Hitler told his military leaders in 1937 that Germany's greatest enemies were France and ~~Russia.~~**
> *Britain*

Example 3

Questions can be designed to cluster several items around the same subject matter. If the subject matter is a diagram, as in the example below, then higher level thinking may be required of the student.

Use the following diagram in answering questions 1 to 5.

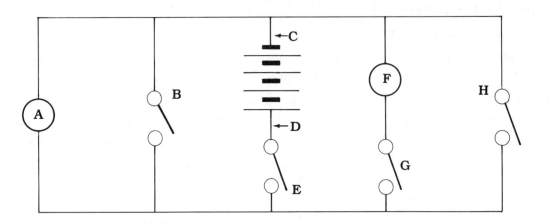

1. A short circuit is caused when switch B is open and switch H is closed.   TRUE   FALSE

2. Switch E only would cause current to flow through lamps A and F.   TRUE   FALSE

3. A short circuit would be created by closing switches B and E.   TRUE   FALSE

4. Light A can be controlled by switch B.   TRUE   FALSE

5. The current in this circuit flows from point D to C.   TRUE   FALSE

(Suitable for Electricity, Grades 7 to 10)

3. THE MATCHING QUESTION

Introduction

Another form of objective-style evaluation is the matching question. Matching questions are made up of lists of words, phrases, statements, symbols or numbers which are to be matched to another list.

Items which the student is asked to match are usually in the left hand column, and are called *premises*. Items from which the selection is to be made, usually the right hand column, are called *responses*.

Advantages and Disadvantages of Matching Questions

Advantages	Disadvantages
• Because of their compact form, matching questions can evaluate a large amount of related factual material quickly. • These questions seem to be easy to construct. • These questions are easy to score. • Because matching questions contain the correct answers, students are assisted in answering correctly.	• Matching questions are usually limited to the evaluation of factual recall. • They often present a difficult reading problem. The matching of two or more columns may make it difficult for students to see how items fit together, though they would be able to show the relationship in another test format. • Giving explicit instructions can be very difficult. • They often require more reading, organizing and thinking skills than assumed, and may not be appropriate for students experiencing difficulties. • The format of these questions can be confusing to students. For example, they may have difficulty matching items in a vertical list with items in a horizontal list. • If matching questions have too many items, they may provide more of an exercise in searching than an evaluation of knowledge. • Because of their apparent simplicity, they tend to be overused. This emphasizes rote memorization rather than thinking. • Construction of good questions requires considerable skill. For example, it is difficult to develop a list of items in which all the choices are a plausible match, but only one of which is correct. • It is difficult to find enough significant and homogeneous material to construct a suitable question. There is a tendency to introduce insignificant material to "pad out" the question.

Guideposts for Constructing Matching Questions

1. Provide clear instructions on how to indicate the correct answers.

2. Indicate whether the same response may be used more than once.

3. Maintain a grammatical consistency within and between columns. For example, within each column all items should be either in sentence form or in point form.

4. Ensure that any matching question appears entirely on one page.

5. Provide an unequal number of premises and responses. In general, the number of responses will be greater than the number of premises. Using an equal number of responses and premises promotes guessing to a further extent than an unequal number. Stating that responses may be used once, more than once or not at all, reduces the guessing factor. Under these circumstances, an equal number of premises and responses is acceptable, but this practice should be used sparingly.

6. Avoid designing questions in which the students are asked to draw connecting lines or arrows from the premise to the response. This format can be confusing to both student and marker. Always provide a clear and adequate space for the letter or number of the appropriate response.

7. Make sure that the lists are homogeneous. For example, do not, in the same column, include separate items dealing with names, dates and events. If there are only dates in one column and only events in the other column, all answers are plausible. On the other hand, if there is a mixture of dates and events in both columns, some items obviously cannot be matched. In such a situation, students can immediately rule out certain choices because of their implausibility.

   The example below uses homogeneous lists:

Directions: 1. On the line to the left of each phrase in Column I, write the letter for the word in Column II that best matches the phrase.

   2. Each word in Column II may be used once, more than once or not at all.

Column I	*Column II*
_____ 1. Name of the answer in addition problems	A Difference
_____ 2. Name of the answer in subtraction problems	B Dividend
_____ 3. Name of the answer in multiplication problems	C Multiplicand
_____ 4. Name of the answer in division problems	D Product
	E Quotient
	F Subtrahend
	G Sum

---

8. Make the wording of the premises longer than the wording of the responses, as illustrated in the preceding example. Students can then read the longer premise first and scan the list of responses quickly in order to make their selection.

9. When using two lists, it is helpful to identify the items in one list with numbers and those in the second list with letters.

10. Consider designing 3-column matching questions in order to encourage higher level thinking. This type of question is best suited for students in Grades 11 and 12.

4. THE SHORT-RESPONSE ITEM

Introduction

Short-response items are a simplified type of essay-style question.
Short-response items include:

        (a) fill in the blanks and / or completion questions;

        (b) short-answer questions;

        (c) interlinear questions.

(a) A *fill in the blank and / or completion* question is one in which words, phrases, numbers or symbols are omitted and must be supplied by the student.

    (i) **The game of _____ was invented by James Naismith.**
                                       (*Answer:* basketball)

                           OR

    The game of basketball was invented by _____.
                                   (*Answer:* James Naismith)

    (ii) **_____ is the turning point in *Romeo and Juliet*.**
                                   (*Answer:* The death of Tybalt)

(b) A *short-answer* question is one which requires a word, phrase, number or one or two sentences to answer the question.

    (i) **Who invented the game of basketball? _____**

    (ii) **In one sentence, identify the turning point in *Romeo and Juliet*.**

(c) An *interlinear* question is one in which incorrect information is embedded in a statement or a series of statements. The student is required to locate the errors and write in corrections above the stroked-out error. In the samples below, the numbers in the right hand column indicate the number of errors.

Sodium combines with chlorine to form sugar.   **(1)**

Between you and I, John is upset about what we did.   **(1)**

**Either the students or the teacher are going to bring
the picture to the gallery next week.**   **(2)**

Advantages and Disadvantages of Short-Response Items

Advantages	Disadvantages
• Short-response items are generally easier to construct than other types of questions.	• Short-response items are better suited to testing factual knowledge than the understanding of abstractions, generalizations or interpretations and may, therefore, encourage rote learning.
• They may lead to more thought among students because students are not simply selecting a correct answer.	• They may be marked more subjectively than multiple-choice or true-false items because some responses may approximate correctness and not be absolutely correct.
• They can be marked relatively quickly.	
• They have a better diagnostic value than the other forms of objective-style questions because students have to provide written answers.	• Judging the correctness of answers may lengthen the time required to mark them.
• The guessing factor present in other kinds of objective-style questions is considerably reduced.	• They must be carefully worded to avoid ambiguity.
	• They are unsuitable for evaluating complex thought or an expanded body of knowledge.

Guideposts for Constructing Short-Response Items

1. Questions must be carefully worded so that all students understand the specific nature of the question asked and the answer required.

   Example:

   Poor   **Wellington defeated Napoleon in _____.**

   This item is ambiguous because it is not clear whether the answer should be "1815" or "the Battle of Waterloo."

   Better   **In what battle fought in 1815 did Wellington defeat Napoleon? _____.**

   OR

   In what year did Wellington defeat Napoleon at Waterloo?

   _____

Example:

Poor   **Correct all errors in the following passage(s).**

> **If we loose the game on Wednesday, alot of people will**
>
> **be unhappy. I know I will not get a moments peace at**
>
> **school.   (3 errors)**

Better   **Imagine you are an editor. Read each sentence in the passage below and stroke out words that are misspelled. Print the word, correctly spelled, above each word you have stroked out.**

> **If we loose the game on Wednesday, alot of people will**
>
> **be unhappy. I know I will not get a moments peace at**
>
> **school.   (3 errors)**

2. When questions require completions or short-answers, word them so that the missing information is at, or near the end of, the sentence. This makes both reading and responding easier.

   Example:

   Poor   **In the _____ , the United States and the Soviet Union agreed to limit the production and stockpiling of nuclear weapons.**
   (*Answer:* Strategic Arms Limitation Treaty I or "S.A.L.T. I")

   Better   **The United States and the Soviet Union agreed to limit the production and stockpiling of nuclear weapons in the**

   _____ .
   (*Answer:* Strategic Arms Limitation Treaty I or "S.A.L.T. I")

3. Both the instructions and the teacher's expectations about filling in blanks should be clear. For example, students should be told whether each blank of equal length represents one word or several words, or whether longer blanks require a missing phrase or clause, or whether synonymous terms are acceptable.

4. Avoid taking statements directly from the student's textbook without changing the wording. Otherwise, there will be an excessive emphasis on rote learning.

5. Where an answer is to be expressed in numerical units, the unit should be stated.

   Example:

   Poor   **If a room measures 7 metres by 4 metres, the perimeter is _____ .**

   Better   **If a room measures 7 metres by 4 metres, the perimeter is _____ metres (or m).**

In the above example, if the area rather than the perimeter had been asked for, the teacher probably would expect the answer "28 square metres" rather than "28." In this case, the teacher would have to decide how many blanks to include.

6. Do not use too many blanks when composing completion items.

7. When designing interlinear questions, the teacher should indicate the number of errors in each sentence or passage.

8. Consider designing questions which require students to make a choice and defend it.

Example:

The following statement has been made concerning the Maritime Provinces of Canada.

> **"From a geographic and economic point of view, it would make better sense for the Maritime Provinces to join the United States than to remain as part of Canada."**

Do you agree with this statement? Indicate your view by circling the appropriate letter from the choices below.

    A. strongly agree

    B. agree

    C. disagree

    D. strongly disagree

In the space provided below, outline *three* reasons why you hold the position you have indicated above. Write your answer in full sentences.

1. _____

_____

_____

_____

2. _____

_____

_____

_____

3. _____

_____

_____

_____

---

9. Consider designing questions which require students to make a choice and then argue for and against the position chosen.

Example:

Below is a list of some suggestions that have been made to help deal with an energy crisis. Choose *two* suggestions, and for *each* choice state *one* argument supporting the suggestion and *one* argument opposing it. State each argument in one sentence.

Suggestions:

1. **Raise the price of gasoline.**

2. **Limit the amount of gasoline each car may use per week.**

3. **Place a tax of $300 to $500 on big, gas-guzzling cars.**

4. **Encourage large businesses and factories to switch from oil to coal.**

5. **Encourage the development of nuclear energy sources.**

6. **Close schools during January and February and extend classes through July.**

First Suggestion: _____

Argument For: _____

_____

Argument Against: _____

_____

Second Suggestion: _____

Argument For: _____

_____

Argument Against: _____

_____

Diagnostic Techniques in Evaluation

Introduction

When planning the evaluation program for the school year, teachers should include all three types of student evaluation: diagnostic, formative and summative. All approaches to evaluation, such as observation, written tests and practical demonstrations, can be used for diagnostic, formative and summative evaluation. Diagnostic evaluation, which is the focus of this section, is integral to an effective and complete evaluation program. For it to be of any value in developing appropriate programs for students, it is essential that teachers follow through with any necessary changes in program for particular individuals, groups or classes. Unless this follow-through occurs, there is little point in diagnostic evaluation.

Many of the approaches and techniques presented in this document can be used for diagnostic purposes. However, the three techniques presented in this section are entirely diagnostic in nature. It is impossible, within the scope of this document, to present all diagnostic evaluation techniques.

Three Examples of Diagnostic Techniques

Three techniques outlined below should be seen only as examples for use in the classroom; teachers are encouraged to consult other resources for additional techniques.

The three techniques are:

Example 1 — Modified Miscue Analysis (Grades 4 to 12);

Example 2 — Cloze (Grades 4 to 12);

Example 3 — Human Figure Drawing (Kindergarten to Grade 6).

Another valuable diagnostic technique, "Evaluating Oral Language," can be found in the section on observation, pages 76-79.

Example 1

Modified Miscue Analysis as a Diagnostic Technique

INTRODUCTION

Miscue analysis was developed by Kenneth Goodman, Yetta Goodman and Carolyn Burke. It is based upon the knowledge that all readers make "errors" when they read, but that some "errors" are better than others. The term "miscue" is preferable to "error" because it implies that we look for and use cues to get the meaning of what we are reading. The term "error," however, implies that the reader's response was wrong and useless.

Miscue analysis is a means of observing and evaluating a person's oral reading. It helps the teacher to know whether or not a reader can make sense of a passage and, if so, how it is done.

The account of miscue analysis presented here is a modified version of the somewhat clinical scheme outlined in Goodman and Burke's *Reading Miscue Inventory Manual — Procedure for Diagnosis and Evaluation.*[17] Modified miscue analysis is valuable for teachers wanting to find out more about students who seem to have trouble gaining meaning from print. Once practiced in the procedure, teachers will be more aware of students' failed attempts to make meaning out of print and will be more able to assist those in difficulty.

This technique can be used for any student and in any subject using reading, from Grade 4 to Grade 12. The technique should be used in a private setting on a one-to-one basis. Its best application would be with students whom the teacher suspects have reading difficulties. Common indications of these difficulties are the inability to answer questions, failure to complete homework assignments satisfactorily, frequent miscues when reading aloud, reluctance to read and undue length of time required to complete a silent reading assignment.

METHOD

1. Choose an appropriate passage for the student to read. It may be a short story or a non-fiction account. It should be somewhat difficult for the student to read, but short enough to finish at a single sitting.

2. If possible, tape-record the reading. However, if the student is intimidated by the recorder, do not use it, but score the reading while the student is reading.

    Before the student begins reading, say:

    "I want you to read this story aloud for me. I will not be marking or grading your reading. I just want to see how you read. After you have finished, I want you to tell me the story in your own words.

    "I won't help you while you are reading. Do the best you can. If you find a word you don't know, you may guess what it is or skip it."

3. After the student reads the story aloud, ask the student to re-tell the story. Do not interrupt the student in the re-telling of the story.

4. Following the unaided re-telling of the story, ask some open-ended questions to probe areas omitted in the re-telling. These questions must not use any specific information which the student has not reported in the re-telling and must not steer the reader to conclusions.

5. Listen to the tape and mark the text for each miscue, using the symbols shown below.

HOW TO INDICATE MISCUES

Sentence in the print: **The big, brown dog ran under the apple tree.**

Type of Miscue	Symbol	What the Reader Reads	How the Miscue Is Marked
Substitution The reader substitutes a word or non-word for the word in print.	run RAN	The big, brown dog run under the apple tree.	The big, brown dog *run* ran under the apple tree.
Insertion The reader inserts something which is not in the print.	∧	The big, brown dog ran under the apple tree.	The big, brown dog ran under the big ∧ apple tree.
Omission The reader leaves out a portion of the text already read.	⬭	The brown dog ran under the apple tree.	The (big,) brown dog ran under the apple tree.
Repetition The reader repeats a portion of the text already read.	Ⓡ	The big...the big, brown dog ran under the apple tree.	Ⓡ The big, brown dog ran under the apple tree.
Correction The reader goes back in an attempt to correct a section of text already read.	Ⓒ Successful Correction ⓊⒸ Un-successful Correction Attempt	The big, blue... brown dog ran under the apple tree. The big, brown dog ran udder...underd the apple tree.	Ⓒ blue The big, brown dog ran under the apple tree. The big, brown dog ran ⓊⒸ 2. underd 1. udder under the apple tree.
Reversal The reader reverses the order of a portion of the print, such as letters, words, or phrases.	∿	The brown, big dog ran under the apple tree.	The big, brown dog ran under the apple tree.

6. Analyze the miscues, using the following questions.

- To what extent does the miscue *look like* the expected response?

- To what extent does the miscue *sound like* the expected response?

- What is the *grammatical function* of the miscue and the expected response?

- Is the miscue *grammatically acceptable* within the text?

- Does the miscue produce a structure that is acceptable in terms of *meaning*?

- To what extent does the miscue *change* the intended *text meaning*?

- Is a different *intonation pattern* involved?

- Is the reader's *dialect* involved in the miscue?

7. In analyzing the miscues, distinguish between high quality and low quality miscues, as described below.

A. High Quality Miscues

Some miscues indicate that the reader is reading for meaning. These are called high quality miscues.

(i) *Familiar Language*

If a reader sometimes uses familiar language when the text uses formal language, the reader is probably deriving meaning from the text.

Example: Text: **He is not here today.**

Reader: **He isn't here today.**

(ii) *Dialect*

If the reader sometimes uses personal dialect which is not present in the text, he or she is probably deriving meaning from the text.

Example: Text: **He bought candy yesterday.**

Reader: **He buy candy yesterday.**

(iii) *Self-correction*

If the reader corrects the miscues of words which are important for meaning, he or she is probably deriving meaning from the text. The correction may occur several sentences or paragraphs after the miscue.

Example: Text: **The little house in the field was white and black.**

Reader 1: **The little horse in the field was....
The little house in the field was white and black.**

Reader 2: **Hey, that wasn't "horse" back there, it was "house."**

(iv) *Omissions*

If the reader sometimes omits words which are not essential or have been used several times before in the text, he or she may be reading for meaning.

> *Example:*   Text: **The big, brown dog ran under the apple tree.**
>
> Reader: **The brown dog ran under the apple tree.**

B. Low Quality Miscues

Some miscues indicate that the reader is insecure in reading and may not be deriving meaning from the print. If the text itself is not too difficult for the reader, then some remedial strategies should be employed.

(i) *Omissions*

A reader who frequently and unintentionally omits important words is not reading for meaning. If the reader frequently and intentionally omits unfamiliar words, then he or she probably thinks that an accurate response is more important than deriving sense from the text.

(ii) *Frequent Self-correction*

A reader who makes *many* successful corrections, is having difficulty with the text. If the reader makes some unsuccessful attempts to correct a miscue, he or she is having difficulty with the text.

(iii) *Reversals, or the Omission or the Addition of Letters*

If the reader confuses words through the reversal of letters (for example, "was" for "saw"), or omits letters ("though" for "through"), or adds letters ("brought" for "bought") and does not correct the miscue, help the student by giving some simple exercises in which these words are emphasized.

> *Note:*   If a student reads a passage with very few miscues, the teacher should not assume that the student has understood what has been read. The student may be "word-calling." On the other hand, a student who makes numerous miscues not only may understand the passage, but also may be able to make perceptive comments about it after only one reading.

8. Analyze the re-telling of the story and the answering of the questions.
   Some students, after reading the selection, will give an elaborate account which includes many details and a statement of theme. Others will give a mere outline. Your questions after the re-telling should be open-ended and should elicit more information than was given in the re-telling. During the re-telling and discussion, the student should volunteer most, but not necessarily all, of the following information:

   (i) *Information to be Derived from a Short Story:*

   Character
   - The names of the principal characters in the story
   - Physical appearance
   - Attitudes
   - Feelings
   - Behavior
   - Relationship to other characters

   Events
   - Actual happenings in order of their occurrence

   Plot
   - Story line
   - General plan upon which sequence of events is organized
   - Overall question, problem or conflict which is central to the story

   Theme
   - Generalized abstraction, message or viewpoint which the author is trying to convey

   (ii) *Information to be Derived from Non-Fiction (Informational or "Content" Material):*

   Specifics
   - Actual happenings, items, instances or pieces of information in the material

   Generalizations
   - General information deduced from an examination of specific items
   - Interrelationship of specific items or facts directly related to the topic of the material

   Major Concepts
   - Universal views or positions abstracted from the generalizations and which indicate concepts which can be applied to diverse topics or across subjects

9. Summarize and make conclusions about the student's reading performance (oral reading, self-correction, comprehension, retention, re-telling).

10. Decide on a course of action, if any, for this particular student.

Case Study — Example of a Miscue Analysis

Student
- Victor (not his real name)
- Born in a southern European country
- Speaks a language other than English at home
- Grade 12 student
- Average achievement in most subjects
- Considered to be a very poor reader by most of his teachers.

Text
- "Ha 'penny," a short story by Alan Paton[18]
- The story is 614 lines long
- The example here is one paragraph from the story, but Victor read the entire story aloud. The excerpt is the third paragraph of the story.
- The excerpt is typical of the reading of the rest of the story.

0208	These secret relations with them were a source of continu-
0209	ous pleasure to me. Had they been my own children I would
0210	no doubt have given a greater expression to it. But often I
0211	would move through the silent and orderly parade, and stand
0212	by one of them. He would look straight in front of him with a
0213	little frown of concentration that expressed both childish
0214	awareness of and manly indifference to my nearness. Some-
0215	time I would tweak his ear, and he would give me a brief
0216	smile of acknowledgement, or frown with still great concen-
0217	tration. It was natural I suppose to confine these outward ex-
0218	pressions to the very smallest, but they were taken as sym-
0219	bolic, and some older boys would observe them and take
0220	themselves to be included. It was a relief, when the reforma-
0221	tory was passing through times of turbulence and trouble,
0222	and when there was danger of estrangement between au-
0223	thority and boys, to make these simple and natural gestures,
0224	which were reassurances both to me and them that nothing
0225	important had changed.

Re-telling of "Ha'penny" by Victor

V: There is this black boy in a reformatory and he has tuberculosis. And he meets this man who wants to be a principal of a reformatory. No, he more or less wants to set up an establishment for an industrial school. And he begins talking to this boy. He has a whole family but which he makes up. But he observes...he seen this lady once Mrs... (what her name) Mrs. Maarman. And he sees she has two sons and two daughters with her. One was Dickie and one was Richard and the two daughters Ann and Mina. And he started telling him about the family but he finally discovered by his mistake once of calling Dickie "Tickie" and he went and investigated more or less and found out the Mrs. Mine wasn't really his mother and they weren't his real sisters. He just made it up because he wanted a family to be with. So he wrote a letter to Mrs. Mine to tell her about the situation and she said o.k. she's come over and adopt Ha'Penny. And, but she started visiting but at the end he ends up dying of tuberculosis.

Questions and Answers

T: What country does it take place in?

V: I think Germany.

T: Why do you think it's Germany?

V: Because there's some German in it.

T: Why do you think that the speaker said his name was Dickie not Tickie near the end of the story?

V: Because he may have misunderstood himself I think at the beginning.

T: Why does the boy come down with tuberculosis at that time?

V: Because he didn't have any family and he was in a reformatory and his health couldn't be really that great. No one really cared for him all that much. So his health just couldn't hold out.

T: Do you think the writer of the story would be a good person in charge of a school like a reformatory?

V: Which person are you referring to?

T: The one who wrote the story, Alan Paton.

V: Oh yeah, I think he'd be.

T: Why?

V: The way he showed sympathy toward Ha'penny more or less. He feels what Ha'penny has that having a family is not a very good thing not to have. He's lonely in the world. There's no one he can throw out his feelings to or communicate with or anything. He just all lonely and that's a terrible feeling.

T: Do you think it's a good story?

V: It is a good story. It may have a moral to it that people should be more considerate to each other and people should have a feelings for other people because they should have an understanding why people feel like that and why people do things...steal like Ha'penny did. He has nothing to hold on so he just keeps searching and he sees, he just falls to crime; it's the only solution he has.

Analysis of the Excerpt and Re-telling and Questioning

Victor, although rated as a very poor reader by his teachers, has many strengths in reading. In the re-telling and questioning after the reading, he was able to recall the names of the main characters; to describe their attitudes, feelings and behaviors; and to analyze their relationships. He also could relate the events of the story to a plot line. Most important, he presented a very sensitive statement about the theme of the story.

Partial Analysis of Victor's Miscues

- Most of Victor's miscues were corrected.

- Some of them could have been caused by his predicting the possible structure of the sentence. For example, in line 0210, the words "but often I" could lead him to expect "have" or "had" to follow in line 0211. This expectation could cause the "ha—" miscue in line 0211. Also, "would have moved" is a common means of expression and the change of tense does not change the meaning. Some other miscues which may have resulted from predicting the way the sentence would develop are:

      0213   that / and
      0219   some older / some of
      0220   It was / It would h—

   This type of miscue shows that Victor is actively applying his knowledge of English to the text. It also shows that he is using one of the most important strategies for reading: *prediction.*

- Two of the miscues occur at the end of lines (0216 and 0218) where words are completed on the next line. The miscues probably result from his need to read ahead to obtain the proper pronunciation of the words.

- The two uncorrected miscues in this passage probably arise from his unfamiliarity with the words. The miscue "tweak / twick" in line 0215 is obviously such an example. The miscue "turbulence / disturb" in line 0221 shows a reading strength. He probably didn't know the word "turbulence," but he knew the concept required and was about to give a synonym for the word when he realized that it wasn't the "right" word. "Disturbance" would have been just fine.

- The correction of "estrangement" (0222) shows that he uses word recognition skills to obtain words because he took the word syllable by syllable: es / trange / ment.

Conclusions

Victor's reputation as a very poor reader is unfounded. He does not read orally with ease, but he does read for meaning and with sensitivity.

Victor needs many opportunities to rehearse and to read aloud in many different settings. Above all, he needs reassurance to overcome his poor self-concept with regard to reading.

Example 2

Cloze as a Diagnostic Technique

INTRODUCTION

Cloze procedure is a technique in which specific words are omitted from a passage and students are asked to fill in as many of the omitted words as possible. This technique can be used effectively in Grades 4 to 12. As a diagnostic evaluation technique, Cloze may be used:

- to provide confirmatory evidence for the placement of students in reading groups;

- to select textbooks and materials appropriate for the class or group;

- to determine whether or not students can read and comprehend the pre-selected textbook;

- to ascertain the comprehension strengths and weaknesses of students.

The procedure outlined below is intended for use with students in Grades 4 to 12. In Kindergarten to Grade 3, the Cloze procedure should be used only as a teaching technique, not as a diagnostic evaluation technique.

CONSTRUCTING THE CLOZE PROCEDURE

1. Select a passage of approximately 250 words.

2. Do a readability study on the passage you intend to use so that its approximate level of reading difficulty is ascertained.

3. Leave the first and last sentences intact. Then delete every fifth word in the passage. Punctuation must be left intact.

   Note: There is some controversy as to whether proper names, dates, sums of money, or numbers should be deleted. In constructing the Cloze exercise, use your discretion. If students have no way of determining the correct response, delete the word following the one in question.

4. Leave each blank exactly the same length (12 typewriter spaces), and type the passage, making sure that approximately *50* words have been deleted. Complete the sentence in which the fiftieth word was deleted and add a final sentence, which is left intact.

   It is suggested that 50 words be deleted for two reasons: first, a sufficient number of blanks are necessary to construct a reliable instrument and, second, it is easy to multiply 50 by 2 to get 100 percent.

5. There should be no time restraints placed upon the completion of this exercise.

Cloze should not be used as a diagnostic technique until students are comfortable with the procedure. Students should have adequate practice with this procedure before it is used formally.

Begin with an easy passage that most students can do successfully. Have students mark their own work. They should first score only words that are exactly the same as the words that were deleted. Then they score all words that make sense in the passage. This activity may be done through group or class discussion *or* by having students work in pairs.

Continue with a more difficult passage or passages and allow students to mark or score their own papers.

The students are now ready for the formal administration of the Cloze procedure.

ADMINISTERING THE CLOZE PROCEDURE

Either orally or in writing, the students should be given the following instructions:

1. Read the entire selection silently to yourself before attempting to fill in the blanks.

2. Write only one word in each blank.

3. Try to fill in every blank. Don't be afraid to guess.

4. You may skip blanks which are difficult and return to them when you have finished. Don't worry if you can't fill in all the blanks.

5. Incorrect spelling will not count against you, if the meaning of the misspelled word is sufficiently clear.

6. Some of the blanks may be filled with contractions such as "isn't" or "can't."

7. Take your time. This is not a speed test.

SCORING THE CLOZE PROCEDURE

Because it is difficult for people who are unfamiliar with the Cloze procedure to interpret scores, teachers should not provide students or parents with Cloze scores expressed as a percentage or as raw scores. In addition, these scores should never be used as part of term or examination marks.

There are two ways of scoring these procedures.

1. In the past, only those words exactly the same as the original words were scored as correct. This method is easier to score, but may be unfair to those students who have a rich vocabulary.

2. The second method of scoring is more time consuming for the scorer. In this method, all suitable words are accepted, but the scorer must consider each word choice carefully and decide upon its suitability.

   In order to score the Cloze procedure, the scorer counts the words which are the same as the words deleted and / or those words which have been accepted as suitable. Ignore spelling errors.

Cloze Score	Rounded Percentages	Levels	Description
0-20	40% or less	Frustration level for the reader of this material.	At this level, little or no information is gained from this particular reading material.
20-30	40% to 60%	Instructional level for the reader of this material.	At this level, information is gained from this reading material, but teacher guidance is recommended.
30-50	60% or more	Independent level for the reader of this material.	At this level, information is gained with ease from this reading material.

INTERPRETING THE RESULTS OF THE CLOZE PROCEDURE

1. *Grouping*

    The results of a Cloze procedure can be used either to establish groups within the class based on reading ability, or to confirm groupings already established.

2. *Matching Students and Material*

    There are many ways to determine the suitability of a text or of selections within a text, basal reader or anthology. The Cloze procedure is one way of determining this suitability. However, teachers must consider not only readability, but also content, concept load, the experience each student brings to the print and his or her personal interests or motivation.

    It must be emphasized, however, that textbooks and basal readers published for a specific grade level may contain selections ranging from three levels below to three levels above the indicated grade level.

3. *Diagnosing Strengths and Weaknesses*

    After administering a Cloze procedure, teachers should be concerned about students with scores below forty per cent. If a student scores below forty per cent, ask the following questions:

    (a) Do most of the words provided by the student make sense in the passage? If they don't, try a Cloze passage based on easier material to see if the student can write words that do make sense. If the words in the easier passage make sense, then the original passage may have been too difficult *or* the student may not have been reading for meaning.

    (b) Did the student use the wrong part of speech in the blanks? If he or she put nouns in verb blanks or verbs in adjective blanks, then syntax was not used to get meaning from the printed page, *or* the material was beyond his or her reading level. If, for example, a student is unable to use prepositions correctly, devise a series of Cloze exercises in which many of the prepositions have been omitted.

(c) Did the Cloze exercise present unfair difficulty to the student? For example, did it contain too many concepts, foreign or archaic words, dialect or unusual syntax?

> Students scoring below 40% should be re-tested on less difficult material in order to determine their instructional level.

EXAMPLE OF A CLOZE PROCEDURE

The following sample is from a Grade 10 history textbook. This passage tests at a difficult Grade 10 reading level, based on a readability graph. However, because the vocabulary, sentence structure and concept load are relatively simple, the passage should be considered as a low to middle Grade 10 readability.

Teachers preparing to teach a textbook could use a passage from it (as illustrated below)[19] to determine whether any students will have difficulty reading it. The numbers in the spaces are included in the example only for the teacher, but would not be included in a passage used with the students.

New technology often leads to changes in people's lives. For example, the

_____[1] was once a new _____[2] of transportation. Only

the _____[3] could afford the high _____[4] of the early

models. _____[5] mass production underway, lower _____[6]

meant many more cars _____.[7] The growth of the _____[8]

industry led to the _____[9] of huge amounts of _____,[10]

the employment of thousands _____[11] auto workers, business

people _____[12] office staff. Automobile dealerships,

_____[13] stations, improved roads, parking _____[14] and

other related services _____[15] developed.

In the early _____,[16] some people resisted the _____[17]

"revolution." These **technophobes** felt _____[18] cars were a

threat _____[19] a way of life _____[20] were comfortable

with. Some _____[21] so far as to _____[22] tacks and broken

glass _____[23] roads and to put _____[24] barriers. Others

simply refused _____[25] buy and learn _____[26] drive a car.

Eventually, _____[27] became a normal part _____[28] the

environment. People grew _____[29] with them. They appreciated

_____[30] mobility, independence and other _____[31] the

automobile had to _____.[32] On the other hand, _____[33]

regretted the injuries and _____[34] caused by automobile

accidents. _____ 35 worried about air pollution _____ 36 noise and junkyards piled _____ 37 rusted cars. They cursed _____ 38 costs of gasoline, _____, 39 repairs and complained about _____ 40 shortcomings of other means _____ 41 travel. But they had _____ 42 hard time imagining their _____ 43 without automobiles.

The widespread _____ 44 of automobiles raised all _____ 45 of questions and arguments _____ 46 problems. Is the same _____ 47 happening in the case _____ 48 micro-computers? We cannot know _____ 49 sure; predicting the future _____ 50 a chancy business. But we can make some careful guesses — in the form of **scenarios** — based on our observations of recent developments, and of the history of other technological changes.

Answer Key:

1. automobile	18. that	35. They
2. kind	19. to	36. and
3. rich	20. they	37. with
4. prices	21. went	38. the
5. with	22. spread	39. insurance
6. costs	23. on	40. the
7. sold	24. up	41. of
8. automobile	25. to	42. a
9. investment	26. to	43. world
10. money	27. automobiles	44. use
11. of	28. of	45. kinds
12. and	29. up	46. and
13. service	30. the	47. thing
14. lots	31. benefits	48. of
15. were	32. offer	49. for
16. years	33. they	50. is
17. automobile	34. deaths	

Example 3

Human Figure Drawing as a Diagnostic Technique

INTRODUCTION

Drawings of human figures can be used as a diagnostic technique from Kindergarten to Grade 6. Analyses of the drawings will provide teachers with information regarding their students' states of cognitive development. That is, by examining a student's drawing of a human figure and by applying the characteristics of the drawing to the detailed chart found on page 201,[20] the teacher can gain an indication as to whether the student's cognitive age is higher than, the same as, or lower than his or her chronological age. This information should not be used by itself, but together with other tests and observations.

The drawings in this section were gathered as part of a human drawing diagnostic procedure conducted in a school system.

METHOD

The human figure drawing task can be administered either as an individual or a group activity. Students' desks should be uncluttered, and a piece of blank paper, 8 1/2" x 11" (21.5cm x 28cm), a pencil and an eraser should be given to each student. The teacher then asks the students to draw a picture of a whole person. This could be any kind of a person they wish, but they should avoid stick figures. There should be no time limit imposed upon this activity.

EXAMPLES OF HUMAN FIGURE DRAWINGS

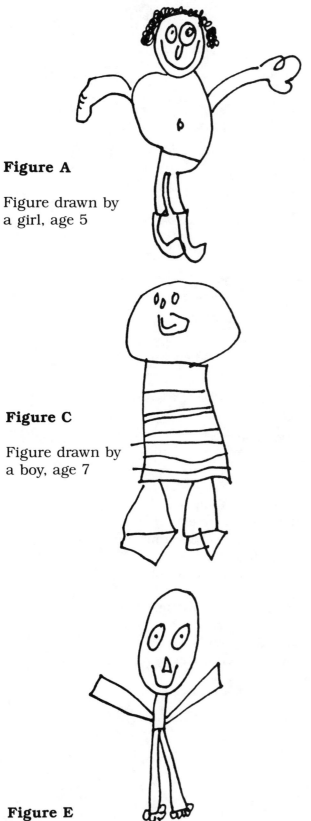

Figure A

Figure drawn by
a girl, age 5

Figure B

Figure drawn by
a boy, age 5

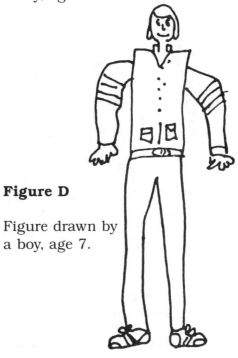

Figure C

Figure drawn by
a boy, age 7

Figure D

Figure drawn by
a boy, age 7.

Figure E

Figure drawn by a girl, age 8.

Figure F

Figure drawn by a boy, age 8.

ANALYSIS OF A HUMAN FIGURE DRAWING

Using the chart on page 201, record each item which appears in the drawing in the expected item chart. For example, looking at Figure C, the teacher would record the following items.

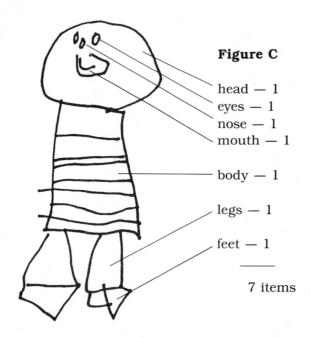

Figure C

head — 1
eyes — 1
nose — 1
mouth — 1

body — 1

legs — 1

feet — 1
———
7 items

Figure drawn by a boy, age seven.

This figure shows seven items which are scored (see illustration above). Referring to the chart on page 201, a seven-year-old boy could be *expected* to draw nine items, which are: a head, eyes, nose, mouth, body, legs, arms, feet, arms in two dimensions. In addition, the boy may draw *exceptional* items such as arms at shoulder, four clothing items, feet in two dimensions, five fingers, pupils in the eyes.

The results of this example of human figure drawing indicate that this student has not reached the expected level of cognitive development for his age. If this information is corroborated by other observations and test results, the teacher could use this information as the basis for providing a suitable program for the student.

Expected Item (N)	Age 5 Boys 128	Age 5 Girls 128	Age 6 Boys 131	Age 6 Girls 133	Age 7 Boys 134	Age 7 Girls 125	Age 8 Boys 133	Age 8 Girls 130	Age 9 Boys 131	Age 9 Girls 134	Age 10 Boys 109	Age 10 Girls 108	Age 11 & 12 Boys 157	Age 11 & 12 Girls 167
Head	X	X	X	X	X	X	X	X	X	X	X	X	X	X
Eyes	X	X	X	X	X	X	X	X	X	X	X	X	X	X
Nose	X	X	X	X	X	X	X	X	X	X	X	X	X	X
Mouth	X	X	X	X	X	X	X	X	X	X	X	X	X	X
Body	X	X	X	X	X	X	X	X	X	X	X	X	X	X
Legs	X	X	X	X	X	X	X	X	X	X	X	X	X	X
Arms	X	X	X	X	X	X	X	X	X	X	X	X	X	X
Feet				X	X	X	X	X	X	X	X	X	X	X
Arms 2 dimensions					X	X	X	X	X	X	X	X	X	X
Legs 2 dimensions						X	X	X	X	X	X	X	X	X
Hair				X		X		X		X	X	X	X	X
Neck						X		X		X	X	X	X	X
Arm down											X		X	X
Arms at shoulders												X		X
2 clothing items														X
Exceptional Items														
Knee	X		X	X	X	X	X	X	X	X	X	X	X	X
Profile	X	X	X	X	X	X	X	X	X	X		X		
Elbow	X	X	X	X	X	X	X	X	X					
Two lips	X	X	X	X	X	X	X	X	X		X			
Nostrils	X	X	X		X		X		X					
Proportions	X	X	X	X										
Arms at shoulders	X	X	X	X										
4 clothing items	X	X	X	X										
Feet 2 dimensions	X	X		X										
Five fingers	X	X												
Pupils	X	X												

Modifying Evaluation Procedures and Methods for Exceptional Students in the Classroom

1. Introduction

In many provinces and states, legislation in the area of special education requires school boards to provide educational programs for all students identified as exceptional. For the purpose of this section, the terms "exceptional student," "special education program" and "special education services" are defined as follows:

Exceptional Student
An exceptional student is one whose behavioral, communicational, intellectual, physical or multiple exceptionalities are such that he or she is considered to need placement in a special education program. In some jurisdictions, a student is deemed to be exceptional only if so determined by a special educational committee.

Special Education Program
A special education program is one which is based on, and modified by, the results of continuous assessment and evaluation, and which includes a plan containing specific objectives and an outline of educational services that will help to meet the needs of the exceptional student.

Special Education Services
Special education services are those facilities and resources, including support personnel and equipment, necessary for developing and implementing a special education program.

> Some of the students identified as exceptional and who will need special education services may be in the regular classroom for part or all of their classroom time. This section of this document applies only to the evaluation of those exceptional students within a regular classroom for all or part of their time. It does not necessarily apply to the evaluation of such students in those parts of the program for which they are withdrawn from the regular classroom.

2. Exceptionalities

There are five categories of exceptional students:

i) Communication Exceptionality:
— Learning Disability
— Autism
— Hearing Impairment
— Language Impairment
— Speech Impairment

ii) Behavioral Exceptionality:
  — Emotional Disturbance
  — Social Maladjustment

iii) Intellectual Exceptionality:
  — Giftedness
  — Slow Learner (Educably Retarded)
  — Trainable Retardation

iv) Physical Exceptionality:
  — Orthopaedic and / or Physical Handicap
  — Visual Impairment

v) Multiple Exceptionalities:
  — Multihandicap

So that most exceptional students can have their needs met in regular classes of their home schools, some jurisdictions provide support systems to assist schools and regular classroom teachers.

In this document, samples of modifications in evaluation have been provided for the following: learning disability, behavioral exceptionality, giftedness and slow learner (educably retarded). These four samples (see pages 208-225) cover the most common exceptionalities likely to be encountered by the teacher in the regular classroom.

3. Modification of Evaluation Procedures for Exceptional Students

BECAUSE

evaluation is closely linked to the course objectives

AND BECAUSE

evaluation is an integral part of the entire education process, not merely a testing of the end product of the student's achievement,

AND BECAUSE

the activities and methods employed in the teaching process must be under constant evaluation by the teacher

AND BECAUSE

many jurisdictions call for a modification of services and programs to meet the needs of exceptional students,

THEREFORE,

it is essential to modify not only objectives and teaching strategies but also procedures and methods used to evaluate exceptional students.

4. Factors to Consider in Evaluating Exceptional Students

For all students, particularly those with exceptionalities, evaluation must focus on the following:

- **Levels of Development**

  It is important to determine the levels of intellectual and emotional development before and during the evaluation of students. To do this, teachers should be fully aware of the stages of development as outlined on pages 35-42 above. Teacher-made tests and standardized tests may also be used to assist in determining students' levels of development.

- **Progress**

  Short-term and long-term objectives should be set, in order to gauge the progress of the students. Teachers should be aware that progress occurs at varying rates and is not necessarily consistent from one competency to another. They also need to be aware that students with exceptionalities may regress academically under stress. For most exceptional students, consolidation of learning requires much practice and review.

- **Specific Strengths and Weaknesses**

  All students, including exceptional students, have strengths as well as weaknesses. Diagnosis of these strengths and weaknesses should be the basis for classroom modifications, individual instruction and evaluation.

  Teachers should have available to them a large quantity of information regarding their students which they should consult before and while evaluating them. A careful analysis of previous school history and background information can reveal patterns of behavior and academic growth which should be of assistance when assessing the individual student's present progress.

5. Factors to Consider When Reporting on the Evaluation of Exceptional Students

When reporting to a parent, whether during an interview or in writing, the teacher should clearly state the student's instructional level, the short-term and long-term objectives, and the progress made by the student.

When a student's program has been modified, both parents and student should be kept fully informed regarding the form and extent of the modification. The report card should indicate the mark or grade, and clearly state that it is the result of a modified program and modified evaluation.

In addition to the formal report card, the following methods may be used to present a clear, fair and accurate assessment of the student.

- **Interviews**

  Prepare for a parent interview by:
  — re-examining the student's permanent record;
  — having available the student's work folder(s);
  — collecting samples of the student's work from the beginning of the year;
  — having available the full record of the student's marks and attendance;
  — having available a statement of course or program objectives;
  — having a detailed account of the specific modifications concerning program and evaluation that have been made for this particular student;
  — arranging the most congenial interview situation possible;
  — deciding whether or not the student will be present at the interview.

  During the interview:
  — show, using specific examples, how the program has been modified for the student, the effect of these modifications on the student's progress and areas that require further improvement;
  — identify areas in which the parent and teacher could work co-operatively, and methods which can be used to meet the concerns identified;
  — ensure that the parent leaves the interview with a positive attitude.

- **Parent Visitation to the Classroom**

  — Observation of the student in the classroom setting may demonstrate to parents their child's abilities and behaviors, and the effectiveness of the program. Teachers and parents should be aware that the presence of another person may change the classroom atmosphere.

- **Written Reports**

  — The student's progress should be communicated to both student and parent in written form by the use of a descriptive report. Honest, positive feedback of progress provides motivation for learning.
  — Frequently use other forms of written communication such as charts, graphs, checklists and short notes, to indicate student progress.

Samples of Modifications in Evaluation for Exceptional Students

On the following pages, four samples of modification in evaluation for exceptional students are provided. These samples cover four of the most common exceptionalities likely to be encountered by the teacher in the regular classroom.

They are:

SAMPLE 1: Communications Exceptionality — Learning Disability

SAMPLE 2: Behavioral Exceptionality

SAMPLE 3: Intellectual Exceptionality — Giftedness

SAMPLE 4: Intellectual Exceptionality — Slow Learner

Each sample includes:

- a definition of the exceptionality;
- identifying traits;
- suggestions for modifications of evaluation procedures;
- implications for reporting;
- considerations regarding the student's self-concept.

Sample 1

Communications Exceptionality — Learning Disability

A. DEFINITION AND IDENTIFYING TRAITS

The students identified as learning disabled are those who are characterized by a condition that results in a significant discrepancy between academic achievement and assessed intellectual ability. They will have deficits in one or more of the following areas:

- receptive language (listening, reading);

- language processing (thinking, conceptualizing, integrating);

- expressive language (talking, spelling, writing);

- mathematical computations.

These deficits are NOT primarily the result of:

- impairment of vision;

- impairment of hearing;

- physical handicap;

- mental retardation;

- primary emotional disturbance;

- cultural difference.

Students with learning disabilities will display some or all of the following indicators or characteristics, which may range from mild to severe.

1. They have problems with short- and / or long-term memory.

2. They have uneven academic development and progress. For example, they may know a fact or process and be progressing one week, but the next week may neither remember nor understand what they apparently knew before.

3. They often have difficulty relating to their peers.

4. They may be able to read well, but unable to write well.

5. They may have specific gaps in skills such as reading, writing and mathematics. For example, they may be very weak spellers.

6. They are very easily distracted.

7. They often lack a sense of time and space and shape; they may also lack an awareness of their body in space.

8. They may lack organizational skills.

9. They often have difficulty in following or creating a sequence.

10. They may have, because of their learning disability, a poor self-concept, and may exhibit negative behavioral patterns caused by their lack of success.

11. They may have co-ordination problems.

12. They may have difficulty following oral directions.

Some students who have been identified as learning disabled and who have subsequently been given a properly modified program, including appropriately modified evaluation procedures, are capable of achieving academic and career success.

B. SUGGESTIONS FOR MODIFICATIONS OF THE EVALUATION PROCEDURES FOR STUDENTS WITH LEARNING DISABILITIES

It is important when evaluating students with learning disabilities to concentrate on the students' strengths while working with them to improve the areas where they have specific needs. To this end, the following suggestions are offered:

1. Provide alternate methods of evaluation, such as oral testing and the use of tapes. For example:

- If a student has difficulty expressing ideas in written form, the student can be withdrawn from the classroom and the questions read to him or her orally. He or she can then dictate the answer into a tape recorder.

- With some students and with some tests, the answer can be dictated to someone else who writes the answer.

- If a student writes fairly well but has a reading problem, the question can be read or provided on tape. The student can then write the answer.

In any of the above situations, the same standards for evaluating information, ideas and thinking should apply as they do for other students.

2. Allow ample time for completion of classroom activities, tests and examinations. For example:

- If the assignment or examination is to be completed in a specified period of time, the student may require more time than that allocated to the rest of the students. The student should know in advance how much additional time has been allowed.

- If the assignment is to cover a longer period of time (for example, a shop project to be completed in 2 to 3 weeks), and is to be done partly outside the classroom, then more time may not be necessary. However, constant checking on the student's progress may be required. Some negotiations with other teachers may be necessary regarding the extension of time for tests and assignments.

3. Re-phrase or repeat oral instructions in an evaluation situation when necessary. Where the instructions are in written form, ask the student to explain his or her understanding of the instructions.

4. Accentuate positive self-concept by avoiding excessive correction of the student's errors. When evaluating a student's written work, concentrate on specific content or on a particular skill which is to be tested, rather than on general corrections.

5. Modify the assignment given to the student in terms of:
   — time;
   — quantity of work expected to be completed;
   — nature of assignment.

6. Have the student verbalize gym, shop or lab procedural steps, before commencing the task to be evaluated.

7. Use illustrative gestures and visual demonstrations while giving oral instructions for a task to be evaluated.

8. Vary the degree of difficulty of assignments to be evaluated and present the task or problem in such a way that students will proceed from the concrete to the abstract.

9. Present manipulative experiences wherever possible. For example, if a student is unable to describe a science experiment in writing,

arrangements should be made to have that student demonstrate the experiment with the proper equipment and describe and explain the experiment. Another example is allowing a history student to create and then discuss a model, collage or poster instead of writing an essay.

10. Consider the following practices when developing an assignment:
    — adequate spacing between items in the printed instructions;
    — size and clarity of print, diagrams, maps, etc.;
    — the color of the paper used (white is recommended);
    — well-organized and uncluttered pages.

11. Provide assistance in developing an individual calendar or schedule outlining dates, places and times that evaluation will occur. Given the complexity of school timetables, and the students' difficulties with organization, such assistance is necessary.

12. Consider avoiding the deduction of marks for errors in spelling and grammar on formal tests and examinations. Such deductions are more appropriate in situations where the student has the opportunity to edit and proofread in consultation with peers and / or the teacher.

C. MARKING STANDARDS

Marking standards for students with learning disabilities should not be set by the teacher alone, but in consultation with at least the principal. Once the standard has been established, parents should be informed and, where applicable, the student.

There are various ways of applying marking standards. For example:

- Even though the student has been given extra time, he or she will still be required to meet the same expectations as for other students regarding content, structure and style.

- If the assignment in the woodworking shop is the construction of a table, a less elaborate structure may be acceptable, but the same skills must be shown and evaluated as in a more elaborate structure.

D. REPORTING

When a student's program is modified, both parents and student should be kept fully informed regarding the form and extent of the modification. The report card should indicate the mark or grade and clearly state that it is the result of modified evaluation within a modified program.

E. SELF-CONCEPT

The development of a positive self-concept is an essential aspect of education. The student with a learning disability may require more help than some other students to acquire and maintain a positive self-concept. This is especially true of evaluation.

Behavioral Exceptionality

A. DEFINITION AND IDENTIFYING TRAITS

Behavioral exceptionality is a learning disorder characterized by specific behavior problems. Exceptional behavior is assessed by the following variables:

- the developmental stage of the student;

- the duration of the behavior;

- the frequency of the behavior;

- the intensity of the behavior.

Behavioral problems adversely affect academic performance and may be accompanied by one or more of the following:

- an inability to build or to maintain personal relationships;

- excessive fears or anxieties;

- a tendency to compulsive reaction;

- an inability to learn which cannot be traced to intellectual, sensory or other health factors, or any combination of these.

Students with a behavioral exceptionality may exhibit some of the following:

1. Behavior which interferes with the rights of others and which indicates problems with interpersonal relationships:
   - aggression
   - defiance
   - attention-seeking
   - stealing
   - lying
   - destructiveness
   - low tolerance for frustration
   - lack of remorse after hurting others
   - inability to accept limits

2. Behavior which suggests a negative self-image and / or personal inner turmoil:
   - self-injury
   - withdrawal
   - offensiveness
   - chronic underachievement
   - over-dependence
   - regression
   - egocentrism
   - inappropriate sexual interest and / or behaviors
   - soiling, wetting
   - setting self up to be a scapegoat

3. Behavior which suggests excessive fears or anxieties:
   - resistance to change
   - school phobia
   - withdrawal
   - over-compliance
   - extreme physical activity
   - infantilism
   - fantasizing or daydreaming
   - inability to concentrate
   - overeating or refusal to eat
   - insomnia

4. Behavior which indicates extreme self-control and a tendency to compulsive reaction:
   - ritualistic behavior
   - resistance to change
   - attempts to control environment
   - excessive need for tidiness or cleanliness

5. Behavior which interferes with the development of academic potential:

- poor concentration
- impulsivity
- distractibility
- withdrawal
- non-completion of tasks
- apathy
- habitual absence
- hyperactive thought processes
- extreme physical activity
- chronic underachievement

Notes:

The above list is not exhaustive.

Behaviors are not categorically fixed.

The same behavior exhibited by different students may indicate different needs.

A student may show, at different times, different behaviors indicating the same need.

Extreme behavior may be a normal reaction to trauma or a life crisis.

These behavioral characteristics may affect academic performance in one or more of the following ways:

— gaps in skill acquisition;

— wide discrepancy in skill acquisition in different subject areas;

— wide fluctuations in attendance and performance;

— loss of previous learning;

— chronic underachievement;

— refusal to risk new learning;

— refusal to work;

— incomplete assignments;

— poor problem-solving strategies;

— lag in cognitive development;

— repertoire of avoidance techniques.

A large percentage of students with behavioral exceptionalities also have learning disabilities. Therefore, the identifying traits and suggestions for modifications described in the section on learning disabilities also apply to many behavior-disordered students. When teachers modify academic programs and evaluation techniques to suit the learning needs of these students, unacceptable behaviors may diminish or disappear.

B. SUGGESTIONS FOR MODIFICATIONS OF THE EVALUATION PROCEDURES FOR STUDENTS WITH BEHAVIORAL EXCEPTIONALITIES

It should be understood that, in evaluating the progress of students with behavioral exceptionalities, it is impossible to separate the evaluation of their behavior from the evaluation of other aspects of their progress. The remainder of this section will deal with these two interlocking aspects.

1. Evaluation of Behavior

Evaluation of the student's social and emotional growth can be obtained from observation and analysis of his or her behavior. Direct observation of specific behaviors may be recorded in anecdotal form, or on checklists, graphs or charts. Daily journals, artwork and the student's writing can also be used to evaluate the current affective state of the student.

(i) *Anecdotal Records*

Significant incidents are often noted by teachers in anecdotal records that describe specific, observable behaviors exhibited by students whose behavior is of concern. Such records include relevant environmental factors such as time, place, other people involved, the antecedents and consequences, as well as a precise account of the incident or behavior. These prior records can be analyzed along with the teacher's current observations and records to provide important information for evaluating the behavior from which the student's development in social skills, self-control and responsibility is inferred.

(ii) *Checklists, Graphs, Contracts*

Data collected in the form of checklists, charts, graphs and contracts provide specific information for the purpose of behavioral evaluation. Examples of each follow.

(a) *Checklists*

In order to determine the specific disruptive behavior that the teacher wishes to modify, a frequency count of behaviors exhibited by the identified student and two or three peers who have not been identified as disruptive can be taken using the following checklist over a set period of time, such as half a day.

Disruptive Behavior	Joel	Kim	Ann
1. Speaks out in class.	卌 //	///	//
2. Argues with teacher.			//
3. Makes rude comments to peers.	//	/	/
4. Interferes with / pokes / hits peers.	/		
5. Out-of-seat.	//	/	///
6. Makes unnecessary noises with voice and / or materials.	////	///	//

Although, on the whole, Joel's behavior in categories 2 to 6 is not greatly different from that of Kim or Ann, his "speaking out" behavior appears significantly more often than that of his peers. As a result, this behavior is selected for modification. A frequency count is obtained by time-sampling, that is, by taking a count of the incidents of behavior during the same two half-hour periods of each day for five days.

Joel Speaking Out In Class					
Time	Mon.	Tues.	Wed.	Thurs.	Fri.
9:30 - 10:00	卌 //	卌 /	////	////	卌 //
2:00 - 2:30	///	卌	卌 /	//	///
TOTAL	10	11	10	6	10

(b) *Graphs*

The results of the tally, when transferred from a checklist to a line graph, provide a baseline from which to evaluate the effectiveness of the intervention during succeeding weeks.

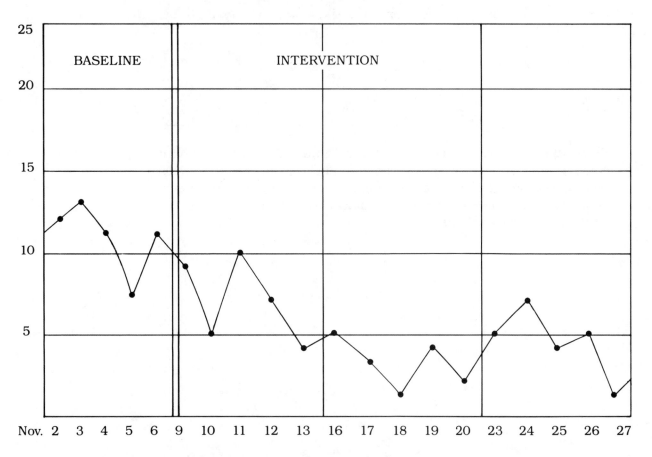

As well as providing concrete evidence of behavior for evaluation purposes, this information can be used for:

• positive reinforcement for the students;
• sharing behavioral information with colleagues;
• reporting to parents.

(c) *Contracts*

A student / teacher contract may be used as a technique for improving a student's behavior. Copies of behavior contracts should be retained in the student's file for evaluation purposes. A sample behavior contract follows.

BEHAVIOR CONTRACT

Name: _____Joel_____   Date: _____Nov. 9 to 13_____

Goal: I will raise my hand and wait to be called on. I will do
this two times in a row if I forget and speak out in class.

Consequence: Each day I fulfill my contract I will .....

Each week I fulfill my contract I will .....

This contract will be in effect for one week, at which time it will be renegotiated.

Student_____Joel_____   Teacher _____Mrs. Rose_____

MON.	TUES.	WED.	THURS.	FRI.

Behavioral checklists, graphs and contracts can be adapted for use with elementary and secondary school students. The student must be involved in setting realistic goals and in choosing the consequences. The student's commitment to achieve the desired change is critical for success and the development of responsibility.

(iii) Self-Evaluation

Self-evaluation should be conducted in a private interview and involve the student in assessing his or her behavior and establishing attainable behavioral goals. Contracts, checklists and graphs can be kept by the students themselves (very young children can use pictograms) to encourage the development of responsibility and self-control and to provide concrete evidence of improvement. Behaviors targeted for improvement should be described in specific observable and positive terms. For example, "speaking-out" behavior is transposed to "raises hand and waits to be called on." A frequency count of the desired behavior can be tabulated on a checklist.

A Grade 4 student whose behavior was described as disruptive and attention-seeking, monitored his own behavior by keeping the records depicted below. At the end of the week, the student and his teacher renegotiated the contract, and doubled the required positive behaviors. As the targeted behavior improved, other disruptive and attention-seeking behaviors disappeared.

Name	Joel	Date	Nov. 9

Time	Raised Hand	Spoke Out
9:00 - 10:30	////	///
10:45 - 12:00	ᵗʰᵗ ////	//
1:00 - 2:30	///	//
2:45 - 3:30	ᵗʰᵗ ///	/
TOTALS	24	8

Week — Nov. 9 - 13

2. Evaluation of Classroom Achievement

When planning evaluation techniques for these students, teachers should take into account the following factors: the regressive effects of stress, the effects of anxiety, the effect of evaluation on student self-concept, and the usefulness of individualized programs.

• Techniques During Periods of Regression

The tendency of people to regress under stress particularly applies to these students because they suffer the stress of previous academic failure, as well as of unmet needs, emotional upsets, and their own inappropriate behavior. Evaluation itself adds further stress. Teachers should be aware of behaviors that indicate regression to earlier developmental stages in emotional and social areas, as well as regression in cognitive areas. Evaluation techniques must take these factors into account. Under severe stress, some students may regress two or three grade levels in basic academic skills, such as reading, writing and mathematics. When serious academic regression is evident, formal testing should be delayed until the student is able to function more normally. Evaluation during periods of regression may be conducted in the following ways.

— Observe daily work and oral contributions in class.

— Present questions orally, in a one-to-one situation.

— Use the chalkboard, manipulative materials, games, puzzles, films or filmstrips, art, dramatization and other activities, as part of evaluation.

— Evaluate students when they act as peer tutors.

• Techniques That Reduce Anxiety

Students may react to the anxiety of being evaluated with "acting-out" or withdrawn behaviors and / or an "I don't care" attitude. The anxiety of students in Grades 7 to 12 may be reduced in the following ways.

— Arrange for evaluation to take place in a familiar setting with adults in charge who are known to the student. If the regular classroom and teacher are not available, the student should be given the opportunity to become familiar with the physical location, and rapport should be established between the new teacher and the student prior to evaluation.

— Prepare the student beforehand by discussing the format, type of questions, time limits, marks to be given for each section and the response expectations.

• Techniques That Enhance Self-Concept

Very frequently, the student with behavioral problems has a poor self-concept. Therefore, it is essential that all evaluation techniques used with these students incorporate successful experiences that will enhance the self-concept and facilitate further learning. The planning and implementation of the necessary modifications should also take into account the need of exceptional students to be seen as normal, able and similar to other students. The sensitive teacher understands and respects this need by creating privacy when necessary, and by maintaining an attitude of warmth, encouragement, and positive expectations. How the modifications are implemented is as important as what the modifications are.

Evaluation procedures enhance the self-concept of students when:

— the purpose of the evaluation is fully explained to and understood by the students;

— the preparation of the evaluation includes, whenever possible, participation of students in decisions regarding format, questions, time limits and marking schemes;

— the responses given by the students are reviewed by the teacher, and his or her comments are stated in positive terms;

— feedback is specific and immediate;

— achievement is recognized;

— the process of self-evaluation is taught to students and practiced by them;

— the learners evaluate their performance against objective standards;

— the results of the evaluation are used to determine future learning objectives;

— records of progress providing visible evidence of achievement are maintained by each student;

— the evaluation method itself is evaluated by analyzing such factors as time, situation, format, required responses and marking scheme;

— the evaluation is based on the individual student's past achievement and present progress;

— practice tests are frequent, and include similar format, questions and response expectations;

— opportunities are provided for re-evaluation of the same material;

— the student's work is monitored during evaluation by giving verbal encouragement and ensuring that he or she understands what is required.

- **Evaluation in Individualized Programs**

  Students with behavioral exceptionalities need individualized programs to encourage learning and enhance self-concept. In these individualized programs, many opportunities should be provided for student self-evaluation to complement the frequent formal and informal evaluation.

  Within the individualized program, the student should be involved in setting specific learning objectives, compete with his or her own past performance, and keep visible records as concrete evidence of progress. Evaluation in the non-threatening situation of a private teacher / student interview is part of the process of setting new objectives and provides an incentive for future learning.

C. REPORTING

When a student's program is modified, both parents and student should be kept fully informed regarding the form and extent of the modification. The report card should indicate the mark or grade and clearly state that it is the result of modified evaluation within a modified program.

D. SELF-CONCEPT

The development of a positive self-concept is an essential aspect of education. The student with a behavioral exceptionality may require more help than some other students to acquire and maintain a positive self-concept. This is especially true of evaluation.

Intellectual Exceptionality — Giftedness

Sample 3

A. DEFINITION AND IDENTIFYING TRAITS

Students identified as gifted have a superior degree of general intellectual ability. Such students are so advanced with respect to the regular class population that they require special provisions beyond the regular program. Gifted students display a wide range of individual combinations of characteristics. These characteristics, although they are difficult to place in exclusive categories and frequently overlap, can be organized as follows:[21]

1. Learning characteristics (intellectual giftedness). The student:
   - has an unusually advanced vocabulary for the age or grade level;
   - has a ready grasp of underlying principles and can quickly make generalizations;
   - has a verbal behavior characterized by richness of expression, elaboration and fluency;
   - reads a great deal at a level well beyond his or her age or grade.

2. Creativity characteristics (aesthetic giftedness). The student often:
   - is a high-risk taker, adventurous and speculative;
   - is very sensitive to beauty;

— generates a large number of ideas or solutions that are often unusual, clever and unique.

3. Motivational characteristics (psycho-social giftedness). The student may:
   — be easily bored with routine tasks;
   — be unusually involved and absorbed in relevant topics;
   — persist in completing tasks and sustain interest over an extended period of time;
   — be concerned with moral issues of right and wrong and make value judgments about people and issues;
   — be sensitive to issues involving the concepts of honor and truth;
   — be constructively critical, directing activities with self-confidence;
   — display intellectual playfulness by fantasizing, imagining and manipulating ideas;
   — demonstrate an unusually sophisticated sense of humor;
   — be concerned with adapting, improving and modifying institutions;
   — have empathy towards others;
   — be interested in social service;
   — be thoughtful and unselfish;
   — be self-controlled;
   — be open to new experiences;
   — be a producer rather than a consumer.

4. Kinesthetic characteristics. The student often:
   — is very well co-ordinated;
   — has a good sense of timing;
   — excels in athletic activities.

B. SUGGESTIONS FOR MODIFICATIONS OF THE EVALUATION PROCEDURES FOR GIFTED STUDENTS

When evaluating gifted students in the regular classroom, avoid the practices of simply assigning them *more* questions or problems and marking these questions or problems more rigorously. For example, it is generally preferable to provide these students with an opportunity to think divergently at higher levels by finding several possible solutions to a single problem than to have them find solutions to *several* problems of similar nature and difficulty. Although gifted students in secondary school must experience the same cross-grade examinations with identical marking standards as the other students at the same grade and level, they should be provided with more challenging, diverse and creative evaluation experiences in the regular classroom program throughout the school year. These evaluation experiences should be assessed with a standard comparable to that of the regular program.

Following are some modifications that can be made in evaluation for the gifted students in the regular program.

1. Beginning at an early age, students should be provided with topics in assignments that require the demonstration of more sophisticated research skills.

2. While all students should encounter higher level thinking in evaluation activities, gifted students must be provided with evaluation activities which demand high intellectual skill development in analyzing, synthesizing and evaluating.

3. Provide evaluation activities which encourage divergent thinking.

4. Because gifted students will have many opportunities for individualized learning activities in the program, contract learning and self-evaluation will be frequent elements of the evaluation.

   (a) *Contract Learning*

   Contract Learning is a particularly valuable technique to use with gifted students in the regular classroom because it allows the student to work independently of the rest of the class.

   It also has the advantage of mutual objective-setting by both teacher and student. Mutual goal-setting has several benefits:

   - it provides an experience of a more personal value and interest, capable of leading to a strong commitment to the learning activity;

   - it provides an opportunity for establishing criteria for evaluation which are especially appropriate to each student's level of ability and stage of development;

   - it can help the student organize work activity. Because of the great diversity of interests and activities, both in and out of the classroom, gifted students can have difficulty organizing efficiently. A contract stipulating which parts of an activity shall be completed at what time can help a student to "manage" work while also providing criteria for evaluating.

   (b) *Self-Evaluation*

   Self evaluation is another particularly valuable technique to use with gifted students in the regular classroom. Because much of their learning will take place through independent activity, it is essential that they develop skills in self-evaluation. Through the practice of these skills, gifted students are able to examine their work objectively and make decisions about its value. They also can decide on a future course of action without awaiting the results of a full and detailed evaluation from the teacher.

5. Encourage gifted students to suggest topics and projects which are related to the program and of particular interest to them. The method of evaluating such topics and projects should be negotiated by the teacher and the student.

6. Although the emphasis may be upon divergent creative activities, the demonstration of fundamental skills and knowledge should not be overlooked in evaluation. In other words, gifted students should also be evaluated for their ability to think precisely, observe carefully, organize and use information wisely and make logical decisions.

7. It is expected that gifted students will be "problem solvers." Therefore, the evaluation program for these students should place emphasis upon their developing problem solving skills. Problem solving should be considered to be an integral part of all learning activities, and not just restricted to mathematics and science.

C. REPORTING

When a student's program is modified, both parents and student should be kept fully informed regarding the form and extent of the modification. The report card should indicate the mark or grade and clearly state that it is the result of a modified program and of evaluation based on "comparable standards" to the regular program in elementary schools and the advanced-level program in secondary schools.

Enriched courses at an advanced level of difficulty should be offered where feasible. Student achievement in such courses should be reported so that all students taking the course, whether it is enriched or not, will receive assessments based on comparable standards. This method of reporting is particularly important when students submit their results to post-secondary institutions.

D. SELF-CONCEPT

Gifted students are not exempt from fears. They can suffer from fear of failure, fear of success (both the potential social consequences and the high expectations for future success) and fears associated with being perceived as "different from" other students. They may have difficulty being accepted socially by students of their own age, because their intellectual peer group is different. Because they tend to think creatively and divergently, they often need the freedom for constructive non-conformity. For all these reasons, gifted students may require considerable help to acquire and maintain a positive self-concept. It is important that evaluation practices and procedures take into account these factors.

Sample 4

Intellectual Exceptionality — Slow Learner

A. DEFINITION AND IDENTIFYING TRAITS

Students identified as slow learners are those who possess the potential for academic learning, independent social adjustment and economic self-support, but who require considerable curriculum modification and support service to function, at best, significantly below expected grade level for their chronological age. Other terms used to describe these students may include "slower learners," "educable retarded" and "students with mild intellectual handicaps."

A student identified as a slow learner will exhibit many of the following characteristics:

- a short attention span;
- poor retention;
- poor verbal skills;
- difficulty transferring a concept from one situation to another;
- difficulty generalizing;
- an academic achievement below the level of his or her peers;
- a low frustration tolerance;
- difficulty competing with peers;

- inadequate work habits and study skills;
- poorly developed physical skills and co-ordination;
- socially inappropriate behavior;
- an aversion to trying new things.

Students who are slow learners will display deficiencies in some or all of the following areas:

1. They have difficulty discriminating in reasoning activities involving auditory, visual and / or tactile experiences.

2. They have difficulty transferring and applying knowledge from one situation to similar or different situations. They also have difficulty generalizing from similar experiences.

3. They cannot attend to a task long enough to gain adequate knowledge or skill, because they are easily distracted and have short attention spans.

4. They have difficulty solving problems in all subject areas, because they have difficulty applying the known to the unknown.

5. They may identify and focus upon an incidental aspect rather than the central important point presented by the teacher.

6. They tend to make more errors than other students in the classroom. As a result, they usually expect failure and often will not attempt a task or will merely guess.

7. They find it hard to develop smooth social relationships.

8. They have trouble learning by observing someone else doing something because they cannot analyze the components of an activity or skill. Similarly, they do not learn efficiently from casual everyday experiences.

B. SUGGESTIONS FOR MODIFICATION OF THE EVALUATION PROCEDURES FOR SLOW LEARNERS

1. It is essential to evaluate their daily work because they need constant, positive reinforcement.

2. Avoid using evaluation procedures which require long-term memory.

3. Provide, for written tests and examinations, the following:
   — more time;
   — appropriately fewer test items for each individual student;
   — a different but familiar test setting to reduce distractions, anxiety and stress;
   — the opportunity to give oral responses, either personally or on tape.

4. Consider using, as frequently as possible, concrete experiences and materials, rather than pencil and paper tasks, for tests and examinations.

5. As frequently as possible, use materials and examples that are meaningful and practical for the students.

6. Ensure that students will have a reasonable measure of success in all evaluation situations.

7. Success with a particular skill in one evaluation setting may not guarantee that these students can transfer that skill to another setting or evaluation experience. For example, they may have a particular arithmetic skill in mathematics and be unable to transfer it to a similar problem in science. Or, they may have an arithmetic skill in the classroom and not be able to transfer it to an activity in the supermarket. Therefore, various kinds of evaluation, all related to the same skill, must take place frequently to determine if the students have acquired the skill.

8. These students frequently cannot evaluate their own performance. Therefore, self-evaluation must be handled carefully to give students practice and support and increase their ability to perform this activity.

C. REPORTING

When a student's program is modified, both parents and student should be kept fully informed regarding the form and extent of the modification. The report card should indicate the mark or grade, and clearly state that it is the result of modified evaluation within a modified program.

D. SELF-CONCEPT

The development of a positive self-concept is an essential aspect of education. The student who is a slow learner will require more help than some other students to acquire and maintain a positive self-concept. This is especially true of evaluation.

Differentiating Evaluation for Different Levels of Ability

Introduction

Just as teachers try to differentiate teaching strategies and learning activities for students working at different levels of difficulty, so they should specify differences in the selection and application of evaluation procedures. This should enable the teacher to support and develop the students' strengths, while working with them in areas in which they have specific needs.

The terms *basic, general* and *advanced* are used in this section to indicate some specific differences in the levels of course difficulty and may be described as follows:

Basic Level

Basic-level courses are designed to focus on the development of personal skills, social understanding, self-confidence and preparation for the world of work. These courses should serve the needs of students who may not participate in post-secondary education and should provide a good preparation for direct entry into employment.

General Level

General-level courses should be considered appropriate preparation for employment, careers or further education in certain programs in colleges of applied arts and technology and other non-degree-granting post-secondary educational institutions.

Advanced Level

Advanced-level courses should focus on the development of academic skills and prepare students for entry to university or to certain programs in colleges of applied arts and technology. Such courses should be designed to assist students to understand the theoretical principles, practical applications and substantive content of a subject.

Evaluation Procedures for Students Experiencing Difficulty in Regular Classroom Programs: Grades 7 to 12

Many of the suggestions in this section offer suitable evaluation strategies for all students, but are particularly applicable to students experiencing considerable difficulty in regular classroom programs, Grades 7 to 12. Some of the areas in which evaluation procedures must be differentiated for various groups of students are: assignments, tests and examinations, formal testing, marking and the implications of results.

A. Assignments

1. Provide students with less "passive listening time" and more "doing time" so that they can learn by doing.

2. When giving assignments, provide step-by-step instructions and allow time for discussion with the class to clarify problems.

3. Provide enough in-class time for students to begin and frequently to complete assignments while help is available. In-class assignments also permit the teacher to monitor progress, speak to individual students and give positive immediate feedback on each step.

4. Help students organize their work by providing outlines and assisting them to develop action plans, notes, summaries or reviews of units or sections of the program.

5. Allow sufficient time for students to complete assignments, especially if the assignments demand a high degree of creativity. Providing enough time will alleviate the tensions and frustration which can lead to discipline problems and incomplete work. Avoid requesting that creative assignments be submitted at the end of the same class period in which they are assigned. Such assignments, because of their complexity and emotional involvement, usually require additional in-class time.

B. Tests and Examinations

> *Weighting of Marks*
>
> **It is recommended that end of term examinations be worth approximately twenty to thirty per cent of the student's final marks for the year.**

1. Ensure that the reading and writing skills demanded on all written tests are reasonable. Review, beforehand, terms and types of questions to be used on the test. Consider asking fellow teachers to examine your questions before you use them.

2. Use some short tests on which most students will do well.

3. Consider establishing a routine in which one of the homework questions sometimes becomes a short test the next day.

4. Let students know, in advance, exactly what the proposed test will cover and the format it will take.

5. Before major texts and examinations, provide copies of previous tests and examinations which cover the same basic work. Have the students answer some of these and discuss them in class.

6. Encourage students to make up questions and tests as if they were the examiners.

7. Consider open-book tests and examinations in which reference books, dictionaries, notebooks and summary sheets, as well as textbooks, can be used. This approach will:

   (a) reduce undue reliance on memorization;

   (b) provide for "real world" practice. Tell students early, and remind them periodically, of the open notebook examinations to encourage them to make good notes. Provide help in organizing a table of contents and index so that students can find information easily and quickly.

   Notes: • Ensure that you have a plan to deal with the student who forgets to bring the necessary materials and requires them.

   • In marking open-book tests, resist the temptation to use a more stringent marking scheme because of the apparent "ease" of this test format.

8. The day before a test, take up the details of how a typical question would be marked.

9. Consider extending the time limit of tests and written examinations, where possible, for those who are good thinkers but slow writers, so that they are not penalized.

10. It is recommended that teachers create examinations in which a large proportion of the students can succeed.

C. Some Alternatives to Formal Testing

1. Consider alternatives to formal written tests and examinations, such as oral testing, observation, classroom assignments, presentations, reviews, notebooks, projects and seminars.

2. Emphasize evaluation of the following: everyday work, practical activities, participation, completion of tasks, effort and co-operation with classmates. *Immediate feedback is essential.*

3. Where appropriate, give short tests frequently. Short quizzes or oral tests can be immediately marked by the teacher or students.

4. Schedule individual interviews to help students evaluate recent performances and to set future goals.

D. Marks

1. Early in the term, clarify for the students the distribution of marks for assignments, term work, tests and examinations.

2. Let students know that a percentage of their mark will be for effort, neat work and class participation.

3. Permit students to rewrite a particular test or assignment with the opportunity to raise their marks.

4. Gather more marks from tests and assignments than will be needed to arrive at a final mark.

5. Provide opportunities for all students to gain bonus marks for extra work, such as assignments or projects.

6. In the secondary school, make sure students can achieve high marks in a basic- or general-level course just as students can achieve high marks in an advanced-level course. If it is possible for some students to get a very high mark in an advanced-level course, it should also be possible for some students to obtain a similar high mark in a basic- or general-level course. Be certain that the range or distribution of marks for all levels of the same course is comparable.

> The most vital ingredient in determining the final mark or grade for a student should be fairness to that student.

E. Implications of Evaluation Results

Use the results of student evaluation as a basis for the reassessment of course objectives, content and methods. If many students are not successful, re-examine and modify, as necessary:

- the original course or unit objectives;

- the teaching methods or learning experiences;

- the evaluation procedures.

Differentiating Evaluation — A Teacher Checklist[22]
A. Everyday Work Assignments and Tests

1. I emphasize everyday work rather than term examinations.

never	seldom	sometimes	usually	always

2. I base a high percentage of my marks (perhaps 70 — 80% or more) upon the continuous evaluation of student work, such as daily assignments, homework, maps, written answers, group activities, oral reports, notebooks and short quizzes or tests.

never	seldom	sometimes	usually	always

3. My assignments and tests focus on highly specific topics, concepts or skills.

never	seldom	sometimes	usually	always

4. I design tests or assignments short enough to be marked and returned to students within one or two days.

never	seldom	sometimes	usually	always

5. As much as possible, I give my students a task for which they are accountable each day. (Students perceive value in a day in which they are accountable for some learning.)

never	seldom	sometimes	usually	always

6. I provide opportunities and encouragement, after a test or assignment, for students to attempt to remedy unsatisfactory or unsuccessful work. I do this as frequently as possible after short-term tasks rather than waiting for long-term evaluation by term examinations.

never	seldom	sometimes	usually	always

B. Tests and Examinations

1. I prepare and provide for students, before tests and examinations, a clear and precise list of course content and skills to be tested.

never	seldom	sometimes	usually	always

2. I design tests and examinations, which will not place a major emphasis on memorization and recall, by:

   (a) using appropriate sight material such as text materials, news-paper or magazine articles, cartoons, illustrations and graphs to test student skills;

never	seldom	sometimes	usually	always

   (b) permitting students to bring notebooks to the examination; (Note that this practice may have the effect of showing the value of carefully recorded and organized notes.)

never	seldom	sometimes	usually	always

   (c) permitting students to bring to the examination a one page summary sheet;

never	seldom	sometimes	usually	always

   (d) providing the students with lists of relevant formulae as part of the question paper;

never	seldom	sometimes	usually	always

   (e) permitting students to use concrete materials in order to create, rather than write, their answers;

never	seldom	sometimes	usually	always

   (f) preparing questions that are based on materials on designated pages in resources such as the text-book. (The students would bring the resource to the test or examination. The teacher would have provided considerable instruction and practice in this "open-book" format before its use in tests and examinations.)

never	seldom	sometimes	usually	always

3. I design tests and examinations so that there is ample time for all students to complete all questions.

never	seldom	sometimes	usually	always

4. I have the students practice in class, or in daily assignments, the various types of questions to be used on tests or examinations.

never	seldom	sometimes	usually	always

C. Marks

1. I explain to the students, early in each term, my evaluation plans regarding the distribution of marks for term work, assignments and term examinations.

never	seldom	sometimes	usually	always

2. I try to design tests which permit and encourage students to be successful, especially at the beginning of the term.

never	seldom	sometimes	usually	always

3. I attempt to ensure that the class averages and grade distribution in basic and general-level classes are similar to those for classes in advanced-level courses.

never	seldom	sometimes	usually	always

4. I have a sufficiently large number of tests and evaluations to permit me to disregard each student's lowest mark, if the tests or assignments are of approximately equal value.

never	seldom	sometimes	usually	always

5. I try to provide opportunities for bonus marks for extra work or improved skill development in assignments and projects.

never	seldom	sometimes	usually	always

6. I permit, where possible, students to re-write a test or assignment in order to raise their marks.

never	seldom	sometimes	usually	always

Additional Considerations for the Evaluation of Students Taking Basic-Level Courses

Although the following considerations are applicable to students taking general-level courses in secondary school and to elementary students encountering difficulty in Grades 7 and 8, they are *absolutely essential* in the evaluation of students taking basic-level courses.

- The most important objective for evaluation is to enhance self-concept by celebrating achievements rather than noting failures.

- Evaluation must be a positive and reassuring process which encourages students to take risks without the fear of failure.

- Evaluation should always be humane and fair. A humane approach invites the student to become part of the learning process in partnership with the teacher and the rest of the class.

- Humane and fair evaluation includes honesty. If students are to have a positive self-concept, they must be able to believe that their evaluation has been honest. If the program, including the evaluation, was appropriate for the students, their achievement, as reflected in marks and comments, must be reported with sympathetic candor. If students are "given" marks, they may feel that they are unable to earn them and, therefore, consider themselves to be inadequate.

- Self-evaluation and peer evaluation should be used frequently. Such practices ensure that students will feel a sense of involvement in their own learning.

- The main emphasis should be on continuous evaluation of on-going classroom work throughout the term rather than on end-of-term examinations. It is recommended that the ratio of term mark to examination mark be approximately 80% to 20%.

- Evaluation of term work must be based upon the continuous evaluation of routine student work, such as daily assignments, maps, written answers, group activities, oral reports, projects and practical demonstrations, and *not* predominantly on tests.

- The term mark must be made up of many and widely varied evaluation experiences to reflect the various strengths of the students.

- Evaluation should recognize such personal skills and attitudes as co-operation, time management, manners, effort, attendance, punctuality and participation.

- Rapid and constant feedback often helps to foster a feeling of achievement and positive self-concept. If the student has not been successful, but is given an opportunity to improve the mark or grade after the immediate feedback, then he or she will maintain a positive self-concept and a positive attitude towards both the teacher and the subject.

- Immediate feedback allows students to monitor and "see" their own progress. When they can "see" their successes clearly, they tend to raise their standards for their own performance. Success breeds success.

- There should be frequent opportunities for students to improve their marks by re-writing tests, re-doing an assignment or producing an additional piece of work for bonus marks.

- Evaluation should take into account the fact that growth in some subject areas may be erratic and non-sequential. In addition, plateaus in learning may occur which last for relatively long periods of time. To accommodate these variations in the rate of learning, there should be a sufficient number of evaluation activities to permit the teacher to disregard some of the lower marks of a student.

- In responding to student work, always respond with some positive comments. Instead of making negative comments on the total piece of work, make specific suggestions for improvement. In doing so, concentrate on no more than one or two major areas of concern.

- In responding to written work, the emphasis should be on the content rather than on the mechanics of the written work. If a piece of work is handed back covered with teacher corrections and comments, the student may become angry and discouraged and ignore even the positive remarks.

- Evaluation should include the observation and assessment of the student as a member of a group and not only as an individual. For example, a mark can be given to a team or group in which the student has participated or to which the student has made a contribution.

- Frequent reporting to students and parents is essential. Frequent reporting provides the teacher with the opportunity to make anecdotal comments and the student with the opportunity to judge his or her own progress on a continuing basis.

- The use of examinations in basic-level courses should not be avoided. However, the examination setting should be comfortable, familiar and, where possible, monitored by the students' own subject teacher.

- The format of tests or examinations should offer the same writing opportunites that the students have in their regular classes. It is fallacious to assume that students taking basic-level courses always find objective-style questions easier than questions requiring a written response. In fact, the opposite may be true.

- Examinations should be designed to enable students to apply their skills and knowledge rather than merely recall factual information.

- It is fallacious to assume that students taking basic-level courses are necessarily incapable of higher level thinking. Test and examination questions should be designed in such a way that they permit students to demonstrate higher level thinking.

- Classes at the basic level have a wide range of skill levels, particularly in reading and writing. Consequently, considerable flexibility, especially regarding time, should be practiced in test and examination situations.

- Because some students have severe difficulties in reading but are still capable of answering test or examination questions, teachers may need to interpret some or all of the questions for some students.

- Because the emphasis should be upon working through the students' strengths in order to overcome their weaknesses, alternatives to formal written tests or examinations should be provided as frequently as possible.

Examples of Evaluation Procedures Differentiated for Different Levels of Ability

It is often difficult to design evaluation activities which are appropriate and fair for students of various levels of ability within a class in an elementary school or for students working at different levels of difficulty in the same grade and subject in a secondary school.

The following pages provide examples of a variety of differentiated evaluation procedures which teachers have developed for such students. They include:

EXAMPLE 1 — Physical and Health Education Project for Grade 7 or 8

EXAMPLE 2 — File Card Assignments for Grade 8 History

EXAMPLE 3 — Secondary School Examinations

EXAMPLE 4 — Preparation for Grade 11 Mathematics Classroom Test — General Level

Physical and Health Education Project for Grade 7 or 8

In this example, the teacher has chosen the topic "personal fitness" for a class project in Grade 7 or 8. Three project assignments have been developed for this topic, each at a different level of difficulty. Note how the objectives and task have been differentiated for the different levels of ability and how the evaluation reflects different objectives and expectations. Each student is given the assignment sheet appropriate to his or her level of ability. The three assignments are arranged in ascending order of difficulty, beginning with the least difficult.

Topic: **The Development of a Personal Fitness Plan**

Objectives:

1. To find out those programs in the school which include physical activity and to make a list of them.

2. To prepare your own fitness plan which includes the fitness components of strength, flexibility, endurance and co-ordination.

3. To become aware of the games or exercises which contribute to your strength, flexibility, endurance and co-ordination.

The Task: **What You Should Include in Your Project**

1. Make up a list of the games and activities in your school which include physical activity.

2. In your own words, explain the terms strength, co-ordination, flexibility, and endurance.

3. Include some pictures, photographs, drawings or diagrams showing examples of strength, co-ordination, flexibility and endurance.

4. Hand in a personal fitness plan for a one-week period that shows what physical activities you are going to do, when you are going to do them and how long you are going to do them.

5. List any references that you used. (People, books, magazines, pictures.)

6. In a sentence or two, write about your feelings about doing this project. Put this statement on a separate sheet and hand it in with your project.

Due Dates:

PRELIMINARY DATES:

A) Classroom work and group discussion   _____

B) 1st Student/Teacher Consultation   _____

C) 2nd Student/Teacher Consultation   _____

FINAL SUBMISSION DATE: _____

It is suggested that you allot the following amounts of time to complete this project:

in class   _____   periods

out of class   _____   hours

HOW YOUR PROJECT WILL BE MARKED

Marks will be awarded for:

40% — giving information that is complete, on topic and accurate for each aspect of your project:
- the list of physical activity programs in the school,
- the fitness plan,
- the games or exercises,
- your explanation of the fitness terms: strength, flexibility, co-ordination and endurance;

30% — including materials such as photographs, drawings, charts, graphs, pictures, models and schedules to support or illustrate the information in your project;

15% — writing in your own words in a way that is clear and easy to understand;

10% — showing originality of content and method of presentation;

5% — achieving attractiveness, neatness and visual impact of the project.

Topic: **The Development of a Personal Fitness Plan Using the Programs Available in the School**

Objectives:

1. To determine the programs available in the school related to physical activity and list them.

2. To list and define the components of physical fitness necessary for a <u>balanced</u> program.

3. To develop a balanced personal fitness program based on the components of physical fitness, using the activities available in the school.

The Task: **What You Should Consider Including in Your Project**

1. A definition of each of the components of physical fitness.

2. The different programs offered in the school related to physical fitness.

3. Activities and programs in the school that you think are most appropriate for developing physical fitness.

4. A realistic long-term plan or program for you to follow in order to develop your own physical fitness. Two important factors to consider are the difficulty of the activity and the time required to do it.

5. A personal weekly schedule of physical activities that you might follow.

6. Ways of determining whether or not your plan is suitable for you.

7. Any references that you used. (People, books, magazines or visuals.)

8. A short account of your feelings about doing this project. Write this statement on a separate sheet and hand it in with your project.

Due Dates:

PRELIMINARY DATES:

    A) Classroom work and group discussion   _____

    B) 1st Student/Teacher Consultation   _____

    C) 2nd Student/Teacher Consultation   _____

FINAL SUBMISSION DATE: _____

It is suggested that you allot the following amounts of time to complete this project:

in class	_____	periods
out of class	_____	hours

HOW YOUR PROJECT WILL BE MARKED

Marks will be awarded for:

25%	— presenting information that is complete, on topic and accurate for each aspect of your project;
20%	— developing a personal fitness plan that is balanced and reflects the appropriate activities and programs in the school;
10%	— presenting ideas that are developed in an organized manner;
20%	— including materials such as charts, graphs, pictures, schedules, models, photographs and drawings to support or illustrate the information in your project;
10%	— indicating that you have done research and that you have presented the information from this research in a manner that is easy to read, brief and to the point;
10%	— demonstrating originality of content and method of presentation;
5%	— achieving attractiveness, neatness and visual impact of the project.

Topic:	**The Development of a Personal Fitness Plan Using the Range of Programs Available in the School**

Objectives:

1. To determine the range of programs available in the school related to physcial activity.

2. To list and define the components of physical fitness necessary for a *balanced* program.

3. To develop a balanced personal fitness plan based on programs available in the school and on the components of physical fitness which you have learned about in your various classes.

The Task:

What You Should Consider Including in Your Project:

1. Activities and programs that you think are appropriate for learning about and developing your physical fitness. Give reasons for your choices.

2. A realistic long-term plan or program for you to follow in order to develop your own physical fitness.

3. A personal weekly schedule of physical activities that you might follow.

4. Direct references to the fitness kit. When making these references, include:
   — the *name* of each instrument;
   — what physical fitness *component* each instrument measures;
   — *how* each instrument measures the fitness component.

5. A pre-test schedule and form.

6. A post-test schedule and form.

7. A bibliography of references (people, books, magazines, visuals) which you used.

8. Your personal feelings about doing this project. (Write on a separate sheet attached to the project.)

Your project assignment, including any schedules, forms, charts, graphs or diagrams, should be submitted according to the dates stated.

Due Dates:

PRELIMINARY DATES:

A) Classroom work and group discussion _____

B) 1st Student/Teacher Consultation _____

C) 2nd Student/Teacher Consultation _____

FINAL SUBMISSION DATE: _____

It is suggested that you allot the following amounts of time to complete this project:

| in class | _____ | periods |
| out of class | _____ | hours |

HOW YOUR PROJECT WILL BE MARKED

Marks will be awarded for:

30% — developing a personal fitness plan which is balanced, reflects the appropriate activities and programs available in the school, includes references to the fitness kit and an example of a pre-test and a post-test;

20% — including information that is complete, on topic and accurate for each aspect of your project;

10% — presenting ideas that are developed in an organized manner;

15% — including materials such as charts, graphs, pictures, schedules, models, photographs and drawings to support or illustrate the information in your project;

10% — indicating that you have done research and that you have presented the information from this research in a manner that is easy to read, brief and to the point;

10% — demonstrating originality of content and method of presentation;

5% — achieving attractiveness, neatness and visual impact of the project.

EXAMPLE 2

File Card Assignments for Grade 8 History

The following four file card classroom assignments could be used with a Grade 8 history class. They are all based on the same topic, "The Building of the C.P.R." (the Canadian Pacific Railway), but have been designed in such a way as to take into account the different levels of ability within the class. It would be necessary, of course, to add specific objectives and evaluation criteria for each of these four assignments. The assignments have been included in this collection of examples because they illustrate effectively one aspect of the design of such assignments, that is, the matching of a task of an appropriate difficulty to a student at a particular level of ability. The file card assignments are presented here in ascending order of difficulty, but would be distributed to students on a basis predetermined by the teacher.

1.

> *Topic:* **The Building of the C.P.R.**
>
> ASSIGNMENT: **"Working on a C.P.R. Construction Gang"**
>
> Examine the pictures on the following pages of the booklet *Building of the Railway:* pages 19, 23, 28, 29, 30-31, 33, 45, 47, 50-51.
> Answer the following questions.
>
> 1. What were 3 things the railway builders had to assist them with the heavy work involved in building the railway?
>
> 2. Identify 4 difficulties that the builders of the railway had to deal with to successfully complete the railway. In which picture did you find each difficulty? How was the difficulty overcome?
>
> 3. Look closely at these pictures. Decide what it would have been like to work on the railway. Imagine that you are a railway worker. Write a one-paragraph description of what it would have been like for you to have worked on building the railway.

This assignment is the least difficult of the four assignments because:

- it is based on a set of pictures given to the students;

- the students are asked to respond to straightforward questions based on the pictures;

- the questions move in a structure from the very literal (1), through the inferential (2), to the imaginative (3);

- the internal directions within each question are very specific, for example,   — "3 things";
                 — "4 difficulties";
                 — "a one-paragraph description."

2.

> *Topic:* **The Building of the C.P.R.**
>
> ASSIGNMENT: **"William Van Horne"**
>
> After consulting the resources listed below, answer the following questions in sentence form.
>
> 1. Who was William Van Horne?
>
> 2. What qualifications did he have for the job he had with the C.P.R.?
>
> 3. What do you admire most about him?
>
> 4. Would you have liked to work for him? Why or why not?
>
> 5. What do you think was his greatest achievement? Why?
>
> *Resources:*
> 1. *Building of the Railway*   p. 17
> 2. *Discovering Canada: Developing a Nation*   pp. 168-169, 179
> 3. *Canada: Builders of the Nation*   pp. 146-148
> 4. *Flashback Canada*   pp. 206-209
> 5. *Canada: Growth of a Nation*   p. 229

This assignment is a little more difficult than assignment 1 because:

- it requires the students to read specific sections of several print resources;

- it requires the students to gather information and make notes on it;

- it requires students to move from factual questions (1 and 2), to evaluative questions (3 to 5).

This assignment is less difficult than assignments 3 and 4 because:

- it focuses on a single person;

- it provides the structure for the students' responses through specific questions.

3.

> *Topic:* **The Building of the C.P.R.**
>
> ASSIGNMENT: **"Jobs Necessary for Building the C.P.R."**
>
> After research in such resources as those listed below, identify 3 different types of jobs involved in constructing the C.P.R.
>
> For each job, describe what the person did, the tools he used, the pay he received and his hours of work. Include also a description of living conditions at "end of track." Each description should be about 2/3 of a page in length.
>
> Which of the 3 jobs would you have preferred to have? Why? Which one would you have liked the least? Why?
>
> *Resources:*
> 1. *Building of the Railway*   pp. 11-59
> 2. *Discovering Canada: Developing a Nation*   pp. 154-179
> 3. *Flashback Canada*   pp. 210-234
> 4. *Canada: Builders of the Nation*   pp. 144-148
> 5. Other resources that you locate.

This assignment is a little more difficult than assignments 1 and 2 because:

- the students are expected to locate some of their own resources;

- the instructions provide less structure for students' responses;

- there is more reading and writing involved;

- there is a greater emphasis upon analysis and evaluation.

This assignment is less difficult than assignment 4 because:

- the first part of the assignment is based upon description of factual information obtained from the resources.

4.

> *Topic:* **The Building of the C.P.R.**
>
> ASSIGNMENT: **"Should the Railway Be Built?"**
>
> Assume you are ONE of the following: A British Columbia politician, a prairie Indian chief, a Metis, or an Ontario business-man. Prepare a presentation for the Members of Parliament in which you outline arguments either for or against the construction of the C.P.R. Your written presentation should be approximately 2 pages in length.
>
> *Resources:*
>
> | | |
> |---|---|
> | 1. *Building of the Railway* | pp. 5, 7-8, 19 22-25,40 |
> | 2. *Discovering Canada: Developing a Nation* | pp. 163-174 |
> | 3. *Flashback Canada* | pp. 202-205 |
> | 4. *Canada: Builders of the Nation* | pp. 140-148 |
> | 5. *Building of the C.P.R., 1871-1885* | pp. 12-58 |
> | 6. Other resources that you locate. | |

This assignment is the most difficult of the four assignments because:

• there is no suggested structure for the response;

• there is a stronger emphasis upon analysis, synthesis and evaluation;

• there is a greater demand for creativity;

• the students will be required to select the most important factors and present them in an argument of approximately two pages.

Note: The suggested length in each of the assignments is merely a guideline. There are both benefits and dangers inherent in stating a definite length for an assignment. One benefit is that students will be aware of the teacher's expectations regarding length. A danger is that the students may write to the specified length and, as a result, either pad or reduce an already effective answer.

EXAMPLE 3

Secondary School Examinations

Secondary school teachers who must prepare differentiated exams for students in the same course and grade should do so only after careful planning. Without this planning, little differentiation may occur, or exams intended to be less difficult may instead be more so.

The following two examinations are actual examples used in Grade 9 history in the same school, in the same term, and in the same school year. The first was for students in an advanced-level course and the second was for students in a general-level course.

Neither can be considered to be the "ideal" examination. When they are compared, they illustrate some of the problems involved in trying to differentiate examinations for varying levels of difficulty.

Second Term	GRADE 9 HISTORY	Time: 1 1/2 hrs.

Marks   **ADVANCED LEVEL**

PART A: **World War One** *(15 marks)*

1. Answer either a) or b) in this question.

3   a) Explain the limitations on the usefulness of airplanes in World War One.

            OR

3   b) Outline the performance of the Canadian Army in World War One.

2. Answer *three (3)* of the 4 parts in this question.

4   a) Explain how Nationalism and the alliances helped start World War One.

4   b) Describe why trench warfare produced such a long stalemate.

4   c) How and why did the Germans use submarine warfare?

4   d) Why did the United States enter the war on Great Britain's side?

PART B: **The Twenties** *(20 marks)*

1. Answer either a) or b), not both in this question.

4   a) Explain why workers were so discontented right after World War One and why the Winnipeg General Strike caused a tremendous amount of trouble.

            OR

4   b) Explain why the farmers chose to form their own political party just after World War One and discuss what success this new party had.

(continued)

2. Answer *four (4)* of the parts in this question.

4   a) Why was Prohibition passed into law?

4   b) Describe why and how Prohibition failed.

4   c) Why did so much change occur in the 1920s?

4   d) Describe how the role of women changed in the 1920s.

4   e) Why would people think that American morality had declined in the 1920s?

4   f) Account for the boom in sports and entertainment in the 1920s.

4   g) Why would it have been so different to live in Canada as compared to the U.S.A. during the 1920s?

PART C: **The Thirties (15 marks)**

Answer *both* questions in this part.

5   1. Explain how the prosperity of the 1920s helped to cause the depression of the 1930s.

10   2. The 1930s are always seen as the time of the Great Depression, and the impact of this on the people who lived then was very great. In a discussion of *two (2)* of the following, show what people faced during that time.

a) life as a farmer

b) life as one of the unemployed

c) life as one of the lucky ones who had a job

d) what a person could expect from the government

e) what entertainment was available to help people forget the depression

---

50 marks total

Marks   **GENERAL LEVEL**

ANSWER ALL QUESTIONS IN COMPLETE SENTENCES
ANSWER TEN (10) QUESTIONS ONLY
EACH QUESTION IS WORTH <u>FOUR</u> MARKS

1. Explain how the murder of Archduke Franz Ferdinand of Austria led to the involvement of each of The Great Powers of Europe *in war* in 1914.

2. Describe the German plan of attack at the beginning of the war and explain why it was *not* successful.

3. Why would you have preferred to have fought on *land* or in the *air* had you been alive and in military service between 1914 and 1918?

4. Describe some of the more important effects of the 1st World War on Canadians, both men and women, on the home front while the war was still going on.

5. Explain the main reasons for so much *unrest* and *violence* in both Canada and the United States in the years immediately following the end of World War I.

6. Describe and explain some of the reasons behind the important changes involving women in North America during the 1920s.

7. What was *Prohibition*? Describe some of its more important *effects* on American society during the 1920s.

8. Why were the mid and late 1920s fairly *prosperous* times for many Canadians?

9. Describe in some detail some of the more popular forms of entertainment in North America in the 1920s.

10. Who were some of the great heroes in Canada and the United States during the Roaring Twenties? Explain why they were admired by so many people.

11. Explain the major causes of the Crash of 1929 and the Great Depression that followed in the 1930s in the United States and Canada.

12. *Why* were people in the Maritimes, Northern Ontario and the Prairie Provinces particularly hard hit by the Great Depression?

13. Describe the efforts of *both* the Federal Government and individual Canadians to try to solve the problems of the Great Depression.

_____
40 marks total

ISSUES REGARDING DIFFERENTIATION RAISED BY THESE TWO EXAMINATIONS

1. Visual Impact

Because the questions in the advanced-level examinations are subdivided into sections, the format appears more open, more organized and less formidable than the relatively dense presentation of the questions in the general-level examination. The student who finds examinations stressful is better served by the more open presentation of the questions in the advanced-level examinations.

When designing an examination paper, careful consideration should be given to the initial visual impact upon the students. One way to create a positive impact is to organize questions in sections so that each section has its own set of instructions and mark distribution. Ample open space should be provided around each question and section.

2. Levels of Thinking

Both examinations, essentially, demand recall of factual information obtained by rote learning. Even in the matter of factual recall, there is little differentiation in what is expected of the students of either level in answering the questions. Neither examination demands much higher level thinking.

Tests and examinations for students in general-level courses should include questions that demand more than factual recall. Examinations for advanced-level courses should have a well-designed component requiring higher level thinking. Examinations for both levels should present situations in which the students can learn. Because the program objectives and classroom activities in general-level courses should place their major emphasis on skill development, the questions designed for the general-level examination should include opportunities for students to exhibit such skills as the interpretation of pictures, cartoons, tables or graphs.

3. Wording of Questions

a) *Use of Directing Words*

Describe and *explain* are the two most common directing words in both examples of general and advanced-level examinations. Neither of these directing words provides much direction; they merely imply that the students should, in effect, tell all they know about the topics. The directing word *why* seems to be used as a variant for *explain* or *describe* and not as a possible demand for higher level thinking. There is no real differentiation in the directing words for either level and, therefore, the questions appear to be of equal difficulty.

b) *Vagueness of Terminology*

Students, especially those taking general-level courses, need to be very clear about the teacher's expectations when answering questions on examinations. Consider the following question (10) on the general-level examination:

> **Who were some of the great heroes in Canada and the United States during the Roaring Twenties? Explain why they were admired by so many people.**

- How many are "some"?

- What is a hero? What is the difference between a great hero and a not-so-great hero?

- Were there no heroines?

- Does the term "heroes" include notorious criminals?

- Is there an expected ratio of Canadian to American heroes? Would a student be penalized for naming three American heroes and one Canadian hero?

- What does "admire" really mean? Does it mean "to capture the interest of," or "to venerate," or "..."?

4. Structure of Questions

Students, especially those in the general-level program, need questions which provide considerable structure and direction. To achieve clarity in structure and direction, the teacher should consider:

- designing questions that are arranged in sub-sections;

- limiting, wherever possible, each sub-section to a single topic of the main theme;

- providing specific expectations, such as "3 reasons for," "2 causes of."

Providing clear directions and specific expectations helps students organize an essay-style answer and properly allocate their time. In addition, the marking of the paper is made easier for the teacher.

Compare the following two questions:

PART B: THE TWENTIES (ADVANCED LEVEL)

Marks

2. Answer *four (4)* of the parts in this question.

4   a) Why was Prohibition passed into law?

4   b) Describe why and how Prohibition failed.

4   c) Why did so much change occur in the 1920s?

4   d) Describe how the role of women changed in the 1920s.

4   e) Why would people think that American morality had declined in the 1920s?

4   f) Account for the boom in sports and entertainment in the 1920s.

4   g) Why would it have been so different to live in Canada as compared to the U.S.A. during the 1920s?

AND

QUESTION 7 (GENERAL LEVEL)

7. What was *Prohibition*? Describe some of its more important *effects* on American society during the 1920s.

Both of these questions present many inadvertent problems for the student. However, because of the structure of the advanced-level question, it is easier to read and answer.

5. Marking Scheme

Advanced-Level Examination

- There seems to be a predetermination on the part of the teacher to have fifty marks, three sections to cover three historical periods, and questions of approximately equal value. This format forces the assignment of equal marks to questions of unequal difficulty. Such a practice causes particular concern when students must choose from among several questions assigned equal marks, but of unequal difficulty. For example, in Question 2, part b), "Why was Prohibition passed into law?", the teacher would likely give four marks for the recitation of four reasons for its passage, while in 2,g), "Why would it have been so different to live in Canada as compared to the U.S.A.," the teacher asks students to make a fairly complex comparison of the lifestyles of two countries. The latter question deserves more marks.

- There are too few marks assigned to most of the questions to permit discrimination between a well-designed and accurate answer and one which merely gives the required number of facts presented in a disconnected manner.

General-Level Examination

- The one hour allowed for the completion of this examination is insufficient. The students must read thirteen questions, select ten, review their choices, write their answers and re-read and revise their responses, all within sixty minutes.

- The format of the examination allows a student to ignore all of one historical period (The Thirties, questions 11 to 13) or most of one of the other two historical periods (World War I and The Twenties). This format may be an advantage or a disadvantage to the students, depending on how they are prepared for the examination.

- There seems to be a predetermination on the part of the teacher to have an examination worth forty marks for ten questions. This format forces the assignment of equal marks to questions of unequal difficulty.

- Constant re-emphasis of the marks for each question should have been provided by placing the marks beside each question, as was done in the advanced-level examination.

- There seems to be an assumption that the students will have very little information for each of these questions. If, however, some students are well-prepared, they will have great difficulty responding to each question in the time allotted and for the minimal marks awarded.

- While the consistency of allotting four marks for each question may make the examination easier to mark, it does not allow the teacher to make a distinction between an excellent answer and a mediocre answer which includes the expected facts.

Example 4

Preparation for Grade 11 Mathematics
Classroom Test — General Level

It is common practice in mathematics, and in many other subjects, to prepare for classroom tests and formal examinations by using review sheets. Teachers might consider an alternative to this practice. Instead of using a review sheet, teachers might consider the occasional use of a pre-test of the same style and format, and covering the same material as the test or examination.

The use of such a pre-test has several advantages:

- it ensures that there will be no surprises on the test or examination;

- it indicates clearly the content and form for the upcoming test or examination;

- it provides practice that is fair and meaningful;

- it provides an opportunity for self-evaluation in preparation for the upcoming test or examination;

- it removes some of the stress associated with tests and examinations, and helps to produce a sense of self-confidence;

- it reduces the potential for an adversarial element in evaluation.

Note in the following example of a pre-test and its subsequent test that the questions are virtually the same in style, format and approximate degree of difficulty, except that letters, numbers and word problems are different.

EQUATION OF A STRAIGHT LINE PRE-TEST

_____

Name

Marks

1. Complete the following table on this page.

	Equation	Slope	Intercept	Intercept
	$X - 2y + 8 = 0$			
(12)	$Y = -\frac{2}{5}X + 5$			
	$X = 51$			
	$4X - 3y = 0$			

(2) 2. Find the slope of the line passing through A $(-3, 5)$ and B $(-6, -7)$.

3. Find the equation of each of the following lines in the form $AX + By + C = 0$.

    a) passing through A $(-7, 2)$ with slope $\frac{5}{4}$

(20)   b) passing through B $(-2, 0)$ and C $(-6, 4)$

    c) parallel to $4X - y + 8 = 0$ and passing through D $(-3, 3)$

    d) perpendicular to $2X + 3y - 17 = 0$ and passing through E $(2, 1)$

4. The cost of publishing a book is $6.00 a copy, plus a fixed cost of $300.00 to set up the type for the press.

    a) Express this relationship in equation form.

    b) Draw the graph of this equation on the graph paper supplied.

(6)   c) From your graph, calculate the cost of publishing 500 copies.

_____

40 marks

EQUATION OF A STRAIGHT LINE

_____

Name

Marks

1. Complete the following table on this page.

Equation	Slope	Intercept	Intercept
$X + 5y + 10 = 0$			
$Y = -\frac{3}{4}X - 7$			
$Y = 21$			
$5X - 2y = 0$			

(12)

(2) 2. Find the slope of the line passing through A (5, −6) and B (6, 9).

3. Find the equation of each of the following lines in the form $AX + By + C = 0$.

   a) passing through A (10, −11) with slope $-\frac{2}{3}$

(20) b) passing through B (0, −4) and C (7, −3)

   c) parallel to $8X - 3y + 7 = 0$ and passing through D (−6, 4)

   d) perpendicular to $5X + y - 6 = 0$ and passing through E (4, 5)

4. The cost of having a party is $3.00 for each guest who attends, plus a fixed cost of $30.00 to rent the hall.

   a) Express this relationship between the cost (C) and the number of guests (N).

(6) b) On the graph paper provided, draw the graph of this linear relationship.

   c) From your graph, find the cost of having a party for 28 guests.

_____

40 marks

In Closing...

No document on student evaluation can ever be considered complete. *Making the Grade* is no exception. Many of the sections in *Making the Grade* could be extended and further developed by writing committees representing specific subjects and / or age bands. The present book could be used as a basis for any subsequent development of programs for student evaluation of a particular nature.

Making the Grade could also be a basis for the development or refinement of evaluation policies for a school, department or individual teacher's program. It is suggested that any policy which is formulated should include a plan for implementation in stages over an appropriate period of time. Such a plan should include those topics from *Making the Grade* which should receive immediate attention and those which could be addressed at a later date or over a longer period. The plan should include specific evaluation practices and procedures based on the sound principles of student evaluation stated throughout the book.

Endnotes

1. Board of Education for the City of Etobicoke, *Student Evaluation in History: An Introduction* (Toronto, Canada: 1982).

2. N.E. Gronlund, *Measurement and Evaluation in Teaching*, 4th ed. (New York: Macmillan, 1981), p. 6.

3. This discussion of the types of evaluation is based partly on information found in the Ontario Ministry of Education's document *Evaluation and the English Program* (Toronto, Canada: 1979).

4. Noted in Neil Graham's *Designing and Marking English Examinations: A Resource Booklet for Scarborough English Teachers* (Scarborough, Canada: 1984), p. 68.

5. The categories for the cognitive domain are taken from B.S. Bloom et al., *Taxonomy of Educational Objectives: Handbook I, Cognitive Domain* (New York: David McKay, 1956).

6. The categories for the affective domain are taken from D.R. Krathwohl et al., *Taxonomy of Educational Objectives: Handbook II, Affective Domain* (New York: David McKay, 1964).

7. The categories for the psychomotor domain are taken from E.J. Simpson, "The Classification of Educational Objectives in the Psychomotor Domain," *The Psychomotor Domain*, Vol. 3 (Washington: Gryphon House, 1972).

8. This material is adapted, with permission, from *Curriculum Guide — Mathematics, K-6* (Toronto, Ontario: Board of Education, 1983).

9. *Listening to Children Talking* (London: Schools Council Publications, 1976).

10. Ibid, pp. 80-86.

11. Graham, loc. cit.

12. This list of directing words is adapted from unpublished material by Dorsey Hammond, "Directing Words."

13. Examples 1 and 2 contain materials derived from *English: A Resource Guide for the Senior Division* (Toronto, Canada: Ontario Ministry of Education, 1980), pp. 76-78.

14. The material on peer evaluation is adapted from *English: A Resource Guide for the Senior Division*, pp. 79-83.

15. Gronlund, op. cit., pp. 166-167.

16. From *Ontario Assessment Instrument Pool: Geography* (Toronto: Ontario Ministry of Education, 1980).

17. In *Reading Miscue Inventory Manual: Procedure for Diagnosis and Evaluation* (New York: Macmillan, 1972).

18. In *Tales From A Troubled Land* (New York: Charles Scribner's Sons, 1961).

19. From Ronald C. Kirbyson et al., *Discovering Canada: Shaping an Identity* (Scarborough, Canada: 1983), pp. 361-362.

20. Adapted from E.M. Koppits' *Psychological Evaluation of Children's Human Figure Drawings* (New York: Grune and Stratton, 1968), p. 330.

21. Adapted from *Curriculum Ideas for Teachers: Gifted / Talented Children* (Toronto, Canada: Ontario Ministry of Education, 1978).

22. This checklist has been adopted from materials prepared by the History Department, Program Department, of the Scarborough (Canada) Board of Education.

Credits

Every reasonable effort has been made to find copyright holders of the following material. The publishers would be pleased to have any errors or omissions brought to their attention.

pp. 2 and 169 Reprinted with permission of Macmillan Publishing Company from *Measurement and Evaluation, 4th ed.* by Norman E. Gronlund. Copyright © 1981 by Norman E. Gronlund.

p. 8 Adapted from *Evaluation and the English Program*, Ontario Ministry of Eduation, 1979. Used by permission of Ontario Ministry of Education.

pp. 12 and 135 Adapted from *Designing and Marking English Examinations: A Resource Booklet for Scarborough English Teachers*, Neil Graham. Used by permission of Scarborough Board of Education.

p. 30 From *Taxonomy of Educational Objectives: The Classification of Educational Goals: Handbook I: Cognitive Domain* by Benjamin S. Bloom et al. Copyright © 1956 by Longman Inc. Reprinted by permission of Longman Inc., New York.

p. 31 From *Taxonomy of Educational Objectives: Handbook II: Affective Domain* by David R. Krathwohl et al. Copyright © 1964 by Longman Inc. Reprinted by permission of Longman Inc., New York.

p. 32 From "The Classification of Educational Objectives in the Psychomotor Domain," in *The Psychomotor Domain, Vol. 3* by E.J. Simpson. Copyright © 1972 by Gryphon House. Reprinted by permission of Gryphon House, Mount Ranier, Maryland.

p. 72 Adapted from *Curriculum Guide — Mathematics, K-6*, Toronto Board of Education, 1983. Used with permission of Toronto Board of Education.

pp. 76 and 77   Adapted from *Listening to Children Talking*, Joan Tough. Used with permission of Ward Lock Educational Publishing Ltd.

p. 138   Adapted from unpublished material by Dorsey Hammond.

pp. 148 and 153   Adapted from *English: A Resource Guide for the Senior Division*, Ontario Ministry of Education, 1980. Used by permission of the Ontario Ministry of Education.

p. 172   From *Ontario Assessment Instrument Pool: Geography*, Ontario Ministry of Education, 1980.

p. 185   Reprinted with permission of Macmillan Publishing Company from *Reading Miscue Inventory Manual — Procedure for Diagnosis and Evaluation*, Yetta Goodman and Carolyn Burke. Copyright © 1972 by the authors. Used by permission of the authors.

p. 190   From *Tales From A Troubled Land.* Copyright © 1961 by Alan Paton. Reprinted with the permission of Charles Scribner's Sons.

pp. 196 and 197   From *Discovering Canada: Shaping an Identity*, Ronald C. Kirbyson et al. Copyright © 1983 by Prentice-Hall Canada Inc. Used with permission.

p. 198   Adapted from *Psychological Evaluation of Children's Human Figure Drawings*, E.M. Koppits. Used by permission of Grune and Stratton, Inc., Orlando, Florida.

p. 232   Adapted from materials originally prepared by the History Department, Program Department, Scarborough Board of Education, Scarborough. Used by permission.

Bibliography

Books

Anastasi, A. *Psychological Testing.* (4th ed.) New York: Macmillan Publishing Co., Inc., 1976.

Andrew, B., Gardner, J., and Hubbard, K. *Student Evaluation...the Bottom Line.* Toronto: Ontario Secondary School Teachers' Federation, 1983.

Becher, T., Eraut, M., and Knight, J. *Policies for Educational Accountability.* London: Heinemann, 1981.

Black, H. and Broadfoot, P. *Keeping Track of Teaching. Assessment In the Modern Classroom.* London: Routledge & Kegan Paul, 1982.

Bloom, B.S., Medaus, G., and Hastings, T. *Evaluation To Improve Learning.* New York: McGraw-Hill, 1981.

Bloom, B.S., et al. *Handbook on Formative and Summative Evaluation of Student Learning.* New York: McGraw-Hill Book Company, 1971.

Bloom. B.S., (ed.). *Taxonomy of Educational Objectives: Handbook I, Cognitive Domain.* New York: David McKay Co. Inc., 1956.

Board of Eduation for the City of Etobicoke. *Assessment Techniques: Cloze.* Toronto: Board of Education for the City of Etobicoke, Revised 1982.

_____ . *Assessment Techniques: Readability Formulas.* Toronto: Board of Education for the City of Etobicoke, 1976.

_____ . *Behaviour Concerns.* Toronto: Board of Education for the City of Etobicoke, 1984.

_____ . *Primary Division Reading Program.* Toronto: Board of Education for the City of Etobicoke, 1982.

_____ . *Strategies for Beginning Reading.* Toronto: Board of Education for the City of Etobicoke, 1978.

_____ . *Student Evaluation in History: An Introduction.* Toronto: Board of Education for the City of Etobicoke, 1982.

Board of Education for the City of North York. *A Marked Improvement: Evaluation of Written English in Secondary Schools.* Toronto: Board of Education for the City of North York, 1982.

Board of Education for the City of Toronto. *Curriculum Guide— Mathematics, K-6.* Toronto: Board of Education for the City of Toronto, 1983.

Boehm, A.E., and Weinberg, R.A. *The Classroom Observer: A Guide to Developing Observation Skills.* New York: Teachers College Press, 1977.

Calderhead, J. (ed.). *Teachers' Classroom Decision-Making.* London: Holt, Rinehart and Winston, 1984.

Chauncey, H., and Dobbin, J.E. *Testing: Its Place in Education Today.* New York: Harper and Row, 1963.

Cohen, D.H., and Stern, V. *Observing and Recording the Behavior of Young Children.* (2nd ed.) New York: Teachers College Press, 1978.

Colwell, R. *The Evaluation of Music Teaching and Learning.* Englewood Cliffs, NJ: Prentice-Hall, Inc., 1970.

Cooper, C.R., (ed.). *The Nature and Measurement of Competency.* Urbana, IL: National Council of Teachers of English, 1981.

Cooper, C.R., and Odell, L., (eds.). *Evaluating Writing: Describing, Measuring, Judging.* Urbana, IL: National Council of Teachers of English, 1981.

Cross, A. *Home Economics Evaluation.* Columbus, OH: Charles E. Merrill Publishing Co., 1973.

Diederich, P.B. *Measuring Growth in English.* Urbana, IL: National Council of Teachers of English, 1974.

Ebel, R.L. *Essentials of Educational Measurement.* (3rd ed.) Englewood Cliffs, NJ: Prentice-Hall, Inc., 1979.

_____, ____. *Measuring Education Achievement.* Englewood Cliffs, NJ: Prentice-Hall, Inc., 1965.

Erickson, R.C., and Wentling, T.L. *Measuring Student Growth: Techniques and Procedures for Occupational Education.* Boston: Allyn and Bacon, Inc., 1976.

Fair, J.W., et al. *Teacher Interaction and Observation Practices in the Evaluation of Student Achievement.* Toronto: Ontario Ministry of Education, 1980.

Farr, R., and Carey, R.F. *Reading: What can be measured?* (2nd ed.) Newark, DE: International Reading Association, Inc., 1986.

Goodman, Y.M., and Burke, C. *Reading Miscue Inventory Manual — Procedure for Diagnosis and Evaluation.* New York: Macmillan, 1972.

Gorow, F.F. *Better Classroom Testing.* San Francisco: Chandler Publishing Company, 1966.

Graham, N. *Designing and Marking Examinations: A Resource Booklet for Scarborough English Teachers.* Scarborough, Canada: Scarborough Board of Education, 1984.

Gronlund, N.E. *Constructing Achievement Tests.* (2nd ed.) Englewood Cliffs, NJ: Prentice-Hall, 1977.

_____. *Improving Marking and Reporting in Classroom Instruction.* New York: Macmillan Publishing Co., Inc., 1974.

_____ . *Measurement and Evaluation in Teaching.* (4th ed.) New York: Macmillan Publishing Co., Inc., 1981.

_____ . *Preparing Criterion-Referenced Tests for Classroom Instruction.* New York: Macmillan Publishing Co., Inc., 1970.

_____ . Stating Behavioral Objectives for Classroom Instruction. New York: Macmillan Publishing Co., Inc., 1970.

Hardaway, M. *Testing and Evaluation in Business Education.* (3rd ed.) Cincinnati: South-Western Publishing Co., 1966.

Harlen, W. (ed). *Evaluation and the Teacher's Role.* London: Macmillan, 1978.

Harris, D.P. *Testing English as a Second Language.* New York: McGraw-Hill Book Company, Inc., 1969.

Holmes, M. *What Every Teacher and Parent Should Know About Student Evaluation.* Toronto: OISE Press, 1982.

Ingram, G.F. *Fundamentals of Educational Assessment.* New York: D. Van Nostrand Company, 1980.

Jones, A., and Whittaker, P. *Testing Industrial Skills.* New York: Halsted Press, 1975.

Kirbyson, Ronald C., et al. *Discovering Canada: Shaping an Identity.* Scarborough, Ontario: Prentice-Hall Canada Inc., 1983.

Kirschenbaum, H., et al. *Wad-Ja-Get? The Grading Game in American Education.* New York: Hart Publishing Company, 1971.

Koppits, E.M. *Psychological Evaluation of Children's Human Figure Drawing.* New York: Grune and Stratton, Inc., 1968.

Krathwohl, D.R., (ed.). *Taxonomy of Educational Objectives: Handbook II, Affective Domain.* New York: David McKay Co. Inc., 1964.

Mathews, D.K. *Measurement in Physical Education.* (5th ed.) Philadelphia: W.B. Saunders Company, 1978.

Mehrens, W.A., and Lehmann, I.J. *Measurement and Evaluation in Education and Psychology.* (2nd ed.) New York: Holt, Rinehart & Winston, 1978.

Morse, H.T., and McCune, G.H. *Selected Items for the Testing of Study Skills and Critical Thinking.* (4th ed.) Washington: National Council for the Social Studies, 1964.

Nelson, C.H. *Measurement and Evaluation in the Classroom.* New York: The Macmillan Company, 1970.

Noll, V.H., et al. *Introduction to Educational Measurement.* (4th ed.) Boston: Houghton Mifflin Co., 1979.

Ontario Ministry of Education. *Curriculum Ideas for Teachers: Gifted / Talented Children.* Toronto, 1978.

_____ . *Education in the Primary and Junior Divisions.* Toronto, 1975.

_____ . *English as a Second Language / Dialect.* Toronto, 1977.

_____ . *English: A Resource Guide for the Senior Division.* Toronto, 1980.

_____ . *Evaluation and The English Program.* Toronto, 1979.

_____ . *Evaluation of Student Achievement: A Resource Guide for Teachers.* Toronto, 1976.

_____ . *French, Core Programs, 1980.* Toronto, 1980.

_____ . *Ontario Assessment Instrument Pool: A General Introduction.* Toronto, 1980.

_____ . *Ontario Assessment Instrument Pool: French as a Second Language.* Toronto, 1980.

_____ . *Ontario Assessment Instrument Pool: Geography.* Toronto, 1983.

_____ . *Ontario Assessment Instrument Pool: History.* Toronto, 1980, 1981.

_____ . *Ontario Schools: Intermediate and Senior Divisions (OSIS).* Toronto, 1984.

Paton, Alan. *Tales From A Troubled Land.* New York: Charles Scribner's Sons, 1961.

Popham, W.J. *Criterion-Referenced Measurement.* Englewood Cliffs, NJ: Prentice-Hall, Inc., 1978.

Rowntree, D. *Assesssing Students. How Shall We Know Them?* London: Harper and Row, 1977.

Ryan, D.W., and Schmidt, M. *Mastery Learning: Theory, Research and Implementation.* Toronto: Ontario Ministry of Education, 1979.

Satterly, D. *Assessment in Schools.* Oxford: Basil Blackwell, 1981.

Scannell, D.P. and Tracey, D.B. *Testing and Measurement in the Classroom.* Boston: Houghton Mifflin, 1975.

Shipman, M. *Assessment in Primary and Middle Schools.* London: Croom Helm, 1983.

Simpson, E.J. "The Classification of Education Objectives in the Psychomotor Domain." In *The Psychomotor Domain.* Vol. 3. Washington, DC: Gryphon House, 1972.

Thorndike, R.L. (ed.). *Educational Measurement.* Washington, DC: American Council on Education, 1971.

Thorndike, R.L., and Hagen, E.P. *Measurement and Evaluation in Psychology and Education.* (4th ed.) New York: John Wiley and Sons, 1977.

Tough, J. *Listening to Children Talking.* London: Schools Council Publications, 1976.

Valette, R.M. *Modern Language Testing.* (2nd ed.) New York: Harcourt, Brace, Jovanovich, Inc., 1977.

Wahlstrom, M.W., and Danley, R.D., *Assessment of Student Achievement.* Toronto: Ontario Ministry of Education, 1976.

Articles

Adkins, A. "Testing: Alternative to Grading." *Educational Leadership.* January 1975, pp. 271-273.

Allen, E.D. "Communicative Competence and Levels of Proficiency." *Canadian Modern Language Review.* V.41, N.6. May 1985, pp. 991-999.

Anderson, L.W., and Anderson, J.C. "Affective Assessment Is Necessary and Possible." *Educational Leadership.* April 1982, pp. 524-525.

Backlund, P.M., et al. "Recommendations for Assessing Speaking and Listening Skills." *Communication Education.* January 1982, pp. 9-17.

Barnes, S. "A Study of Classroom Pupil Evaluation: The Missing Link in Teacher Education." *Journal of Teacher Education.* V.36, N.4. July-August 1985, pp. 46-49.

Bloom, T.K. "Peer Evaluation — A Strategy for Student Involvement." *Man/Science/Technology.* February 1974, pp. 137-138.

Brown, L.B. "What Teachers Should Know About Standardized Tests." *Social Education.* November-December 1976, pp. 509-516.

Clarke, E.G. "Grading Seminar Performance." *College Teaching.* V.33, N.3. Summer 1985, pp. 129-133.

Cohen, A.M. "Objectives, Accountability, and Other Unpleasantries." *English Journal.* April 1972, pp. 565-570.

Cohen, K.C. "Some Workable Evaluation Strategies." *Today's Education.* January-February, 1976, pp. 60-62, 95.

Evans, P.J.A. "Canadian Activity in Large Scale Assessment of Writing." *English Quarterly.* V.18, N.2. Summer 1985, pp. 33-37.

Flint, D. "Evaluating Written Assignments." *History and Social Science Teacher.* Summer 1977, pp. 247-249.

France, N. "Evaluation in the High School: Fact or Fiction?" *Education Canada.* March 1971, pp. 14-18.

Francis, J. "A Case for Open-Book Examinations." *Educational Review.* V.34, N.1. 1982, pp. 13-26.

Fraser, B.J. "Evaluation of Inquiry Skills." *The Social Studies.* May-June 1978, pp. 131-134.

Hammond, D. "Directing Words." Unpublished material. 1983.

Hartman, C.L. "Describing Behaviour: Search for an Alternative to Grading." *Educational Leadership.* January 1975, pp. 274-277.

Harvey, A. "Student Contracts: A Break in the Grading Game." *Education Canada.* September 1972, pp. 41-44.

Herlihy, M.T., and Herlihy, J.G. "Report Cards." *Social Education.* November-December 1976, pp. 574-575.

_____ . "Report from the Classroom." *Social Education.* November-December 1976, pp. 576-581.

Herrington, A.J. "Writing to Learn: Writing Across the Disciplines." *College English.* April 1981, pp. 379-387.

Hoffman, R.E. "Student Evaluation and Principles of Learning." *Journal of Business Education.* May 1974, pp. 333-334.

Holmes, M. "Alternative Method for Presenting Student Evaluation Grades in Secondary School." *School Guidance Worker.* March-April 1972, pp. 45-52.

_____ . "The Case For and Against Criterion-Referenced Tests." *School Guidance Worker.* March-April 1974, pp. 11-16.

_____ . "Competency Based Education — Is It Time? Can It Work?" *School Guidance Worker.* March-April 1980, pp. 5-11.

Hughes, A.L., and Frommer, K. "A System for Monitoring Affective Objectives." *Educational Leadership.* April 1979, pp. 521-523.

Hurst, J.B. "Product and Performance Checklists in Social Studies Education." *The Social Studies.* July-August 1979, pp. 158-162.

Johnson, W.D. "We Teach Best What We Test Best." *The Social Studies.* October 1969, pp. 217-224.

Lecroix, W.J. "Evaluating Learner Growth." *Man/Science/Technology.* February 1974, pp. 133-136.

Ladas, H. "Grades: Standardizing the Unstandardized Standard." *Phi Delta Kappan.* November 1974, pp. 185-188.

Leary, J.L. "Assessing Pupil Progress: New Methods are Emerging." *Educational Leadership.* January 1975, pp. 250-252.

McConaughy, S.H. "Using the Child Behavior Checklist and Related Instruments in School-Based Assessment of Children." *School Psychology Review.* V.14, N.4. 1985, pp. 479-494.

Millman, J. "Reporting Student Progress: A Case for a Criterion-Referenced Marking System." *Phi Delta Kappan.* December 1970, pp. 226-230.

Neel, T.E. "Classroom Performance Standards." *Thrust for Educational Leadership.* October 1972, pp. 17-20.

O'Hanlon, J. "A Guide to Grading: Pass — Incomplete." *Clearing House.* November 1973, pp. 138-141.

Prock, L.M. "The Ethical Implications of Evaluating Students." *B.C. Teacher.* May-June 1972, pp. 295-297, 315.

Robson, B. "Through The Education Looking-glass or Alice in Criteria-land." *Use of English.* V.37, N.1. Autumn 1985, pp. 1-6.

Shankman, W. "Testing for Interpretation and Analysis." *History and Social Science Teacher.* Fall 1977, pp. 56-59.

Simon, S.B., and Hart, L. "Grades and Marks: Some Commonly Asked Questions." *The Science Teacher.* September 1973, pp. 46-48.

Tucker, J.A. "Curriculum-Based Assessment: An Introduction." *Exceptional Children.* V.52, N.3. November 1985, pp. 199-204.

Wahlstrom, M., Regan, E., and Jones, L. "Teacher Beliefs and the Assessment of Student Achievement." In K. Leithwood (ed.) *Studies in Curriculum Decision-Making.* Toronto: OISE, 1982, pp. 27-34.

Westcott, G. "Teaching and Evaluating Discussion Skills." *English Journal.* January 1982, pp. 76-78.

Williams, R.G. and Miller, H.G. "Grading Students: A Failure to Communicate." *Clearing House.* February 1973, pp. 332-337.

Wise, R.I., and Newman, B. "The Responsibilities of Grading." *Educational Leadership.* January 1975, pp. 253-256.

Wood, R., and Napthali, W. "Assessment in the Classroom: What Do Teachers Look For?" *Educational Studies.* V.1, N.3. 1975, pp. 151-161.

Index

Advanced-level courses, defined, 228
Affective aspects of job performance, evaluation checklist for, 85-86
Affective domain, 29
    taxonomy for, 31-32
Anecdotal records
    on students with behavioral exceptionalities, 214
Assignments
    differentiated file card assignments for Grade 8 history, 244-247
    differentiated physical and health education project for Grade 7 or 8, 238-243
    for students experiencing difficulty, 229, 232
Assisted reading, 69

Basic-level courses
    definition of, 228
    evaluation of students in, 235-237.
        See also Differentiating evaluation for different levels of ability.
Behavioral exceptionality, 205, 212-220

definition and identifying traits of, 212-213
and development of self-concept, 220
modifying evaluation procedures for, 213-220
    evaluation of behavior, 213-217
    evaluation of classroom achievement, 218-220
    reporting on, 220

Calendar for tests, examinations and assignments, 53
Checklists
    on behavioral exceptionalities, 214-215
    observational, 62
    for students. See Student handouts.
Classroom work and study habits, 46
Cloze procedure, 193-197
    example of, 196-197
Cognitive development, stages of, 36-42
Cognitive domain, 29
    taxonomy for, 30
Communication exceptionality, 204
    learning disability, 208-211
Completion questions, 178

Concrete operational stage, 40-41
Contract learning: use with gifted students, 222
Contracts: for improving behavior, 216
Cultural background, and evaluation, 11, 12-13

Developmental domains, 29-33
Diagnostic evaluation, 8-9, 184-201
    Cloze procedure, 193-197
    human figure drawing, 198-201
    modified miscue analysis, 184-192
Dictated material, 66
Differentiating evaluation for different levels of ability, 228-257
    a checklist for teachers, 232-234
    definitions, 228
    evaluation of students experiencing difficulty in regular programs, 229-232
    examples, 237-257
        file card assigments for Grade 8 history, 244-247
        physical and health education project for

Grade 7 or 8, 238-243
pre-test, Grade 11
mathematics, 255-257
secondary school
examinations, 248-254
"Directing" words, 12, 251
in formulating essay-style
questions, 128,
135-139
and levels of thinking,
140-142
"Discuss," ambiguity of, 12,
135-137
Discussions, observational
checklist for, 88
Drafting, 93
Dramatic arts, observation
in, 82
Drawings of human figures,
as a diagnostic
technique, 198-201

Electricity, 91
example of true-false
question in, 174
Electronics, 92
Essays, 144-153
assignments and
objectives, 144
different types of, 153
example of an effective
assignment, 147
frequent, short, 145
instructions re purpose,
audience and format
for, 146-147
and levels of ability, 145
marking, 148-151
objectives and evaluation
criteria, 144-145
peer evaluation of, 153
revision process for,
147-148
selective evaluation of, 145
Essay-style questions,
120-142
advantages and disadvan-
tages of, 120-122
constructing, 127-130
"directing" words in, 128,
135-139
marking, 131-132
planning the use of, 127
preparing the students for,
123-126
student checklist for
answering, 132

using information
obtained from
marking, 133-134
Evaluation
characteristics of an
effective program, 7-8
defined, 2
differentiating, for different
levels of ability,
228-257
factors to consider after,
15
factors to consider
before, 14
learning objectives and,
2, 28-34
pitfalls during, 10-12
planning for, 110
policy, developing for a
grade, subject or
department, 20-26
example: student
evaluation in music,
20-26
post-evaluation activities,16
purposes of, 3-4
questions to consider
when developing
programs, 18
reactions of students to, 16
school policy for, 19
significant factors
affecting, 4-6
three types of, 8-10. See
also
Diagnostic evaluation;
Formative evaluation;
Summative
evaluation.
Examinations. See Tests and
examinations.
Exceptional students,
evaluation of, 204-225
categories of exceptional
students, 204-205
definitions, 204
factors to consider, 206
reporting on evaluation,
206-207
statement of purpose, 205
"Explain," as a directing
word, 138, 141

Feedback: importance of,
235-236
Fill-in-the-blank questions,
178

Formal operational stage,
41-42
Formative evaluation, 9

General-level courses,
defined, 228
Geography
example of short-response
question in, 181
example of true-false
question in, 172
Gifted students, 220-223
definition and identifying
traits of, 220-221
modifying evaluation
procedures for,
221-223
reporting on, 223
self-concept of, 223
Graphs
on behavioral exception-
alities, 215
"Guessing factor," with true-
false questions, 169

Higher-level thinking
and multiple-choice
questions, 165-166
History
differentiated examinations
for Grade 9, 248-254
differentiated file card
assignments for Grade
8, 244-247
example of essay-style
question for, 129
example of true-false
question in, 173
project assignment sheet,
107-108
Homework
and study habits, 46
Homework and assignment
chart, 51

Informal print experiences,
as observational
technique, 65
Instructions, 10
Intellectual exceptionality,
205
Interlinear questions, 178

Laboratory work, evaluating,
89
Language differences, and
evaluation, 12, 13

Learning disabled, 208-211
  definition and identifying
    traits of, 208-209
  marking standards for,
    211
  modifications of evaluation
    procedures for,
    209-211
  reporting on, 211
  self-concept of, 211
Learning objectives and
  student evaluation,
  28-34
  the three domains, 29-33
Level of abstraction of
  evaluation activity, 11
Levels of ability: differing
  evaluation procedures
  for different, 228-257
Levels of thinking: directing
  words and, 140-142

Marking
  of essays, 148-151
  marking scheme for
    Grade 9 history
    examination, 254
  standards for learning
    disabled students, 211
  of students experiencing
    difficulty in regular
    programs, 231, 234
  of tests, 117
Matching questions, 175-177
  advantages and disadvan-
    tages of, 175
  guideposts for construc-
    ting, 176-177
Mathematics
  multiple-choice question
    in senior algebra, 166
  pre-test for Grade 11
    mathematics, 255-257
  project assignment sheet,
    105-106
  record for individual
    students, 72-75
Memory, vs. understanding, 11
Miscue analysis, 184-192
  case study, 190-192
  method, 185-189
Multiple-choice questions,
  159-166
  advantages and disadvant-
    ages of, 159
  guideposts for construc-
    ting, 160-164

and higher-level thinking,
  165-166
Multiple exceptionality, 205
Music, student evaluation
  in, 20-26
  opportunities for evalua-
    tion, 22-25
  rationale for, 20-21

Note taking, 48

Objectives, suggestions on
  writing, 33-34
Objective-style questions,
  156-182
  advantages of, 157
  disadvantages of, 157-158
  factors to consider when
    using, 156-157
  matching questions,
    175-177
  multiple-choice questions,
    159-166
  preparing, 158
  short-response items,
    178-182
  true-false questions,
    167-174
Observation, 60-93
  advantages and disadvant-
    ages of, 60
  as a method of evaluation, 61
  examples of techniques in,
    63-93
    affective aspects of job
      performance, 85-86
    assisted reading, 69
    class or small group
      discussions, 88
    dictated material, 66
    dramatic arts, 82
    informal print experi-
      ences, 65
    laboratory work, 89
    mathematics record,
      individual, 72-75
    oral language, evalua-
      ting, 76-79
    physical and health
      education, 80-81
    play, evaluation of, 70-71
    practical demonstrations,
      90-93
    record sheet — reading
      strategies, 68
    service-oriented shops
      or classrooms, 87

trade books, 67
    visual arts, 83-84
  guideposts for construc-
    ting observational
    checklists, 62
Open-book tests, 230
Oral language, evaluating,
  76-79

Parent interviews, 207
Parents: of exceptional
  students, reporting to,
  206-207
Peer evaluation, 9
  of essays, 153
Performance test in music,
  25
Personal study inventory,
  46-47
Physical and health education
  differentiated project
    for Grade 7 or 8,
    238-243
  observation in, 80-81
  project assignment sheets,
    103-104
Physical exceptionality, 205
Piaget, Jean, 38, 42
Play activities, evaluation of,
  70-71
Practical demonstrations,
  observational check-
  lists for, 90-93
Pre-operational stage, 39-40
Pre-tests, 110
  for general-level Grade 11
    mathematics, 255-257
Projects, 96-108
  advantages of, 96
  assignment sheet for, 100
    examples, 102-108
    sample outline, 100
  defined, 96
  disadvantages of, 97
  evaluation criteria for,
    101-102
  guideposts for assigning
    and marking, 98-99
  in music, 24-25
Psychomotor domain, 29
  taxonomy for, 32-33

Reading strategies record
  sheet, 68
Report card
  for slow learners, 225

Report cards
  for exceptional students,
    206
Reporting
  on exceptional students,
    206-207
  on learning-disabled
    students, 211
  marks or grades in music,
    26
  on students in basic-level
    courses, 236
  on students with behav-
    ioral problems, 220

Science, example of essay-
  style question for, 129
Self-concept, developing
  gifted students, 223
  learning-disabled students,
    211
  students with behavioral
    problems, 219, 220
Self-evaluation, 9
  by gifted students, 222
  in music, 21
  by students with behavioral
    exceptionalities, 217
Sensori-motor stage, 38
Service-oriented shops or
  classrooms, observation
  in, 87
Short-response items,
  178-182
  advantages and disadvan-
    tages of, 179
  guideposts for construc-
    ting, 179-182
  types of, 178
Slow learners
  definition and identifying
    traits of, 223-224
  modifying evaluation pro-
    cedures for, 224-225
  reporting on, 225
  self-concept of, 225
Special education program,
  defined, 204. *See also*
  Exceptional students,
  evaluation of.
Special education services,
  defined, 204
Stages of cognitive development, 36-42
Stress, 11

and exceptional behavior,
  218
Student handouts
  calendar for tests,
    examinations and
    assignments, 53
  essay-style questions:
    checklist for
    answering, 132
  homework and assignment
    chart, 51
  improving performance on
    essay-style questions,
    125-126
  personal study inventory,
    46-47
  personal work habit
    inventory, 45
  techniques for improving
    study skills, 48-50
  weekly study schedule
    chart, 52
Studying for tests and
  examinations, 49-50
Study methods, 49
Study schedule, 48, 52
Study skills
  personal inventories for,
    45-47
  and student evaluation,
    44-53
  suggestions for teaching, 44
  techniques for improving,
    48-50
  and time management,
    51-53
Summative evaluation, 9-10

Taxonomy, 29
  for the affective domain, 31
  for the cognitive domain, 30
  for the psychomotor
    domain, 32
Technical subjects
  affective aspects of job
    performance in, 85-86
  practical demonstrations
    in, 90-93
Terminology used in
  instructions. *See*
  "Directing" words.
Tests and examinations,
  110-118
  88 key questions about,
    112-117

balance in, 111
  building a particular test,
    114-115
  differentiated secondary
    school examinations,
    248-256
  essay-style questions on.
    See Essay-style
    questions.
  examinations, defined, 110
  giving a test, 116
  integration between
    learning and testing,
    111
  levels of thinking called
    for by, 251
  marking a test, 117
  marking scheme for,
    253-254
  objective-style questions
    on. *See* Objective-style
    questions.
  planning for, 110, 113
  post-test activities, 118
  providing criteria for
    evaluation of, 128-129
  structure of questions on,
    252-253
  for students experiencing
    difficulty in regular
    programs, 230, 231,
    233-234
  studying for, 49-50
  surprises, avoiding, 17, 118
  testing, defined, 110
  visual impact of tests
    papers, 251
  wording of questions on,
    251-252
Textbooks, studying, 47
Trade books, 67
True-false questions, 167-174
  advantages and disadvant-
    ages of, 168-169
  criticisms of, 167
  guideposts for construc-
    ting, 170-171
  variations on, 172-174

Variety in evaluation
  approaches, 56-57
Visual arts, observation in,
  83-84

Work habit inventory, 45